Networks Social Studies

United States Early Years

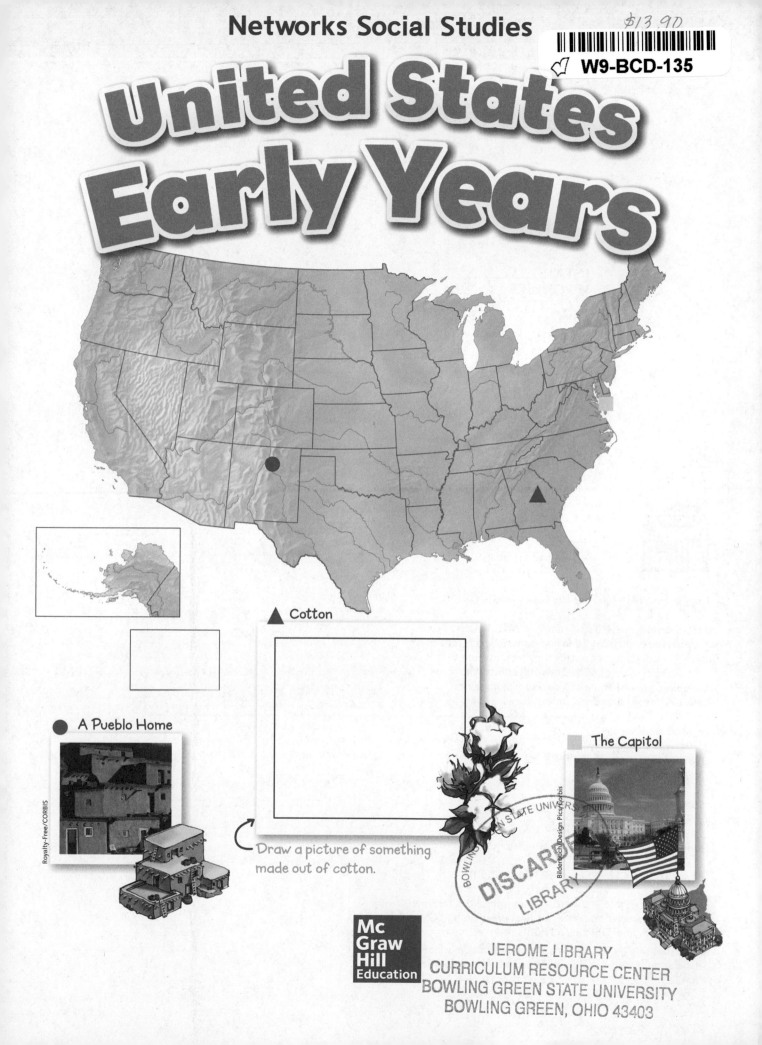

▲ Cotton

Draw a picture of something made out of cotton.

● A Pueblo Home

The Capitol

Mc Graw Hill Education

Send all inquiries to:
McGraw-Hill Education
8787 Orion Place
Columbus, OH 43240

ISBN: 978-0-02-130469-1
MHID: 0-02-130469-6

Printed in the United States of America.

1 2 3 4 5 6 7 8 9 QLM 22 21 20 19 18 17 16 15 14

PROGRAM AUTHORS

James A. Banks, Ph.D.
Kerry and Linda Killinger Endowed
    Chair in Diversity Studies and
    Director, Center for Multicultural
    Education
University of Washington
Seattle, Washington

Kevin P. Colleary, Ed.D.
Curriculum and Teaching Department
Graduate School of Education
Fordham University
New York, New York

Linda Greenow, Ph.D.
Associate Professor and Chair
Department of Geography
State University of New York at
    New Paltz
New Paltz, New York

Walter C. Parker, Ph.D.
Professor of Social Studies Education,
    Adjunct Professor of Political Science
University of Washington
Seattle, Washington

Emily M. Schell, Ed.D.
Visiting Professor, Teacher Education
San Diego State University
San Diego, California

Dinah Zike
Educational Consultant
Dinah-Might Adventures, L.P.
San Antonio, Texas

CONTRIBUTING AUTHORS

James M. Denham, Ph.D.
Professor of History and Director,
    Lawton M. Chiles, Jr., Center for
    Florida History
Florida Southern College
Lakeland, Florida

M.C. Bob Leonard, Ph.D.
Professor, Hillsborough Community
    College
Director, Florida History Internet Center
Ybor City, Florida

Jay McTighe
Educational Author and Consultant
McTighe and Associates Consulting
Columbia, Maryland

Timothy Shanahan, Ph.D.
Professor of Urban Education &
    Director, Center for Literacy
College of Education
University of Illinois at Chicago

ACADEMIC CONSULTANTS

Tom Daccord
Educational Technology Specialist
Co-Director, EdTechTeacher
Boston, Massachusetts

Joe Follman
Service Learning Specialist
Director, Florida Learn & Serve

Cathryn Berger Kaye, M.A.
Service Learning Specialist
Author, *The Complete Guide to
    Service Learning*

Justin Reich
Educational Technology Specialist
Co-Director, EdTechTeacher
Boston, Massachusetts

Explore! UNIT 1 Geography

BIG IDEA Location affects how people live.

My Book

My Computer

networks™

Go online and find this interactive map of the Southeast region.

My Cover

Find a geographic feature on your cover. Describe what you found.
What fun things might you do there?

iv

Explore! UNIT 2 — Native Peoples of North America

BIG IDEA Culture influences the way people live.

My Book

My Computer

networks™

Go online and find this video about Native American cultures.

Keep going!
Next we'll explore the Age of Exploration!

My Cover

Find an artifact from Native American cultures on your cover.
Tell what it is and in what region you found it.

_____

_____

EXplore! UNIT 3 The Age of Exploration

BIG IDEA People's actions affect others.

My Book

My Computer

networks™

Go online and find this interactive main idea and details chart. It can help you write a summary.

Graphic Organizer
Main Idea and Three Details

My Cover

Find the Spanish ship exploring North America. Its sails are shaped like triangles. What state is it sailing near? Where do you think it is going?

_____

_____

_____

_____

Explore! UNIT 4 Colonial America

BIG IDEA 💡 Location affects how people live.

My Book

My Computer

networks™

Go online and find this interactive map of the Middle Colonies.

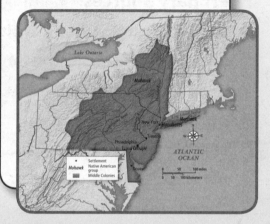

Keep going!
Next we'll explore the American Revolution!

My Cover

Find the colonial town. It's in the Northeast.
Why do you think it has walls?

_____

_____

_____

My Book

My Computer

networks™

Go online and find this video about the Revolutionary War.

My Cover

Find the man on horseback. He's carrying a white flag. What do you think he might say? Write his words in the speech bubble below.

EXplore! UNIT 6 Founding the Nation

BIG IDEA Rules provide order.

My Book

My Computer

networks™

Go online and find this interactive word web. It can help you organize information before you analzye it.

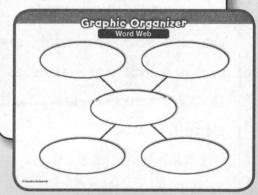

Graphic Organizer
Word Web

Keep going!
Next we'll explore westward expansion!

My Cover

On the cover, find the buildings with domes. Which one is the U.S. Capitol? How do you know?

_____

_____

EXplore! UNIT 7 Westward Expansion

BIG IDEA Relationships affect choices.

My Book

My Computer

networks™

Go online and find this interactive map of the Indian Removal Act.

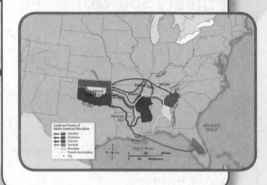

My Cover

Find an example of overland transportation on your cover. Think about how you travel over land today. Draw how you travel.

EXplore! Skills and Maps

Skills

Reading Skills

Primary and Secondary Sources

Chart and Graph Skills

My Computer

networks™

Go online and find an activity to help you build social studies skills.

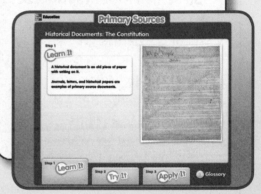

Keep going! Next we'll explore maps!

My Cover

Count the number of buildings, ships, people, and animals on your cover. Draw a chart or graph to show this information.

EXplore! Skills and Maps

Maps

My Computer

networks™

Go online and find this interactive map about Florida schools.

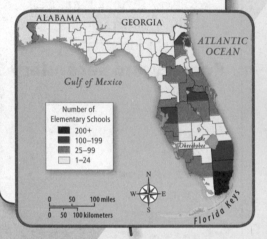

My Cover

There are many landforms and bodies of water on your cover. Name as many of them as you can.

_____

_____

Explore! Skills and Maps

New France and New England in 1750

Maps

Explore! Skills and Maps

Maps

Reference Section

UNIT 1

Geography

The physical features of North America greatly influenced the growth of the United States. These physical features also determined the outcomes of many of the most significant events in U.S. history. In order to understand this history, you must first understand the land on which it took place. In this unit, you will learn about the physical and political features of the United States. As you read, think about how these features affect life in our country today. This will help you understand the past as well.

Lake Okeechobee ▶

As you read this unit, add major physical features, labels, and symbols to the map and map key. Here are some things you will want to do:

☐ Add a title.
☐ Label the following on the map:
- The Atlantic and Pacific oceans
- The Gulf of Mexico
- The Great Lakes (Be sure to label all five!)
- The Rio Grande
- The Appalachian and Rocky mountains

After you finish labeling your map:
☐ Outline and shade each geographic region of the United States. Be sure to choose a different color for each region.
☐ Complete the map key by shading the box for each region the color used on your map.

Show As You Go!

As you read this unit, use this page to record details about the geographic regions of the United States on the map. These details will help you complete a project at the end of the unit.

Fold page here

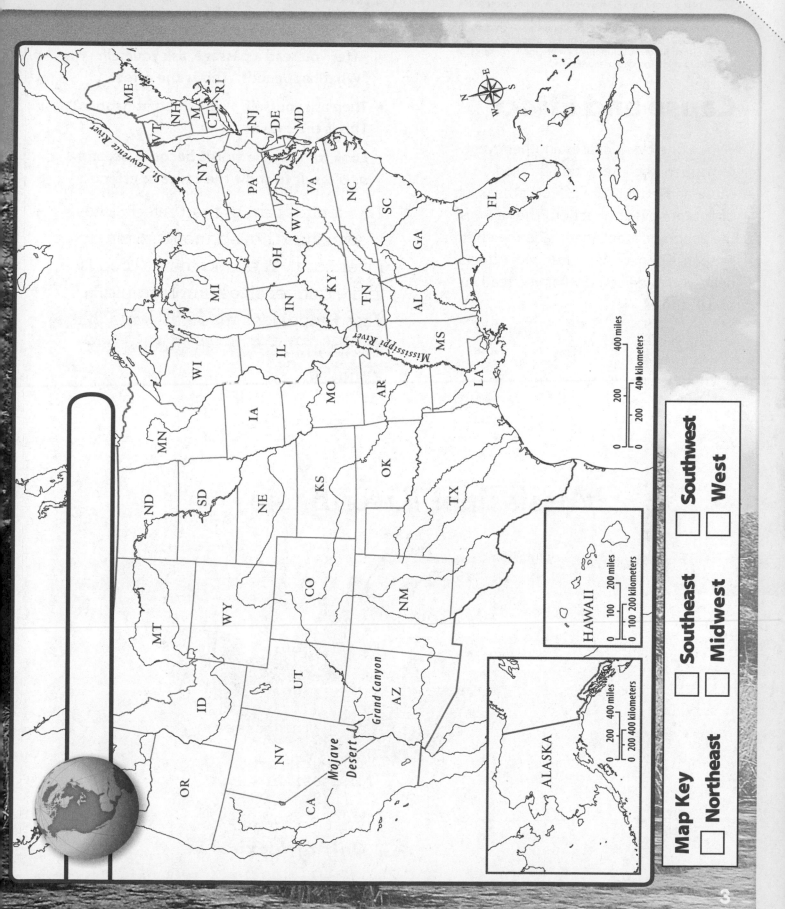

Map Key

☐ Northeast
☐ Southeast
☐ Midwest
☐ Southwest
☐ West

Common Core Standards
RI.3: Explain the relationships or interactions between two or more individuals, events, ideas, or concepts in a historical, scientific, or technical text based on specific information in the text. **RI.5:** Compare and contrast the overall structure (e.g., chronology, comparison, cause/effect, problem/solution) of events, ideas, concepts, or information in two or more texts.

Cause and Effect

When one event causes another event to happen, the interaction is called cause-and-effect. The effect is the result of another event or action. The cause is the action or event that made the effect happen. Connecting causes with effects helps you understand what you read in social studies.

Cause

Effect

LEARN IT

To identify cause and effect:

- After you read a passage, ask yourself, "What happened?" This is the effect.

- Then ask yourself, "Why did that happen?" This is the cause.

- Look for the clue words *because, so,* and *as a result* to show the cause or effect.

The central part of the United States is sometimes called the Mississippi River Basin. The land in this area is fertile and receives ample rainfall. These conditions make the land of the Mississippi River Basin excellent for farming.

Mississippi River Basin

Lake Itasca

Missouri

Upper Mississippi

Ohio

Arkansas Red-White

Tennessee

Lower Mississippi

Delta

Gulf of Mexico

TRY IT

Use the graphic organizer below to keep track of causes and effects.
Fill in the cause and effect from the passage on page 4.

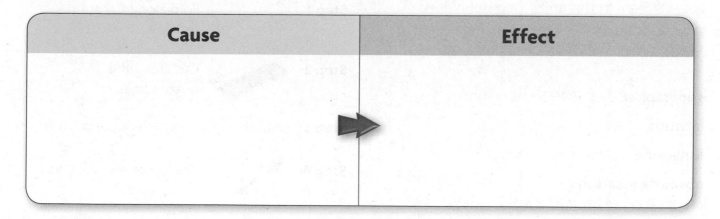

Cause	Effect

APPLY IT

- Review the steps for identifying cause and effect.

- Read the passage below. Then circle the cause and underline the effect.

As water flows over land, it wears away soil and rock in a process called erosion. Over many millions of years, the waters of the Colorado River wore away soil and rock in the desert of northwestern Arizona. This formed the Grand Canyon—a natural wonder that draws tourists and adventurers from all over the world.

© Corbis

The Grand Canyon ▶

Words to Know

Common Core Standards
RI.4 Determine the meaning of general academic and domain-specific words and phrases in a text relevant to a grade 5 topic or subject area.

The list below shows some important words you will learn in this unit. Their definitions can be found on the next page. Read the words.

geographer (jee • AWG • ruh • fuhr)

latitude (LA • tuh • tood)

longitude (LAHN • juh • tood)

absolute location
   (ab • soh • LOOT loh • KAY • shuhn)

relative location
   (REH • luh • tihv loh • KAY • shuhn)

contiguous (kuhn • TIH • gyuh • wuhs)

territory (TEHR • uh • tawr • ee)

canyon (KAN • yuhn)

The **Foldable** on the next page will help you learn these important words. Follow the steps below to make your Foldable.

Step 1   Fold along the solid red line.

Step 2   Cut along the dotted lines.

Step 3 Read the words and their definitions.

Step 4   Complete the activities on each tab.

Step 5 Look at the back of your Foldable. Choose ONE of these activities for each word to help you remember its meaning:

- Draw a picture of the word.
- Write a description of the word.
- Write how the word is related to something you know.

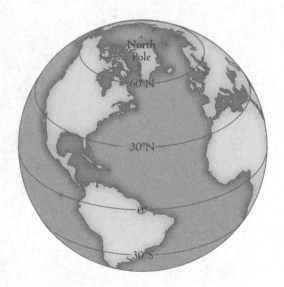

▲ Lines of Latitude

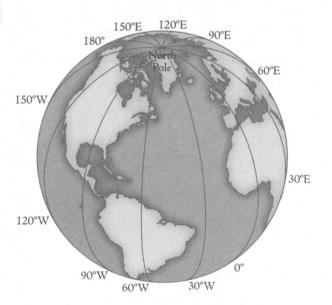

▲ Lines of Longitude

	FOLD	

A **geographer** is someone who studies geography.

Write the root word of *geographer*.

_____ _____

Latitude is an imaginary line on Earth that goes from east to west and shows a location's distance from the Equator.

Circle the key words in the definition of *latitude*. Write those words here:

_____ _____

Longitude is an imaginary line on Earth that goes from north to south and shows a location's distance from the Prime Meridian.

Underline two key words in the definition of *longitude*. Write those words here:

_____ _____

The exact location of a place is its **absolute location**.

Use *absolute location* in a sentence.

_____

_____

The location of a place in relation to other landmarks is its **relative location**.

Circle the words or phrases that can be used to describe *relative location*.

near   across from   at

on   next to   by

Contiguous means to be touching or connected in an unbroken series.

The opposite of *contiguous* is *noncontiguous*. Explain what it means.

A **territory** is an area of land controlled by a nation.

Write the plural form of *territory*.

A **canyon** is a deep valley with steep sides.

Write the definition of a *canyon* in your own words.

geographer	geographer
CUT HERE	
latitude	latitude
longitude	longitude
absolute location	absolute location
relative location	relative location
contiguous	contiguous
territory	territory
canyon	canyon

Primary and Secondary Sources

Learn about U.S. history through primary and secondary sources. Primary sources are written or created by someone who witnessed an event. Secondary sources are written or created by someone after an event occurs. Both types of sources teach us about people, places, and events.

Graphs

Graphs show many different types of information. They can show changes over time, differences between groups, or the way parts fit into a whole. A graph can be either a primary or a secondary source. If a graph is made at the time data is collected, it's a primary source. If a graph is made years later with old data, it's a secondary source.

A graph is one tool that you can use to study geography. The graph on this page shows information about the **climate** of a location. Climate is the weather in an area over a long period of time. The climate of an area is a part of its geography. This graph combines a line graph showing the average monthly temperature and a bar graph representing the average amount of precipitation, or rainfall, each month.

 Document-Based Questions

Study the graph. Then complete the following activities:

- In one color, circle the part of the graph that tells how wet it was in March.

- In another color, circle the part of the graph that tells how warm or cold it is throughout the year.

- Put a box around the part of the graph that tells in what years the data was collected.

Climate of Jacksonville, 1971–2000

Legend: Precipitation — Temperature

Precipitation (in.) scale: 0–10
Temperature (°F) scale: 0–100
Months: JAN FEB MAR APR MAY JUN JUL AUG SEP OCT NOV DEC

Month

netw⚡rks
There's More Online!
- Skill Builders
- Resource Library

The World in Spatial Terms

? Essential Question

How do we show location? What do you think?

_____

_____

_____

_____

_____

_____

_____

Words To Know

Write a synonym for each of the words below.

*intersect _____

relative location

_____

absolute location

_____

The Basics of Geography

You've probably looked at a globe or map before. Globes are models of Earth. Maps are flat representations of Earth. Since Earth isn't flat, size and distance on a map sometimes are distorted, or no longer accurate. Both maps and globes use a grid system to help us locate specific locations on Earth. This grid is a series of **intersecting** vertical and horizontal lines.

Draw a map of your bedroom from above. Include a compass rose, map key, and simple grid system (ABC/123). Write two questions about your map and have a partner use the map to find the answers.

1. _____

2. _____

Parallels and Meridians

Long ago, **geographers**, or people who study geography, created a grid system of intersecting lines to help us find places more easily on maps. Lines of **latitude** go from east to west. Lines of **longitude** run north to south.

Lines of latitude are called parallels. They are an equal distance apart. These lines are numbered from 0 degrees (°) at the Equator to 90° North at the North Pole and 90° South at the South Pole.

Lines of longitude, or meridians, circle Earth from pole to pole. These lines measure distance from the Prime Meridian, at 0° longitude. Meridians are not parallel. Latitude and longitude can be used to make observations about location and generalizations about climate.

Location, Location, Location!

When giving directions, you probably use what is called **relative location**. This is the location of a place in relation to landmarks.

Absolute location, on the other hand, is a very specific way of telling where a place is. Absolute location is the exact location of any place on Earth. Each location has a unique number where one line of latitude intersects a line of longitude. Each spot on Earth has an absolute location.

Map Skills

1. Label the Prime Meridian, the Equator, and the unlabeled continents.

2. Highlight one line of longitude.

3. Circle the degrees for two lines of latitude.

4. What continent lies southeast of Africa? _____

5. Place a star on the continent that is west of North America.

11

Geography and Technology

Maps have long helped people solve problems at the local, state, and national levels. Today, people also use new technologies. One of these technologies is the Geographic Information System (GIS). GIS uses data to manage, analyze, and share geographic information.

GIS helps people analyze and interpret geographic relationships, patterns, and trends in different ways. This geographic information is shared through maps, graphs, and charts. The information helps people solve problems.

How do people use this information? Take, for example, a fire station that wants to know the fastest emergency routes. Firefighters can see which roads to avoid at busy times of day by placing a map layer showing traffic patterns over a city map. Businesses also use GIS. They might, for example, use GIS to layer data about population, housing, and taxes to find the best location for a new store.

The Global Positioning System (GPS) is a GIS that uses radio signals from satellites to find the absolute location of places on Earth. GPS was originally used by the U.S. military for navigation, map-making, and guiding missiles. Today, many people use GPS devices instead of traditional maps when traveling by car. Cell phone technology even allows people to use GPS when traveling by foot!

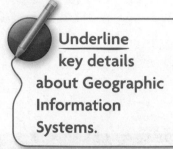

Underline key details about Geographic Information Systems.

GIS combines data to provide information that can be viewed one layer at a time, or all together (below left). This 3-dimensional physical map shows the bottom of the ocean off the west coast of Central America (below right).

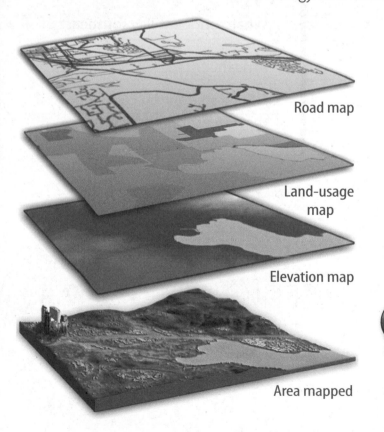

Road map

Land-usage map

Elevation map

Area mapped

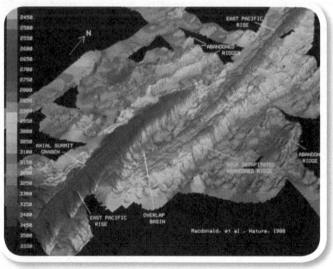

© Dr. Ken MacDonald / Photo Researchers, Inc.

Look at the maps on the next page. Imagine that you and your partner work for the state government. Your job is to analyze GIS data and decide which counties are in need of more elementary schools. Base your decision on population and the number of existing schools.

Putting GIS to Use

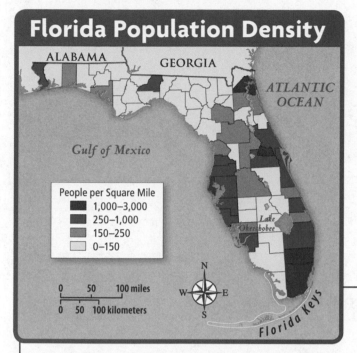

Florida Population Density

ALABAMA
GEORGIA
ATLANTIC OCEAN
Gulf of Mexico
Lake Okeechobee

People per Square Mile
- 1,000–3,000
- 250–1,000
- 150–250
- 0–150

0   50   100 miles
0   50   100 kilometers

N W E S

Florida Keys

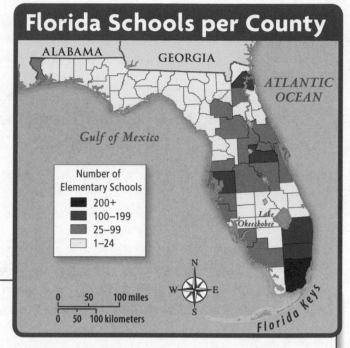

Florida Schools per County

ALABAMA
GEORGIA
ATLANTIC OCEAN
Gulf of Mexico
Lake Okeechobee

Number of Elementary Schools
- 200+
- 100–199
- 25–99
- 1–24

0   50   100 miles
0   50   100 kilometers

N W E S

Florida Keys

1. Create a bar graph for each map showing the number of counties that fall within each data range. Use the graph frames at the bottom of the page.

2. How many counties have the highest number of elementary schools?

_____

3. How many counties have between 25 and

99 elementary schools? _____

4. How many counties have the largest

populations? _____

5. How many counties have both the largest populations and 100 or more elementary schools?

_____

6. Place stars on the counties you think should receive new elementary schools. Explain how you made your decision.

_____

_____

_____

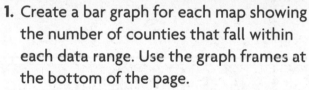

Solve Local Problems with GIS

Suppose you are a city planner responsible for choosing a location for a new park in Anytown, State. Use the GIS data below to help you choose the location.

How does Anytown's **population** affect where the park should be placed?

Find locations of **available land** in areas that make the park easy to access. Describe the area of each area in relation to the population.

Look at the **geographic features** of the available locations. How do they affect the type of park that can be built?

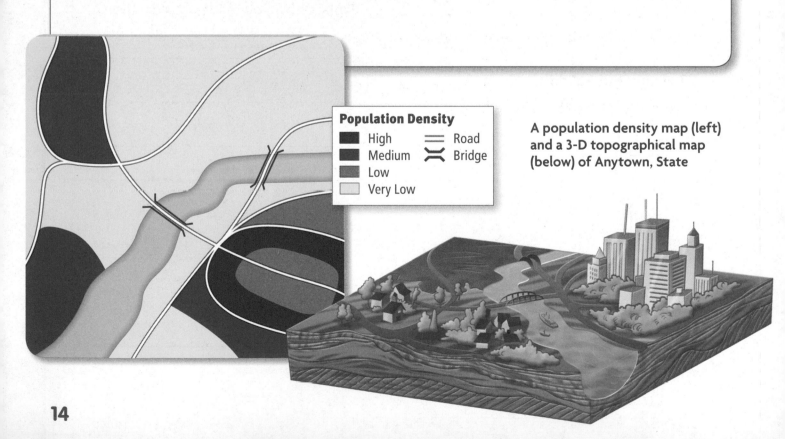

Population Density

■ High	═ Road
■ Medium	✕ Bridge
■ Low	
□ Very Low	

A population density map (left) and a 3-D topographical map (below) of Anytown, State

Once you have analyzed the GIS data and chosen a location, draw a map of the city that includes the new park. Add a title, compass rose, and map key.

Map Key

Explain why you chose this site for the new park. Be sure to explain how the GIS data influenced your decision.

_____

_____

Lesson **1**

 Essential Question   How do we show location?

_____

_____

_____

Go back to _Show As You Go!_ on pages 2–3.

Geography of the United States

? Essential Question

How do we describe location?
What do you think?

_____

_____

_____

_____

_____

Words To Know

Write the definition of each word in your own words.

*influence _____

_____

contiguous _____

_____

navigable _____

_____

tributary _____

_____

Think about the area where you live. Are there any hills, plains, lakes, or rivers nearby? Is there a bay, gulf, or ocean? These are all physical features. You may not think about it a lot, but geography affects how your family lives. For example, people living along a lake may fish for a living. They may also boat or swim for fun.

Identify a physical feature near your home. Then explain how it **influences** your daily life. Draw a picture of this physical feature.

Physical Feature: _____

How it affects my life: _____

_____

_____

_____

_____

_____

_____

The United States

Later in this lesson you will learn about the geographic regions of the United States. But first, let's find out more about our country in general. The United States is the world's third-largest country in size. Forty-eight of the country's fifty states stretch across the middle of North America. Two states lie elsewhere. Alaska lies in the northwestern part of the continent. Hawaii is in the Pacific Ocean.

The western coast of the United States faces the Pacific Ocean. The eastern coast faces the Atlantic Ocean. In the north, the very cold Arctic Ocean borders Alaska. The southern United States enjoys the warm waters of the Gulf of Mexico.

The states located in the central part of North America are **contiguous**, or connected by shared borders. Alaska and Hawaii don't share a border with any other states, so they are noncontiguous. The United States is divided into five regions: the Northeast, Southeast, Midwest, Southwest, and West. Alaska and Hawaii are considered part of the West region.

U.S. Territories

The United States has several **territories**, or areas of land that are under its control and protection. These territories are not part of the country. Puerto Rico and the U.S. Virgin Islands are territories in the Caribbean, southeast of Florida. Guam and American Samoa are territories in the Pacific Ocean, west of Hawaii.

U.S. Territories

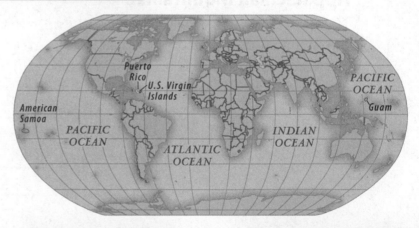

Map and Globe Skills

Locate and circle Puerto Rico, the U.S. Virgin Islands, Guam, and American Samoa on the world map.

Lowlands and Highlands

As you read, underline the details that describe where each geographic region is located. Circle details that describe the major physical features of each geographic region.

Many different landforms shape North America. These physical features create geographic regions in the United States. Read about these physical features. You will later learn about the geographic regions they create.

Atlantic Coastal Plain

A broad area of lowland called the Atlantic Coastal Plain runs along the Atlantic coast. In the northeastern areas of the plain, the soil is thick and rocky. Farming is limited here. However, an area called the Piedmont has rich soil. The Piedmont lies just east of the Appalachian Mountains.

Appalachian Mountains

The Appalachian Mountains are west of the Atlantic Coastal Plain. These highlands run from eastern Canada to Alabama and separate the East Coast from the Midwest. The Appalachians include several mountain ranges, including the Blue Ridge, the Great Smoky, and the Allegheny mountains.

The Gulf Coastal Plain

Another lowland, the Gulf Coastal Plain, lies along the Gulf of Mexico. It is wider than the Atlantic Coastal Plain. Soil in this region is richer than in the Atlantic Coastal Plain and is excellent for farming. Cotton is a major crop of the Gulf Coastal Plain.

Central Lowlands

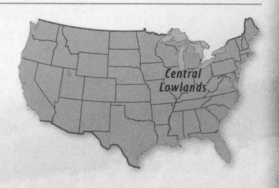

West of the Appalachians is an area full of grassy hills, rolling flatlands, thick forests, and rich farmland. This area is called the Central Lowlands. The Great Lakes, the Mississippi River, and other waterways influence life here.

Great Plains

West of the Mississippi stretch the Great Plains. Here the land begins to rise. At the river's edge, the land is relatively low. Going west, over many miles, the elevation rises quite a bit. Most of the Great Plains region consists of prairies, or flat, rolling lands covered with grass. Here, farmers grow crops and ranchers raise cattle. The Great Plains are also rich in resources such as coal, oil, and natural gas.

Waterways, Mountains, and Plateaus

Highlight text that describes where each geographic feature is located. Then complete the map below by adding the missing lake and river names.

The United States has many amazing physical wonders, such as the Great Lakes, Rocky Mountains, and Grand Canyon. These physical features shape life in the country.

The Mississippi River

North America has many lakes and rivers. Many of these rivers are **navigable**, or wide and deep enough to allow the passage of ships. One of these rivers, the Mississippi, begins in Minnesota where it is too narrow for ships. As it heads south to the Gulf of Mexico, it enlarges and becomes navigable.

The central part of the United States is sometimes called the Mississippi River Basin. The land in this area is fertile and receives ample rainfall, making it excellent for farming. Over one million square miles of land in this basin drains off into the Mississippi and its **tributaries**. A tributary is a river that flows into another river.

Mississippi River Basin

Lake Itasca

Missouri

Upper Mississippi

Ohio

Arkansas Red-White

Tennessee

Lower Mississippi

Delta

Gulf of Mexico

The Great Lakes and St. Lawrence Seaway

Giant blankets of ice called glaciers carved out the Great Lakes about 10,000 years ago. Lakes Huron, Ontario, Michigan, Erie, and Superior are located in the central part of North America and are the world's largest group of freshwater lakes. Lake Superior is the largest of the Great Lakes, while Lake Erie is the smallest.

The Great Lakes drain into the St. Lawrence River, which flows to the Atlantic Ocean. The St. Lawrence was unnavigable due to rapids, waterfalls, and uneven water levels. A series of canals and a system of locks have made the river navigable. A lock is a part of a canal where water is pumped in or out in order to raise or lower ships.

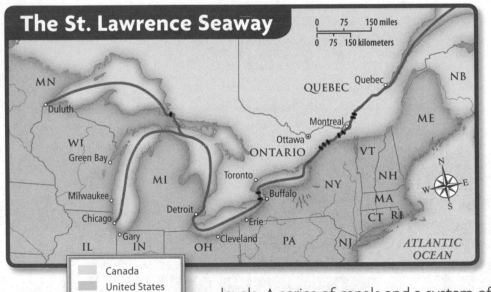

The St. Lawrence Seaway

0   75   150 miles
0   75   150 kilometers

MN
Duluth
WI
Green Bay
MI
Milwaukee
Chicago
Gary
IL   IN
OH
Cleveland
Detroit
Erie
Buffalo
Toronto
ONTARIO
Ottawa
Montreal
QUEBEC
Quebec
NB
ME
VT
NH
NY
MA   RI
CT
PA
NJ
ATLANTIC OCEAN

Canada
United States
St. Lawrence Seaway
○ City
━ Lock

Western Mountain Ranges

West of the Great Plains is a group of mountain ranges. The Rocky Mountains begin in Alaska and run south to New Mexico. The Rockies are younger and higher than the Appalachians.

Between the Rockies and the Pacific Coast are the Pacific Coastal ranges. These include several smaller mountain chains, including the Cascade and Sierra Nevada mountains.

Highlight the text that describes where each geographic feature is located.

The Continental Divide

The Continental Divide runs along the Rocky Mountains. The Divide separates the flow of water in North America. East of the Divide, rivers drain into the Arctic Ocean, the Atlantic Ocean, and the Gulf of Mexico. To the west, rivers flow into the Pacific Ocean and the Gulf of California.

LOVELAND PASS
ELEVATION 11,990
CONTINENTAL DIVIDE
ATLANTIC   PACIFIC

West   East

River

The Plateaus and Canyons

Between the Pacific Ocean and the Rockies is a stretch of dry basins and high plateaus. The Mojave Desert makes up a large part of this area. The Mojave is located in southeastern California, southwestern Utah, southern Nevada, and western Arizona.

In Northwestern Arizona, rivers have worn through rock to create magnificent **canyons**, or deep valleys with steep sides. One of the most beautiful is the Grand Canyon of the Colorado River.

(l) Sigrid Dauth/Stock Photography/Alamy. (r) © Corbis

21

The Northeast

Now that you've learned about the physical features of the United States, let's learn more about the regions. The Northeast region includes eleven states and the nation's capital, Washington, D.C. The region has two areas: New England and the Middle Atlantic States. The Appalachian Mountains, the Piedmont, and the Atlantic Coastal Plain run through the Northeast.

Image Ideas / PictureQuest

Use the information on pages 16–21 and the Atlas to label the following on the map.

Physical Features	States	Capitals
☐ Atlantic Coastal Plain	☐ Rhode Island	☐ Hartford, CT
	☐ Maryland	☐ Montpelier, VT
☐ Atlantic Ocean	☐ New Hampshire	☐ Harrisburg, PA
	☐ New Jersey	☐ Albany, NY
	☐ Delaware	☐ Augusta, ME
		☐ Boston, MA

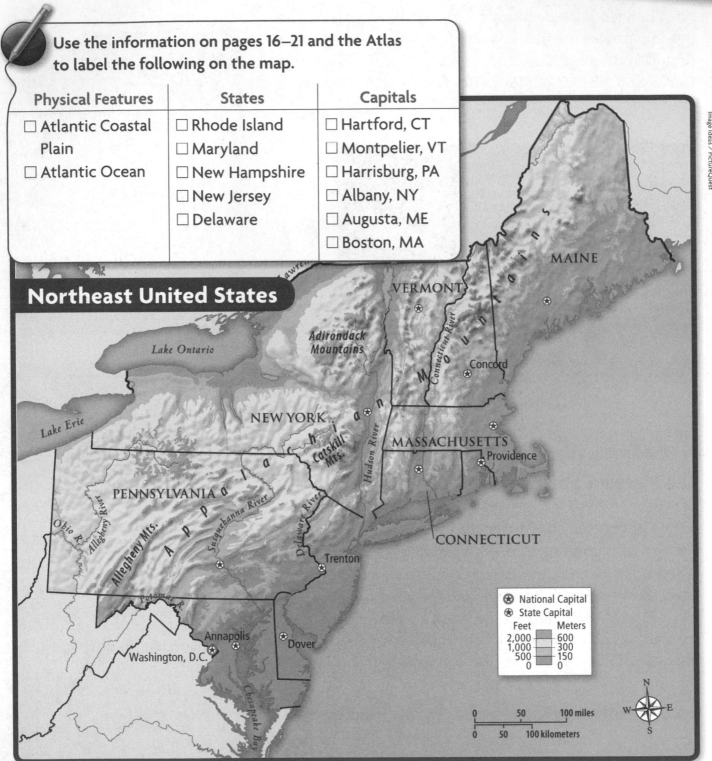

Northeast United States

Lake Ontario
Lake Erie
Adirondack Mountains
Lawrence
VERMONT
MAINE
Concord
NEW YORK
Ohio R.
Allegheny River
PENNSYLVANIA
Allegheny Mts.
Susquehanna River
Catskill Mts.
Hudson River
Delaware River
MASSACHUSETTS
Providence
CONNECTICUT
Trenton
Potomac R.
Annapolis
Dover
Washington, D.C.
Chesapeake Bay

National Capital
State Capital

Feet	Meters
2,000	600
1,000	300
500	150
0	0

0   50   100 miles
0   50   100 kilometers

N W E S

The Southeast

The twelve states of the Southeast include Florida. In this region, part of the Atlantic and Gulf Coastal Plains wrap around the southern end of the Appalachians. Five southeastern states border the Atlantic Ocean. Four states line the Gulf of Mexico.

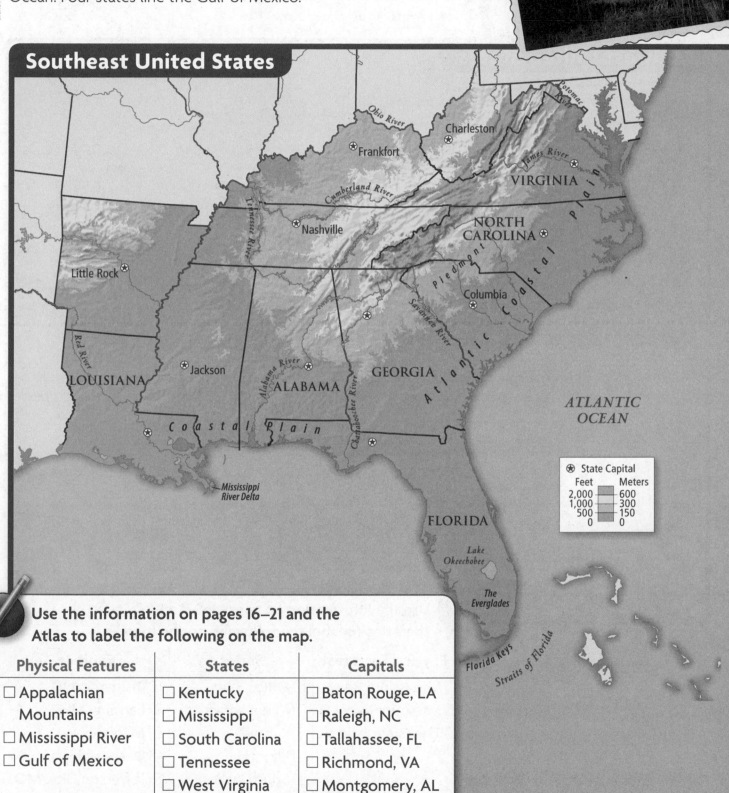

Southeast United States

Ohio River

Charleston

Frankfort

VIRGINIA

Potomac River

James River

Cumberland River

Tennessee River

Nashville

NORTH CAROLINA

Piedmont

Little Rock

Columbia

Savannah River

Red River

Jackson

Alabama River

ALABAMA

Chattahoochee River

GEORGIA

Atlantic Coastal Plain

ATLANTIC OCEAN

LOUISIANA

C o a s t a l P l a i n

Mississippi River Delta

FLORIDA

Lake Okeechobee

The Everglades

Florida Keys

Straits of Florida

State Capital

Feet		Meters
2,000		600
1,000		300
500		150
0		0

Use the information on pages 16–21 and the Atlas to label the following on the map.

Physical Features	States	Capitals
☐ Appalachian Mountains	☐ Kentucky	☐ Baton Rouge, LA
	☐ Mississippi	☐ Raleigh, NC
☐ Mississippi River	☐ South Carolina	☐ Tallahassee, FL
☐ Gulf of Mexico	☐ Tennessee	☐ Richmond, VA
	☐ West Virginia	☐ Montgomery, AL
	☐ Arkansas	☐ Atlanta, GA

23

The Midwest

The Midwest is a region of plains. The twelve states in this region experience extreme weather conditions. From spring through autumn, thunderstorms and tornadoes are a constant danger. During winter, this region experiences low temperatures and snow.

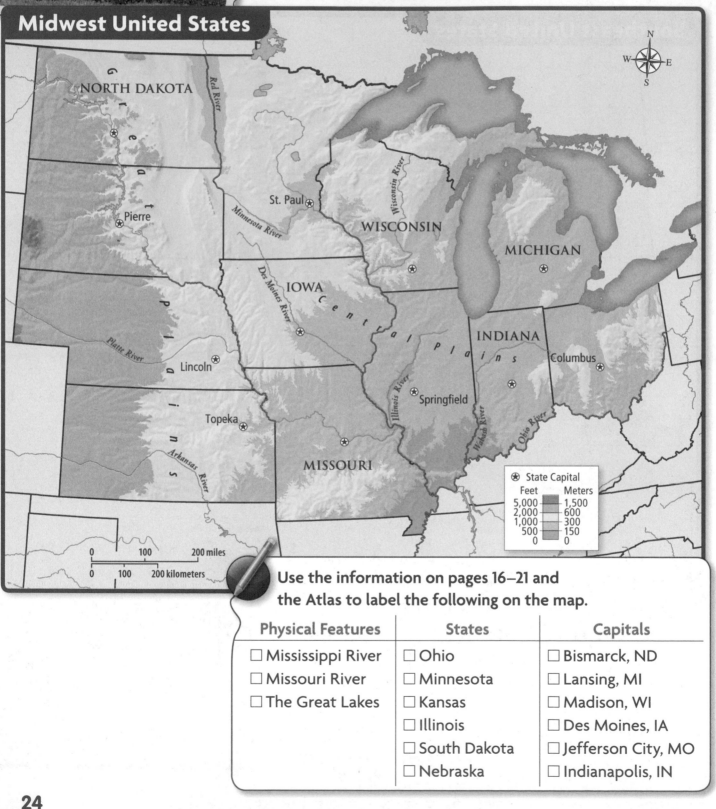

Midwest United States

Use the information on pages 16–21 and the Atlas to label the following on the map.

Physical Features	States	Capitals
☐ Mississippi River	☐ Ohio	☐ Bismarck, ND
☐ Missouri River	☐ Minnesota	☐ Lansing, MI
☐ The Great Lakes	☐ Kansas	☐ Madison, WI
	☐ Illinois	☐ Des Moines, IA
	☐ South Dakota	☐ Jefferson City, MO
	☐ Nebraska	☐ Indianapolis, IN

The Southwest

The Southwest has only four states. The Rio Grande separates this part of the United States from Mexico. The region also includes the southern end of the Rocky Mountains.

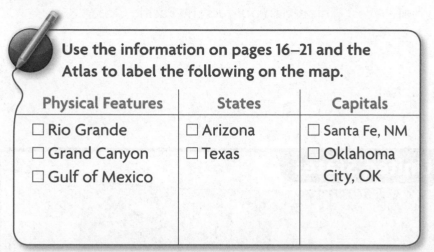

Use the information on pages 16–21 and the Atlas to label the following on the map.

Physical Features	States	Capitals
☐ Rio Grande	☐ Arizona	☐ Santa Fe, NM
☐ Grand Canyon	☐ Texas	☐ Oklahoma City, OK
☐ Gulf of Mexico		

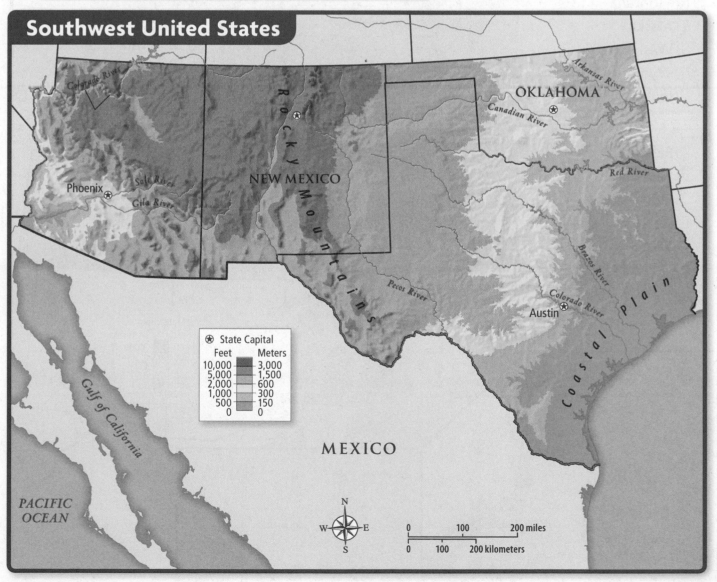

Southwest United States

The West

The West region includes eleven states. Two states, Alaska and Hawaii, do not share borders with any other states. The Rocky Mountains run north and south through the West. This region borders the Pacific Ocean.

Use pages 16–21 and the Atlas to label the following on the map.

Physical Features
- ☐ Pacific Ocean

States
- ☐ Colorado
- ☐ Montana
- ☐ Alaska
- ☐ Washington
- ☐ Wyoming
- ☐ Idaho

Capitals
- ☐ Salem, OR
- ☐ Sacramento, CA
- ☐ Honolulu, HI
- ☐ Carson City, NV
- ☐ Salt Lake City, UT

West United States

Draw a map of an imaginary country that includes states, capitals, and at least five physical features similar to those on pages 17–21. Don't forget to include a map key and title!

Lesson 2

Essential Question **How do we describe location?**

Go back to ***Show As You Go!*** on pages 2–3.

networks There's More Online!
- Games
- Assessment

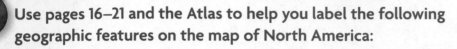
Use pages 16–21 and the Atlas to help you label the following geographic features on the map of North America:

1. **Rocky Mountains**   4. **Great Lakes**   7. **Lake Okeechobee**
2. **Appalachian Mountains**   5. **Great Plains**   8. **Mojave Desert**
3. **Mississippi River**   6. **Rio Grande**

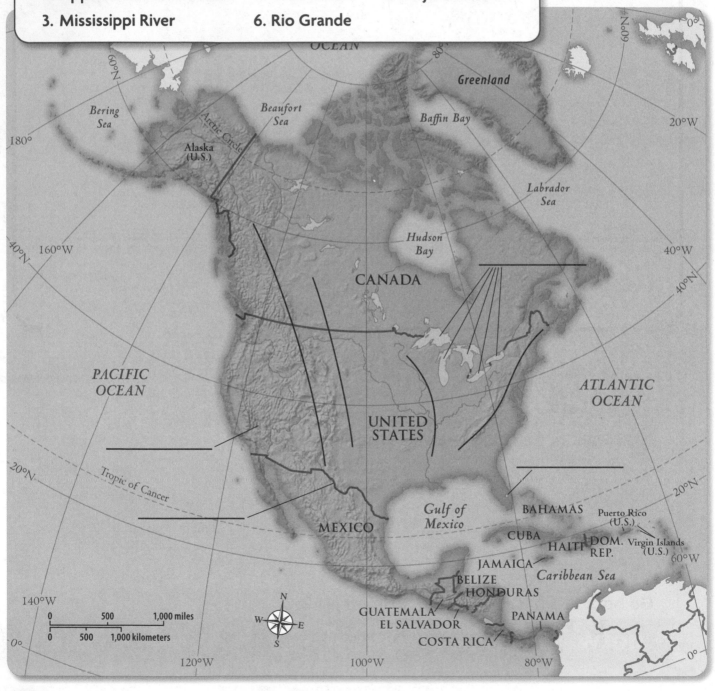

BIG IDEA

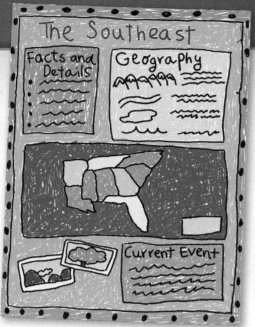

Unit Project

With a team, you will create a poster featuring one region of the United States. Before you begin, look back at pages 2–3 to review your notes and brainstorm ideas. Do additional research in the library or on the Internet to learn more about your region. Read the list below to see what you should include on your poster. Check off the tasks you have completed.

Your poster should include...   **Yes, it does!**

accurate facts and details about the region ☐

the major geographic features of the region ☐

all states and capitals in the region ☐

a map of the region with a map key ☐

images representing the region ☐

an explanation of a specific current event in the region ☐

few errors in spelling, grammar, and punctuation ☐

Think about the Big Idea

BIG IDEA Location affects the way people live.

What did you learn in this unit that helps you understand the BIG IDEA?

_____

_____

_____

The Climate of the United States

By Gabriel Sanchez

Climate is the weather in a place over a number of years. The weather of a place includes its wind pattern, temperature, and amount of precipitation, or rain and snow, that falls. Climate is mainly determined by latitude. Other factors, such as mountains or bodies of water, also influence climate.

The movement of air and water helps create Earth's climates. The sun's heat is moved around the globe by streaming waters and moving air. In the ocean, the moving streams of water are called *currents*.

Most of the United States is located in a *temperate* climate, which has changing seasons and mild weather that is neither too hot nor too cold. For example, the Northeast experiences snowy winters, rainy springs, and hot, wet summers. The Southeast has mild temperatures due to regular rainfall. The climate in the West varies with elevation.

The warmest parts of the country are nearest the Equator. The air and water here are heated and travel from the tropics toward Earth's poles. Areas near the tropics, such as Florida and Hawaii, are warm all year. The Gulf Stream is one of the strongest, warmest ocean currents in the world. It flows north from the Gulf of Mexico through the cool Atlantic Ocean.

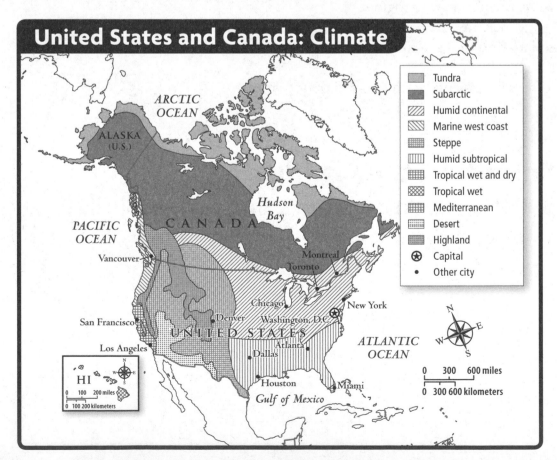

United States and Canada: Climate

1 What is the theme of this article?

Ⓐ Climate influences the movement of air and water.

Ⓑ The United States has one climate.

Ⓒ Currents have the greatest influence on climate.

Ⓓ Many factors influence the climate of the United States.

2 Which detail from the article helps show the reasons why areas near the tropics are warm all year?

Ⓕ Frequent rainfall causes mild temperatures.

Ⓖ The air and water near the tropics are heated.

Ⓗ The sun's heat is moved around the globe.

Ⓘ Climate in the West varies by elevation.

3 The mild temperatures of the Southeast are created by

Ⓐ ocean currents.

Ⓑ moving streams of air.

Ⓒ regular rainfall.

Ⓓ elevation.

4 By reading the article and looking at the map, you can tell that the climate of Florida is affected by

Ⓕ the Pacific Ocean.

Ⓖ the Gulf Stream.

Ⓗ elevation.

Ⓘ its location in the Northeast.

5 Read these sentences from the article.

> **For example, the Northeast experiences snowy winters, rainy springs, and hot, wet summers. The Southeast has mild temperatures due to regular rainfall.**

What does the word *mild* mean?

Ⓐ humid

Ⓑ mostly cold

Ⓒ not too hot or too cold

Ⓓ never the same

6 Which word means *changing seasons and mild weather*?

Ⓕ elevation

Ⓖ climate

Ⓗ current

Ⓘ temperate

Native Peoples of North America

BIG IDEA Culture influences the way people live.

Native Americans thrived in North America long before Europeans arrived. Each group developed unique ways of life based on the place and time in which they lived. In this unit, you will learn about the lives and cultures of Native Americans in different geographic regions of North America. As you read, think about how each culture was influenced by the environment.

NATIVE AMERICAN EXHIBIT ➡

networks

connected.mcgraw-hill.com
● Skill Builders
● Resource Library

Show As You Go! After you read each lesson, draw something that represents a cultural aspect from that region in one of the display cases or frames. Be sure to label each of your exhibit pieces. You will use this information to help you complete a project at the end of the unit.

Reading Skill

Common Core Standards
RI.5: Compare and contrast the overall structure (e.g., chronology, comparison, cause/effect, problem/solution) of events ideas, concepts, or information in two or more texts.

Compare and Contrast

When you compare, you notice how things are alike. When you contrast, you look at how they differ. Comparing and contrasting helps you understand the people and events you read about in social studies.

LEARN IT

As you read, do the following to compare and contrast:

- **To compare two things, note how they are similar. The words** *like, same,* **and** *both* **are clues to similarities.**

- **To contrast two things, note how they are different. The words** *different, however,* **and** *unlike* **show differences.**

> **This explains how the towns were different. <u>Underline</u> other differences between the towns.**

> **This explains how the towns were similar.**

To protect themselves from enemies, the Creek formed the Creek Confederacy. They divided Creek towns into war towns (red) and peace towns (white). Red towns declared war, planned battles, and held meetings with enemy groups. White towns passed laws and held prisoners. During periods of war, however, even the people in the peace towns joined in the fighting.

A meeting of the
Creek Confederacy ▶

34

TRY IT

Fill in the diagram below to compare and contrast the information from the passage on page 34.

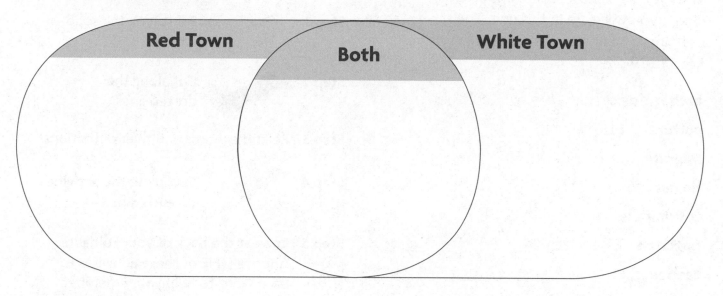

Red Town · Both · White Town

APPLY IT

- Review the steps to compare and contrast in Learn It.
- Read the passage below. <u>Underline</u> sentences that compare similarities among groups. (Circle) sentences that show differences among groups.

In order to survive, the Navajo adapted ideas and practices from their Pueblo neighbors. Unlike the Pueblo, the Navajo built dome-shaped family homes. Like the Pueblo, the Navajo used dry farming to grow crops in the dry land. They also wove cotton to make cloth. However, it is the Navajo who are well known as shepherds. Both the Navajo and the Pueblo are known for their fine silver and turquoise jewelry.

▲ A silver and turquoise ring

Common Core Standards
RI.4: Determine the meaning of general academic and domain-specific words and phrases in a text relevant to a grade 5 topic or subject area.

The list below shows some important words you will learn in this unit. Their definitions can be found on the next page. Read the words.

archaeologist (ahr • kee • AH • luh • jist)

culture (KUHL • chuhr)

migrate (MY • grayt)

hogan (HOH • guhn)

totem pole (TOH • tuhm POHL)

potlatch (PAHT • lach)

teepee (TEE • pee)

longhouse (LAWNG • hows)

The **Foldable** on the next page will help you learn these important words. Follow the steps below to make your Foldable.

Step 1 Fold along the solid red line.

Step 2 Cut along the dotted lines.

Step 3 Read the words and their definitions.

Step 4 Complete the activities on each tab.

Step 5 Look at the back of your Foldable. Choose ONE of these activities for each word to help you remember its meaning:

- Draw a picture of the word.
- Write a description of the word.
- Write how the word is related to something you know.

	FOLD
An **archaeologist** is a scientist who looks for and studies artifacts.	*Archaeologists* are scientists. What other kinds of scientists can you think of?
Culture is a people's way of life.	List two examples of culture. _____ _____
To **migrate** means to move from one place to another.	Write a sentence using the word *migrate*.
A **hogan** is a dome-shaped home that is made of log frames or stick frames that are covered with mud or soil.	Circle two key words in the definition of *hogan* that help you understand the meaning.
A **totem pole** is a tree trunk that is carved with sacred images.	Write the definition of *totem pole* in your own words.
A **potlatch** is a feast in which the guests receive gifts.	Explain the purpose of a potlatch.
A **teepee** is a cone-shaped tent made from animal hides.	Teepees were temporary shelters. Write an antonym, or opposite, for the word *temporary*.
A **longhouse** is a home shared by several related Iroquois families.	Circle the words that belong with *longhouse*. large Iroquois families small Navajo home

archaeologist

archaeologist

CUT HERE

culture

culture

migrate

migrate

hogan

hogan

totem pole

totem pole

potlatch

potlatch

teepee

teepee

longhouse

longhouse

Artifacts

Objects created by humans long ago are called artifacts. Scientists called **archaeologists** study artifacts to learn about how people lived in the past. To understand artifacts, you must know the geography of the area where it was found. You then need to study the design of the artifact. Next, think about how someone might have used it in the past.

In this unit, you will learn about how different Native American groups lived and expressed their cultures. Examine the Anasazi and Mound Builder artifacts on this page. What clues do they give you about each culture?

▲ **Anasazi artifacts**

 DBQ Document-Based Questions

Study the artifacts. Then complete the activities.

1. **Choose an artifact and describe how it was most likely used in the past.**

_____

_____

_____

▲ **Mound Builder artifact**

2. **Imagine that scientists in the future are studying our culture. Draw an artifact from your life that would give them clues about how you live.**

(t) George H.H. Huey / Alamy; (c) Peter Visscher/Getty Images

networks
There's More Online!
● Skill Builders
● Resource Library

Ancient Cultures

? Essential Question

What makes a civilization? What do you think?

_____

_____

_____

_____

_____

_____

_____

_____

Words To Know

Write a number to show how much you know about the meaning of each word.

1 = I have no idea!
2 = I know a little.
3 = I know a lot.

____ *develop

____ civilization

____ slavery

____ empire

____ irrigation

Suppose you lived thousands of years ago. How would you travel? What would you eat? Where would you live?

_____

_____

_____

The First North Americans

Archaeologists study the **cultures** of people from the past. Culture is the way of life, including the customs, beliefs, and language of a group of people. The research of archaeologists helps us understand what life was like long ago.

There is some debate about how ancient peoples came to North America. Many Native Americans believe that they have always been here. Archaeologists believe that they came to North America from Asia. Tens of thousands of years ago, there was a period of cold weather called the Ice Age. During this time a land bridge formed, connecting Asia and the Americas. Archaeologists believe ancient peoples followed the animals they were hunting across this land bridge. Some archaeologists think these people reached the Americas between 15,000 and 30,000 years ago. Some people may have traveled by boat along the coast as well.

◄ Archaeologists use special tools when uncovering artifacts.

Carlos Carrion/Sygma/Corbis

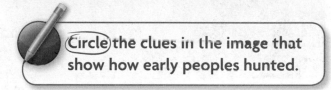
Circle facts and underline opinions on pages 40–41 about how ancient peoples came to the Americas.

The Growth of Civilizations

As the Ice Age ended, Earth's climate warmed. Many animals couldn't survive in warm weather. As food sources disappeared, people had to figure out how to get food in order to survive.

People in Mesoamerica began farming around 5500 B.C. Mesoamerica is the part of North America that stretches from Mexico to Costa Rica. Here, people grew three crops: maize (or corn), beans, and squash.

Farming changed life in Mesoamerica. Hunting wasn't a priority anymore. With more time, people were able to do other things such as trade, build, and create art. Over time, large societies **developed** and became **civilizations**. A civilization is a culture with systems of government, education, and religion.

▲ Hunter-gatherers attack an Ice Age mastodon.

Circle the clues in the image that show how early peoples hunted.

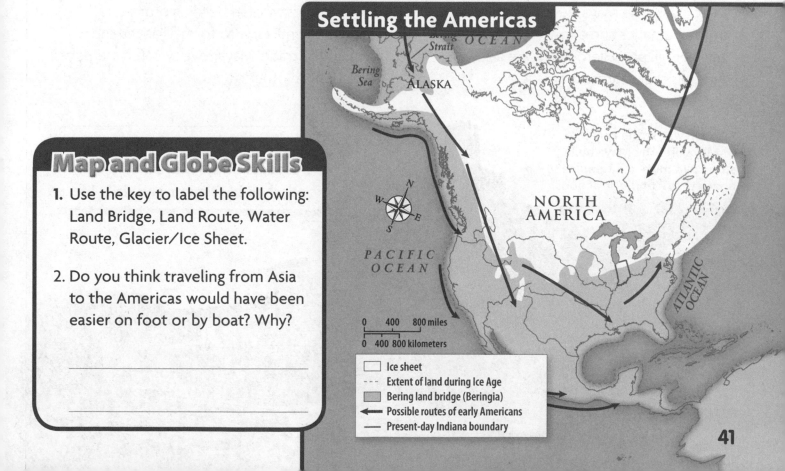

Settling the Americas

Map and Globe Skills

1. Use the key to label the following: Land Bridge, Land Route, Water Route, Glacier/Ice Sheet.

2. Do you think traveling from Asia to the Americas would have been easier on foot or by boat? Why?

_____

_____

OCEAN
Bering Strait
Bering Sea
ALASKA
NORTH AMERICA
PACIFIC OCEAN
ATLANTIC OCEAN

0   400   800 miles
0   400 800 kilometers

☐ Ice sheet
- - - Extent of land during Ice Age
☐ Bering land bridge (Beringia)
← Possible routes of early Americans
— Present-day Indiana boundary

© Art Archive

41

The Maya

The development of farming in Mesoamerica led to the growth of some of the first North American civilizations. The Maya were one such group. In about 2500 B.C., the Maya arose in southeastern Mexico and Central America. From about A.D. 250 to 900, they became a powerful civilization. Read about their culture and ways of life.

The Maya
■ Maya lands, A.D. 300–A.D. 900

0   250   500 miles
0   250   500 kilometers

Maya scientists created a 365-day calendar to help with farming and predicting events such as eclipses. The Maya developed a system of mathematics and a form of writing we call hieroglyphs. Hieroglyphs are a series of symbols that represent words.

Maya cities were ruled by kings who claimed to have been chosen by Maya gods. Maya leaders oversaw large building projects and led the military. To form alliances and strengthen trade, Maya royalty often married royalty from other cities.

Religion was at the center of Maya life. The Maya built stone pyramids and temples to honor their hundreds of gods.

Underline different cultural aspects of the Maya including food, shelter, religion, and daily life.

The Decline of the Maya

Maya cities such as Chichén Itzá, Tikal, and Copan had populations of several thousand people. Over time, the population outgrew the food supply. People moved out of the cities in search of food. The Maya lost power by A.D. 900, but the people did not disappear. Today more than 6 million Maya live in Mexico, Belize, and Guatemala.

A popular game in Mesoamerica was a ballgame called pok-a-tok. Let me tell you all about it!

This was a dangerous game! Check out all of the protective stuff we had to wear!

The goal of the game was to hit a ball through a stone ring. We passed the ball by using a stick called a manopla, by using our bodies, or by kicking it.

Games drew large crowds. We played to please our gods. Winners were rewarded with clothing and riches. Many times, the losing team was sacrificed to our gods.

Label the pok-a-tok player. Write the number for each item on the lines.
1. **Yugito:** knee guard
2. **Headdress:** head protection
3. **Yoke:** hip protector
4. **Manopla:** used to bat the ball

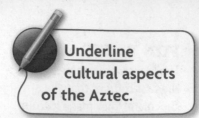
The Aztec

To the west of the Maya, the Aztec settled on the shores of Lake Texcoco around A.D. 1325. They built their capital, Tenochtitlán, on an island in the lake. The Aztec connected the island to the surrounding land with wide roads and bridges.

The large markets of Aztec cities were full of excitement. Dancers, musicians, and other performers often entertained the crowd. Other people sold food such as peppers, squash, tomatoes, corn, and beans.

The most highly prized items for sale were the colorful feathers of the quetzal bird. Wealthy Aztec often used quetzal feathers or gold to decorate their clothing. Most Aztec men wore loincloths and cloaks or capes, while women wore simple blouses and skirts.

Religion

The Aztec had many gods and built large temples to honor them. One god they worshipped was Huitzilopochtli, the god of war and the sun. The Aztec believed that the sun god required human blood in order to make the sun rise. Therefore, every day the Aztec would sacrifice slaves or other prisoners to the sun god.

DID YOU KNOW?

Tenochtitlán was built on watery, swampy land. The Aztec developed floating gardens called *chinampas* They stuck rows of thick posts into the swamp. Then they filled the spaces between the posts with mud.

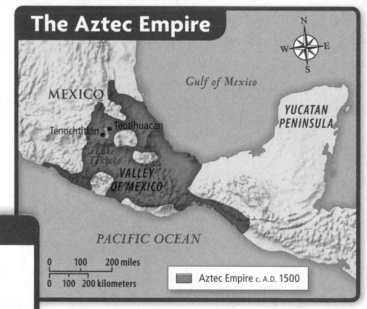

The Aztec Empire

Gulf of Mexico

MEXICO

Tenochtitlán • Teotihuacan

YUCATAN PENINSULA

Lake Texcoco

VALLEY OF MEXICO

PACIFIC OCEAN

| 0 | 100 | 200 miles |
| 0 | 100 | 200 kilometers |

▬ Aztec Empire c. A.D. 1500

Gianni Dagli Orti/CORBIS

Map and Globe Skills

1. Shade in the area on the map in which the Maya settled. Tip: Use pages 42–43.

2. What major bodies of water bordered Aztec land to the north and south?

_____

_____

The Aztec and War

War played an important part in the lives of the Aztec. From an early age, Aztec boys were trained as soldiers. In battle, they captured the enemy. Some of these prisoners were forced into **slavery**. Slavery is the practice of owning people and forcing them to work without pay.

The Aztec were often at war with their neighbors. They conquered hundreds of cities in central Mexico. By A.D. 1440, the Aztec had established a powerful **empire**. An empire is a large area of different groups of people controlled by one ruler or government.

▲ Some Aztec soldiers wore suits made to look like animals that were meant to terrify the enemy.

Reading Skill

Compare and Contrast Think about different cultural aspects of the Maya and the Aztec. How were they similar? How were they different?

_____

_____

_____

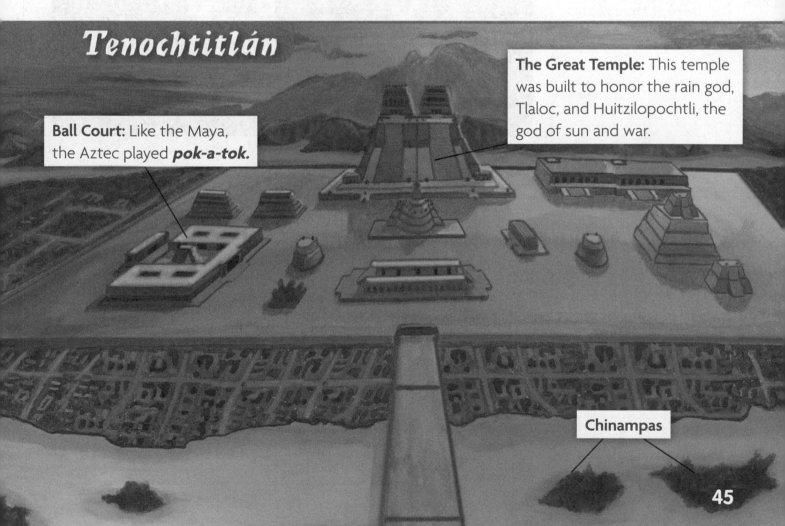

Tenochtitlán

Ball Court: Like the Maya, the Aztec played *pok-a-tok.*

The Great Temple: This temple was built to honor the rain god, Tlaloc, and Huitzilopochtli, the god of sun and war.

Chinampas

Early North American Civilizations

▲ Anasazi bowls

The Anasazi

In about A.D. 700, the Anasazi settled in the "Four Corners" area where Utah, Colorado, Arizona, and New Mexico meet. The Anasazi are known as the first "cliff dwellers." They lived in homes that look like large apartment buildings built into the sides of cliffs. Their homes were made of adobe, a sun-baked clay brick. Special underground rooms called *kivas* were used for meetings or religious purposes.

The Four Corners area is a very hot, dry place. As you can imagine, this made farming difficult. The Anasazi adjusted to the heat and dryness by using **irrigation** to bring water to their crops. The Anasazi irrigation system guided rain water through a series of ditches. The Anasazi planted crops such as maize, beans, and squash.

▼ Ruins of an Anasazi dwelling at Mesa Verde

Look at the image of the home on page 47. How is it different than Mesa Verde?

_____

_____

_____

_____

Map and Globe Skills

1. Label the states that make up the Four Corners. Use the Atlas if you need help.

2. Mesa Verde is located in what state?

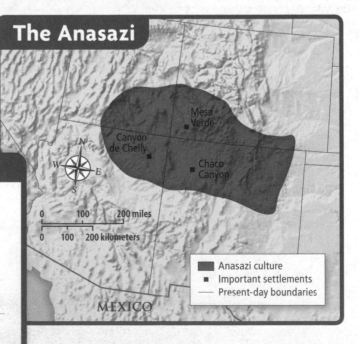

The Anasazi

Mesa Verde
Canyon de Chelly
Chaco Canyon

0   100   200 miles
0   100   200 kilometers

■ Anasazi culture
■ Important settlements
— Present-day boundaries

MEXICO

The Inuit

Living in the desert is certainly difficult. But so is living in the bitterly cold Arctic! The Inuit settled in Alaska and Northern Canada as early as 3000 B.C. They kept warm by building pit houses made of stones covered with earth. On winter hunting trips, men used snow blocks to build temporary shelters called igloos. In warm weather, hunters made tents from wooden poles and animal skins.

The Inuit hunted caribou, walruses, seals, fish, and whales. On land many traveled by dog sled. On water they paddled single-person boats made of sealskin called kayaks.

The Inuit believed that all living things had souls. For this reason, they showed great respect for the animals they hunted by not wasting anything. The meat provided food. Several parts of animals were used for clothing. Boots were made from skin. Animal fur became warm coats called parkas. To sew, the Inuit used bone to create needles. Tools and weapons were carved from bone as well.

Think about the cultural aspects of the Anasazi and the Inuit. <u>Underline</u> similarities and (circle) differences.

Igloos protect people from the harsh winter weather conditions of the arctic. ▼

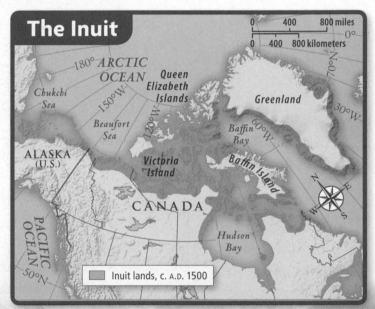

The Inuit

Inuit lands, c. A.D. 1500

◀ This decorative bird was made of copper, which was plentiful in the region.

Mound Builders

Other North American civilizations developed in the river valleys of the Midwest. Over a period of about 1,000 years, civilizations arose in the Ohio and Mississippi River valleys. These people are called Mound Builders because they built cone- and animal-shaped mounds of earth. The earliest of these cultures were the Adena and Hopewell. The Adena settled in the Midwest in about 1000 B.C. About 800 years later, the Hopewell settled in the Mississippi River Valley.

At first, mounds were used to bury people with their possessions, such as weapons, jewelry, and tools. Archaeologists believe this was done to honor the dead. Mound builders often built one mound on top of another. As time passed, these mounds grew larger. Other mounds were used for religious ceremonies.

The Mound Builders were mainly hunters and gatherers. They grew sunflowers and gourds. By about A.D. 100, corn was an important crop. The Mound Builders were known for creating pottery, jewelry, and other artwork out of materials such as clay, limestone, and copper.

Think about the crops grown by the Anasazi and the Mound Builders. Underline similarities and circle differences on this page.

The Great Serpent Mound in Southern Ohio measures over 1,000 feet in length! ▼

Cahokia

Another mound-builder culture developed along the Mississippi around A.D. 700. Their largest city was Cahokia, built near present-day St. Louis, Missouri. Nearly 400 years later Cahokia's population of 30,000 people made it one of the largest cities in the world. Villages stretched around the city in all directions. High log fences, called palisades, protected the villages.

▲ Cahokia

 Compare and contrast cultural aspects of any two cultures discussed in this lesson.

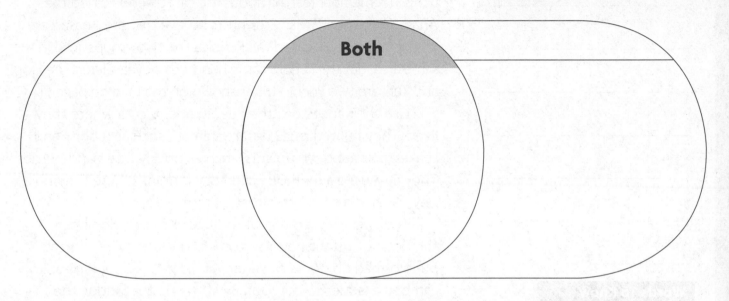

Both

Lesson 1

? **Essential Question**   **What makes a civilization?**

_____

_____

_____

Go back to *Show As You Go!* on pages 32–33.

 networks   **There's More Online!**
● Games ● Assessment

Native Americans of the Southwest

Essential Question

How does location affect the way people live? What do you think?

_____

_____

_____

_____

_____

_____

_____

Words To Know

Write the definition of each word in your own words.

migrate _____

_____

*translate _____

_____

THINK · PAIR · SHARE *Can you imagine living in a place where it almost never rains? Work with a partner and make a list of ways your life would be different with limited rain and water.*

The Pueblo

Do you remember reading about the cliff dwellers called the Anasazi in Lesson 1? Many scientists believe that the Anasazi are related to a people called the Pueblo. The two groups lived in the same area, but the Pueblo came hundreds of years later. The Hopi and Zuni are two Pueblo tribes shown on the map on page 51.

Like their ancestors, the Pueblo adapted to where they lived. They hunted small desert animals, such as rabbits and snakes, and ate desert plants, such as prickly pears and berries. They also used a method called dry farming where they built tiny dams and canals to direct water to crops.

The Spanish used the word *pueblo* to describe both the people and their adobe homes. The first floor of most pueblos had no doors or windows. To get in or out, people climbed a ladder to the roof. By lifting up the ladder, the Pueblo protected themselves from unwanted guests.

Library of Congress Prints and Photographs Division [LC-DIG-ppmsca-17890]

▼ **The Taos Pueblo in New Mexico, shown here around 1900, is now a historical site.**

The Kachinas

Many Pueblo beliefs and traditions continue today. The Pueblo believe in spirits called **kachinas**. According to Pueblo beliefs, kachinas bring rain and help crops grow. The Pueblo believe that kachinas show people how to live and behave.

Kachinas are believed to live in the Pueblo villages for six months each year. During this time, the Pueblo hold kachina ceremonies to gain the favor of the spirits.

Kachina dances are an important part of these ceremonies. People train for years to be kachina dancers. Each dancer wears decorative costumes, sometimes covered in jewelry and feathers, in order to represent different kachina spirits. Dancers are accompanied by music played on flutes, rattles, and whistles.

Dancers sometimes give out colorful dolls that look like the kachina the dancer represents. The Pueblo use these kachina dolls to teach their children about the powers and abilities of each of the hundreds of different kachinas.

Getty Images

▼ Kachina dancers

Reading Skill
Main Idea and Key Details
Underline the purpose of kachina ceremonies.

Draw your own kachina doll and explain what it represents.

Native Americans of the Southwest, 1700s

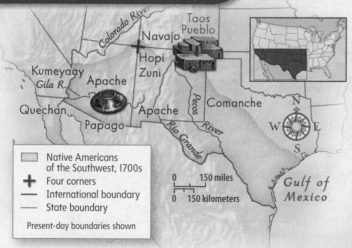

Colorado River
Taos Pueblo
Navajo
Hopi
Zuni
Kumeyaay
Gila R.
Apache
Quechan
Papago
Apache
Pecos River
Comanche
Rio Grande
N
W E
S
Gulf of Mexico

☐ Native Americans of the Southwest, 1700s
✛ Four corners
— International boundary
— State boundary
Present-day boundaries shown

0   150 miles
0   150 kilometers

Map and Globe Skills

1. (Circle) Taos Pueblo on the map.

2. The Navajo live closest to which rivers?

_____

_____

Compare and Contrast

Underline ways the Navajo were similar to the Pueblo. Circle ways they were different.

The Navajo

Another tribe in the Southwest are the Navajo, or Diné. Thousands of years ago, they were hunter-gatherers in parts of present-day Alaska and Canada. The Navajo began to **migrate**, or move from one place to another. By the 1400s, they had migrated to northern New Mexico. Today the Navajo are the largest non-Pueblo people in the Southwest. Many live in the Four Corners area of the United States.

▼ A Navajo woman

A Navajo ring ▼

Shared Practices and Arts

In order to survive, the Navajo used many of the ideas and practices of their Pueblo neighbors. Like the Pueblo, the Navajo used dry farming to grow crops in the desert. They also both wove cotton to make cloth. Both the Navajo and the Pueblo are known for their silver and turquoise jewelry. Turquoise is a blue stone that is found only in the Southwest of North America and in western South America.

What farming style was shared by the Navajo and Pueblo?

_____

Navajo Living

The Navajo lived in **hogans**, or dome-shaped homes large enough for one family. Hogans are made with log or stick frames covered with mud or sod. A smoke hole in the roof releases smoke from a fire used for heat and cooking inside the hogan. Traditional hogans face east to catch the first rays of dawn.

The Navajo believe in *hozho*, which roughly **translates** to "walking in beauty." This means living in balance and harmony. To gain *hozho*, the Navajo pass knowledge through stories and songs. One song says, "All is beautiful before me, All is beautiful behind me, All is beautiful above me, All is beautiful around me."

Rob Crandall/The Image Works

▲ A Navajo hogan

Compare and contrast a pueblo and a hogan.

_____

_____

_____

Lesson 2

 Essential Question How does location affect the way people live?

_____

_____

_____

_____

Go back to *Show As You Go!* on pages 32–33.

 netw⚪rks There's More Online!
○ Games ○ Assessment

Native Americans of the Pacific Northwest

Lesson 3

Essential Question

How does location affect the way people live? What do you think?

Words To Know

Write the plural form of each word on the line.

totem pole _____

potlatch _____

THINK • PAIR • SHARE *Imagine that it was your birthday party, but YOU had to give gifts to all of your guests! How would you feel? What would you give everyone?*

Life in the Pacific Northwest

Like Native Americans in other regions, those in the Pacific Northwest survived by using natural resources. Food in this region was so plentiful that people there **typically** didn't need to farm. As a result, the Pacific Northwest had one of the highest populations of Native Americans in North America.

The rocky, narrow Pacific coastline and offshore islands provided wild plants, berries, and fish, especially salmon. Every year, millions of salmon return to the rivers of the Pacific Northwest for a few months in order to lay eggs. During this time, it was not uncommon for families to catch hundreds of pounds of fish! People also hunted animals such as deer, elk, beaver, and bears.

Native Americans in the Pacific Northwest used stone axes to cut cedar trees. They hollowed out logs to make canoes as long as 60 feet—perfect for hunting seals and whales in the ocean. Logs were also carved into boxes, dishes, spoons, and masks.

W. Langdon Kihn/National Geographic Society/Corbis

▲ Canoes arriving for a potlatch

Totem Poles

Pacific Northwest tribes also used wood to make **totem poles**. Totem poles are logs that are carved and then painted with symbols, called totems, of animals or people. Totem poles often tell stories of important family members or celebrate special events. Totem poles can be very tall. Totem poles can measure 40–60 feet in height. Som are as tall as 150 feet!

Totem Pole ▶

Celebrations

When totem poles were raised, a family sometimes held a **potlatch**. Potlatches are special celebrations at which guests, not hosts, receive gifts. The host might give hundreds of gifts at the potlatch. In return, the host received the respect of the community. These celebrations could sometimes last for days. Potlatches also feature feasts, singing, and dancing. As in the past, potlatches today bring people together for important family events such as the birth, death, or marriage of a family member.

Potlatch dancers ▶

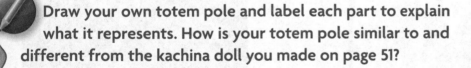

Draw your own totem pole and label each part to explain what it represents. How is your totem pole similar to and different from the kachina doll you made on page 51?

FUN FACTS

Native Americans of the Pacific Northwest wore skirts, loincloths, or blankets made from the soft inner bark of a cedar tree. Jewelry was worn in pierced lips, ears, or noses. Tattoos were also common.

The Tlingit and Kwakiutl

The Tlingit and Kwakiutl are two tribes that settled in the Pacific Northwest. Like other tribes in the area, most of their food came from the sea. Canoes made trade between tribes easy.

In the 1700s the Tlingit lived along the coast between Alaska and what is now the Portland Canal in British Columbia, Canada. The many islands nestled between Vancouver, British Columbia, and the mainland were home to the Kwakiutl.

The mild and wet weather of the Pacific Northwest allows thick forests to grow. The Tlingit and Kwakiutl were skilled craftworkers. They used tree bark and other materials to make baskets and weave colorful blankets. Their wooden plank houses were large enough for several related families. The Tlingit also used their woodworking skills to make dams and traps for catching large amounts of salmon.

DID YOU KNOW?

People of the Pacific Northwest believe the natural world is full of powerful spirits that affect everyday life. Groups of singers and dancers perform to communicate with spirits during ceremonies. Most often they give thanks or to ask spirits to provide help.

IndexStock / SuperStock

▲ A Tlingit woman in tribal clothing

Native Americans of the Pacific Northwest

Inuit
Koyukon
Yukon River
Inuit
Ingalik
Tanana
Inuit

Tlingit

Haida
Tsimshian

Pacific Ocean

Kwakiutl
Nootka
Makah
Chinook *Columbia River*
Tillamook

Totowa
Yurok Modoc Shoshone
Hupa
Yuki Nisenan Shoshone Cheyenne
Pomo
Miwok Shoshone
Washo Paiute
Yokuts Mojave
Chumash Cahuilla
Luiseño Kumeyaay

0   250   500 miles
0   250   500 kilometers

N
W   E
S

Native Americans of Alaska
Native Americans of the West
— International boundary
— State boundary
Present-day boundaries shown

Map and Globe Skills

1. Locate and (circle) the Tlingit and Kwakiutl tribes on the map.

2. (Circle) the group that lives in present-day Idaho.

Imagine you are a traveler heading from the Southwest to the Pacific Northwest. Write a letter comparing and contrasting people and their cultures along your journey. You can also include illustrations with your letter.

Dear _____

_____

_____

_____

_____

_____

_____

Sincerely,

_____

Lesson 3

? **Essential Question** How does location affect the way people live?

_____

_____

_____

Go back to *Show As You Go!* on pages 32–33. «««

netwrks There's More Online!
● Games ● Assessment

Lesson 4

Native Americans of the Great Plains

? Essential Question

How does location affect the way people live? What do you think?

_____

_____

_____

_____

_____

_____

_____

Words To Know

Tell a partner what you know about these words.

prairie

nomad

teepee

lodge

*characteristic

THINK • PAIR • SHARE *Imagine that you had to move at a moment's notice. Each time you moved, only a short time would pass before you had to move again. How would it make you feel? What things would you need to bring with you?*

Grass and Sky for Miles

The Great Plains is a vast region made up of **prairies**. A prairie is a flat or gently rolling land covered mostly with grasses and wildflowers. Powerful winds, blistering summer heat, and cold winters are **characteristic** of the region.

Native Americans first settled the Great Plains around A.D. 1300. Some of these people moved constantly as they followed the animals they hunted. These **nomads** had no permanent home and moved in search of food. Hunting on foot with bows and arrows, they chased animals into traps. Other tribes lived permanently near rivers where they farmed.

Taming Wild Horses

By the 1700s, Native Americans had discovered a tool that changed their lives forever: wild horses. Once tamed, horses allowed people to hunt on horseback. Tribes could also travel great distances for trade. As a result, tribes such as the Lakota, Crow, Pawnee, and Cheyenne prospered on the Plains.

▼ **This painting shows the excitement of a bison hunt.**

Superstock

Different Food, Different Homes

During this time, as many as 100 million bison roamed the Great Plains. They provided plenty of food. Some tribes used bison hides, or skin, to make clothing such as shirts, dresses, robes, and shoes called moccasins.

They also used hides to make **teepees**. Teepees are cone-shaped homes made with long poles covered by animal hides. Teepees were portable and could be put up or taken down quickly. This made it easier for nomadic Native Americans to follow bison or other animals.

Some Great Plains tribes farmed and hunted for food near their permanent communities. Instead of teepees, these groups lived in large earthen **lodges**. Lodges are homes made of logs covered with grasses, sticks, and soil. A fire in a central fireplace provided heat and light.

> **How are these teepees similar to and different from the Navajo hogan on page 53?**
>
> _____
>
> _____
>
> _____

Stockbyte

Teepees were decorated in many ways using dyes from plants, animal fur, hooves, and porcupine quills. ▼

> **DID YOU KNOW?**
> When the Spanish came to North America in the 1500s, they brought horses with them. Some horses got away and lived in the wild. A few hundred years later, wild horses had spread to the Great Plains.

Native Americans of the Great Plains, 1700s

Blackfoot

Mandan
Crow
Cheyenne Lakota

Pawnee

Mississippi River
Missouri River

0   150   300 miles
0   150 300 kilometers

▮ Native Americans of the Plains, 1700s
— International boundary
— State boundary
Present-day boundaries shown

Kiowa   Osage   Arkansas River
Seminole
Red River   Seminole
Comanche

Natchez

Gulf of Mexico

Map and Globe Skills

1. Identify and label the present-day states of the Great Plains. Use your reference atlas if you need help.

2. Most groups settled near what type of geographic feature?

Life on the Plains

Bison were important to people living on the Plains. In preparation of each bison hunt, they held ceremonies honoring the spirit world and the bison. They believed that without the support of the spirit world, the hunt would be unsuccessful and they could not survive.

Plains Art

The people of the Great Plains often tied their art to everyday life. For example, people decorated everyday items—such as pipes, shields, and clothes—with beads, feathers, and porcupine quills.

Another example of this was the winter count. A winter count was an illustrated calendar that was usually painted on an animal hide. Every year, tribal leaders met to decide the most important events of the past year. These events were painted as picture symbols in a circle on bison hide. The winter count you see below was created by a Lakota named Lone Dog.

Primary Source

Winter Count by Lone Dog, 1800–1871

Examine the artifact and read the translations below. Then complete the activity.

 1800–1801: Europeans bring striped blanket

1853–1854: 30 Lakota killed by Crow Indians

1845–1846: There is plenty of buffalo meat

1. Draw lines from the translations to the symbols on the artifact.

2. Circle the symbols you think are related to food or hunting.

3. What is the purpose of the winter count?

_____

_____

Learning Responsibilities

Great Plains children were taught about their culture through stories and songs. They also learned skills that prepared them for the tasks of adulthood. Read below to learn about the education of boys and girls.

▲ Today, children are still taught traditions at an early age.

A Boy's Life

Young boys were taught to hunt and shoot using bows and arrows made especially for children. Older boys took part in shooting contests. During bison hunts and practice battles, boys learned the value of courage.

A Girl's Life

Girls learned to sew by making doll clothes, using sinew from bison as thread. Sinew is the fibers that connect muscles to bone. Girls were also taught to build teepees. Older girls learned to use scraping tools to clean animal hides.

Similarities	Differences

Reading Skill

Compare and Contrast

Use the chart to list similarities and differences between religious beliefs of Native Americans of the Great Plains and the Pacific Northwest.

Lesson 4

 Essential Question How does location affect the way people live?

_____

_____

_____

Go back to *Show As You Go!* on pages 32–33. ◀◀

 networks **There's More Online!** ● Games ● Assessment

Warren Morgan/CORBIS

Native Americans of the Eastern Woodlands

Essential Question

How does location affect the way people live? What do you think?

_____

_____

_____

_____

_____

_____

_____

Words To Know

Write a number in each box to show how much you know about each word.

1 = I have no idea!
2 = I know a little.
3 = I know a lot.

____ *conduct

____ longhouse

____ wampum

____ confederacy

THINK · PAIR · SHARE *How do you get the things you need to survive? What if you had to find your own food, clothing, and shelter? Where would you get them?*

Living in the Forest

The Eastern Woodlands stretch from the Mississippi River to the Atlantic Ocean. In the past, most of this area was covered in thick forests. People of the woodlands used forest animals, such as deer, bear, and rabbit, for food and clothing.

Farming the Land

The region is divided into two parts: the northeast and the southeast. The southeast is thinly wooded, has a mild climate, and a long growing season, which are all good for farming.

The thicker forests of the northeast made farming more difficult. There, many tribes practiced a type of farming called **slash-and-burn**. They cut down and burned the trees in the forest. Ash from the burned vegetation helped make the soil fertile. In autumn the tribes harvested, dried, and stored the crops for the winter. After the harvest, they let the land rest several years before replanting the crops.

▼ **The homes of Native Americans of the Eastern Woodlands were often surrounded by the thick forests of the region.**

The "Three Sisters"

One Eastern Woodlands group, the Iroquois, includes five tribes: the Cayuga, the Mohawk, the Oneida, the Onondaga, and the Seneca. Each spring most Iroquois planted what they called the "Three Sisters": corn, squash, and beans. These crops were grown together and were often eaten together.

Religion

People in the Eastern Woodlands believed that spirits were involved in everyday life. They believed that good spirits helped those in need, and that evil spirits caused sickness and conflict.

Native Americans **conducted** ceremonies to communicate with spirits. Dancing was important to these ceremonies. People also sang and played instruments, such as wooden flutes and drums. The hope was that these ceremonies would either invite in good spirits or drive out the bad.

Label the "Three Sisters" on the illustration.

Native Americans of the Eastern Woodlands, 1600s

Great Lakes
Penobscot
Hudson River
Huron Oneida
Cayuga Mohawk Wampanoag
Seneca Onondaga
Narragansett
Pequot
Mohegan
Shawnee
Ohio River
Mississippi River
N W E S
Cherokee Tuscarora
Chickasaw Catawba Atlantic Ocean
Tennessee River Creek
Choctaw
Natchez
Timucua
Seminole
Gulf of Mexico

Native Americans of the Eastern Woodlands, 1600s
International boundary
State boundary
Present-day boundaries shown

0 150 300 miles
0 150 300 kilometers

THINK · PAIR · SHARE
Work with a partner to compare and contrast the major beliefs and practices of Native Americans of the Eastern Woodlands and Native Americans of the Great Plains.

Map and Globe Skills

1. Circle the Iroquois tribes on the map.

2. What river forms the western border of the Eastern Woodlands?

_____

People of the Eastern Woodlands

The Eastern Woodlands cover a large area. So, while the people there shared **aspects** of their lives, there were many differences as well. On the next few pages, you will learn about two tribes from the Eastern Woodlands, the Creek and the Iroquois.

Both the Creek and Iroquois celebrated the Green Corn Festival in honor of the summer's first maize crop. During this festival people offered thanks to the spirits through music, song, and dance.

Creek

Communities
The Creek arranged their towns around a large council house, or "chokofa." Family homes were wattle-and-daub huts, which are made from poles and covered with grass, mud, or thatch.

Art
The Creek decorated their pots with wooden stamps. They pressed the carved stamps into pottery while it was still wet.

Look at the images on this spread. In what ways are the clothes worn similar and different to the clothing of other Native American groups you've already learned about?

_____

_____

_____

_____

Both the Iroquois and the Creek played lacrosse. Lacrosse is a team sport played with a rubber ball and a stick with a net pocket. The object of the game is to shoot the ball into the other team's goal. Native Americans sometimes played lacrosse to settle disagreements among tribes.

Clothing among the people of the Eastern Woodlands was similar as well. Most clothing was made from animal hides. In the winter, furs were used for warmth. To decorate clothing, tribes used everything from feathers and beads to detailed sewing and shells.

Iroquois

Communities

The Iroquois call themselves *Hodenosaunee*. In the Iroquois language, this means "people of the **longhouse**." Longhouses were homes large enough for several families and were made of bent poles covered with sheets of bark.

Art

The Iroquois made fine beadwork, called **wampum**. Wampum is polished beads made from shells that are woven together. It was used in ceremonies or as gifts.

Reading Skill

Compare and Contrast

Underline ways the Creek and Iroquois differed. Circle their similarities.

Government in the Woodlands

The people of the Eastern Woodlands worked together to solve their problems. Some tribes formed **confederacies**. A confederacy is a group of people who work together for a common purpose.

Creek Government

To protect themselves from enemies, the Creek formed the Creek Confederacy. They divided towns into war towns (red) and peace towns (white). Red towns declared war, planned battles, and held meetings with enemies. White towns passed laws and held prisoners captive. During periods of war, however, even the people in the peace towns joined in the fighting.

Iroquois Government

When the Iroquois were a small group, they worked together to solve disagreements. But as their numbers began to grow, the Iroquois began arguing among themselves. The Iroquois saw that this fighting was destroying their people. They had to take action.

Around 1570, five Iroquois tribes joined together to form the Iroquois Confederacy, also known as the Iroquois League. Its goal was to maintain peace among the five Iroquois tribes, or nations. The Confederacy later added another tribe, and it was then called Six Nations. The Confederacy is still active today.

Explain the purpose of Native American confederacies.

_____

_____

_____

Compare cultural aspects of Native Americans in each region. Use the information from Lessons 2–5 to complete the chart.

Group	Environment	Religion	Food Source	Art and Daily Life
Southwest				
Pacific Northwest				
Great Plains				
Eastern Woodlands				

Lesson 5

? Essential Question How does location affect the way people live?

_____

_____

_____

Go back to *Show As You Go!* on pages 32–33. ≪

networks There's More Online!
• Games • Assessment

Write the name of the tribe in the space provided. Then place the numbers of the tribes in the correct region on the map.

Color in the map key and the corresponding regions on the map.

Key

◯ Eastern Woodlands

◯ Great Plains

◯ Southwest

◯ Pacific Northwest

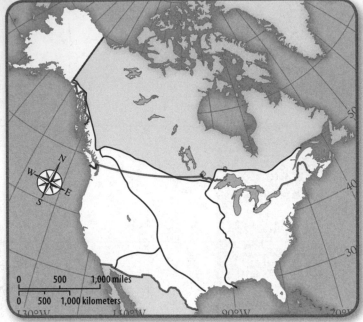

1. This group created a confederacy that is still active today. It is known as the Six Nations. _____

2. It is believed that this group is related to the Anasazi. _____

3. Lone Dog, a man from this tribe, created a winter count from 1800–1871. _____

4. These skilled craftworkers lived between Alaska and the present-day Portland Canal in the Pacific Northwest. _____

5. Also known as the *Diné*, this tribe was known for being shepherds. _____

6. The traditional home of this tribe were the islands between Vancouver, British Columbia, and the mainland of Canada. _____

7. The towns of this tribe were arranged around a large council house called a "chokofa." _____

Unit Project

Choose a Native American tribe or region you learned about in this unit. Imagine that you have been hired by a museum to create a display about that tribe or region. Draw the layout of your museum exhibit. Before you begin, turn back to pages 32 and 33 to review your illustrations. You may want to use them as part of your display. You should also write a few paragraphs that explain what is in your display, and why. Read the list below to see what you need to include in your display and your writing. As you work, check off each task.

Your museum display should include . . .   **Yes, it does!**

the name and location of the tribe or region you chose   ☐

artifacts from the tribe or region you chose   ☐

information about how your tribe or region interacted with their environment   ☐

cultural aspects of the tribe or region you chose, including clothing, shelter, food, major beliefs, music, and art   ☐

a written summary of what you chose to put in your display   ☐

· ·

Think about the Big Idea

BIG IDEA 💡 Culture influences the way people live.

What did you learn in this unit that helps you understand the BIG IDEA?

_____

_____

_____

_____

Read the passage "The Pottery of Nampeyo" before answering Numbers 1 through 8.

The Pottery of Nampeyo

by Elyse Maddox

The Pueblo people live in the American Southwest. In the past, their land stretched into many present-day states, such as Utah, Colorado, California, Arizona, Texas, and New Mexico. The Hopi are a Pueblo people that live in present-day Arizona.

Art has long been an important part of Hopi daily life. The Pueblo are known for their beautiful pottery. Ancient Pueblo pottery often included designs that were tied to nature. Some favorite designs included birds, insects, and water.

One important Hopi potter was a woman named Nampeyo. As a young girl, Nampeyo watched her grandmother make beautiful pottery. Soon, Nampeyo began making her own pottery. In 1895 Nampeyo heard of ancient pottery being uncovered at an archaeological site near her home. When she saw the pottery that had been found there, Nampeyo admired its beauty. She thought the ancient designs were even better than current designs.

At first, Nampeyo used the ancient designs in her work. Later, she created her own designs using the ancient style. Determined to spread interest in the traditional Hopi pottery, Nampeyo taught the skill of pottery making to others. Today, many Hopi potters carry on Nampeyo's work.

1 What is this passage mostly about?

Ⓐ the importance and beauty of Hopi pottery

Ⓑ why traditional pottery is better than modern

Ⓒ the main design elements of Hopi pottery

Ⓓ how archaeologists discover artifacts

2 Read the sentence from the passage.

When she saw the pottery that had been found there, Nampeyo admired its beauty.

What does the word *admired* mean in this passage?

Ⓕ disliked very much

Ⓖ liked very much

Ⓗ ignored

Ⓘ copied and made your own

3 What happened in 1895?

   Ⓐ The Hopi flourished in Arizona.

   Ⓑ Nampeyo spread the interest of traditional pottery.

   Ⓒ Archaeologists found ancient pottery near Nampeyo's home.

   Ⓓ Nampeyo was born.

4 Which two words from the passage have nearly OPPOSITE meanings?

   Ⓕ beautiful, nature

   Ⓖ ancient, current

   Ⓗ favorite, admired

   Ⓘ art, pottery

5 Which detail from the passage helps show what influenced Nampeyo to start making pottery?

   Ⓐ The Pueblo people lived in the American Southwest.

   Ⓑ Today, many Hopi potters carry on Nampeyo's work.

   Ⓒ Nampeyo heard of ancient pottery being uncovered at an archaeological site near her home.

   Ⓓ As a young girl, Nampeyo watched her grandmother make beautiful pottery.

6 Which of the following was NOT a favorite design item used in Hopi art?

   Ⓕ birds

   Ⓖ trees

   Ⓗ water

   Ⓘ insects

7 After Nampeyo saw the ancient pottery found near her home, how did this affect her own pottery designs at first?

   Ⓐ She taught others how to make pottery.

   Ⓑ She created her own designs using the ancient style.

   Ⓒ She copied the designs of the ancient pottery.

   Ⓓ She made pottery using current designs.

8 Where do the Hopi traditionally live?

   Ⓕ present-day Texas

   Ⓖ present-day California

   Ⓗ present-day Utah

   Ⓘ present-day Arizona

UNIT 3
The Age of Exploration

During the 1400s, European explorers traveled east to Asia by land and sea. There they found exotic spices, fabrics, and jewels. The trip to Asia was very long, very dangerous, and very expensive. Some people thought it might be faster to get to Asia by traveling west across the Atlantic Ocean. In this unit, you will learn about the explorers who headed west and the results of their journeys. As you read, think about how the actions of Europeans affected the land and people of both the Americas and Europe.

networks

connected.mcgraw-hill.com
○ Skill Builders
○ Vocabulary Flashcards

Who: Juan Ponce de León

Sponsor: _____

Goal: _____

Location: _____

Results: _____

This symbol is used to show a long period of time that is not covered in a time line.

_____

1450   1460   1490   1500

Describe a technology that improved European travel.

_____

_____

_____

Who: _____
Sponsor: Spain
Goal: Find a western sea route to Asia
Location: Bahamas, Central and South America
Results: Claimed land for Spain; Columbian Exchange

Show As You Go!

After you read each lesson in this unit, use these pages to record important details about the explorers. You will use your notes to help you complete a project at the end of the unit.

Fold page here

Who: _____

Sponsor: France

Goal: Find a northwest passage

Location: Gulf of St. Lawrence and St. Lawrence River

Results: Claimed land for France

Who: Henry Hudson

Sponsor: Dutch East India Company

Goal: Find a northwest passage

Location: Hudson Bay and Hudson River

Results: Abandoned at sea by crew

Connect this box to the correct year on the time line.

Hernando de Soto

_____

1520   **1540**   **1600**   **1610**   **1620**

Francisco Pizarro

Samuel de Champlain

_____

Who: Étienne Brûlé

Sponsor: _____

Goal: _____

Location: _____

Results: _____

Who: Hernán Cortés

Sponsor: Spain

Goal: Find gold and claim land

Location: Central America

Results: Caused the fall of the Aztec Empire

Connect this box to the correct year on the time line.

73

Reading Skill

Common Core Standards
RI.2 Determine two or more main ideas of a text and explain how they are supported by key details; summarize the text.

Summarize

Summarizing is a good way to remember what you read. A summary is a brief statement about the topic of a passage. After you read a paragraph or section in your book, make a summary of it. A summary includes the main ideas of a text. It leaves out minor details and includes only key details.

LEARN IT

To summarize a passage:

- **Find its main ideas.**
- **Include only key details.**
- **Restate the important points in your summary.**

The first people of the Middle Ages to travel to distant regions were the Norse, or "north people," who lived in what are today Denmark, Sweden, and Norway. To gain wealth, they sailed throughout the seas and rivers of Europe trading goods. Some people knew them as Vikings, a Norse word for "raiders."

Around A.D. 1000, Viking explorers were the first Europeans to reach North America. But their settlements there did not last. As a result, the Viking settlements in North America were forgotten for many years.

Detail

Main Idea

© Ivy Close Images / Alamy

TRY IT

Complete the chart. Fill in the top boxes with main ideas and their key details from page 74. Write a summary in the bottom box.

Main Idea and Detail(s)	Main Idea and Detail(s)

Summary

APPLY IT

- Underline two main ideas. Circle their key details as you read.
- Then summarize the passage on the lines.

In 1095 European soldiers began a long journey to Jerusalem. The city had great religious importance to Jews, Christians, and Muslims. European Christians hoped to capture the city from Muslim Turks who ruled the city at the time. These journeys were called Crusades.

The Crusaders captured Jerusalem but were driven out after about 100 years. Many Europeans returned home with products, such as silk or spices, that were unknown in Europe. Traders soon found that Europeans were willing to pay a lot for these new products such as cotton, pepper, and cinnamon.

_____

_____

_____

Words to Know

Common Core Standards
RI.4 Determine the meaning of general academic and domain-specific words and phrases in a text relevant to a grade 5 topic or subject area.

The list below shows some important words you will learn in this unit. Their definitions can be found on the next page. Read the words.

merchant (MER • chuhnt)

navigation (nah • vih • GAY • shuhn)

enslave (in • SLAYV)

missionary (MIH • shuh • nehr • ee)

ally (AL • eye)

The Foldable on the next page will help you learn these important words. Follow the steps below to make the Foldable.

Step 1 Fold along the solid red line.

Step 2 Cut along the dotted lines.

Step 3 Read the words and their definitions.

Step 4 Complete the activities on each tab.

Step 5 Look at the back of your Foldable. Choose ONE of these activities for each word to help you remember its meaning:

- Draw a picture of the word.

- Write a description of the word.

- Write how the word is related to something you know.

▲ Samuel de Champlain founds the city of Quebec. Quebec became a center of French trade in North America.

Ambroise-Louis Garneray/Getty Images

76

FOLD

Write the definition of _merchant_ in your own words.

A **merchant** is a person who makes a living from buying and selling goods.

Write the root word of _navigation_.

Navigation is the science of determining a ship's location and direction of travel.

Write the root word of _enslaved_.

To be **enslaved** means to be forced to work for no pay and without the freedom to leave.

Put a box around two key words in the definition of _missionary_. Write those words here:

A **missionary** is a person who tries to persuade people to accept new religious beliefs.

Write the plural of _ally_.

An **ally** is a person, group, or nation that unites with another in order to do something.

merchant

navigation

enslave

missionary

ally

CUT HERE

merchant

navigation

enslave

missionary

ally

Primary and Secondary Sources

Maps

Maps help us examine and understand the geography of a specific area. A map can be a primary source or a secondary source.

If a map was created and used by someone in the past, it is a primary source. Primary source maps show us where people lived and how they saw their world. We also use these maps to learn how people in the past interacted with the geography of an area.

If a map was created and used after the time period it shows, then it is a secondary source. These maps are often called historical maps. They help us understand how the geography of an area influenced people or events in the past.

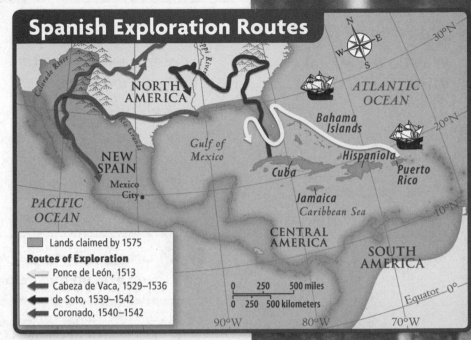

Spanish Exploration Routes

Lands claimed by 1575

Routes of Exploration
- Ponce de León, 1513
- Cabeza de Vaca, 1529–1536
- de Soto, 1539–1542
- Coronado, 1540–1542

0   250   500 miles
0   250   500 kilometers

McGraw-Hill Education

DBQ Document-Based Questions

Examine the map to answer the questions and complete the activities.

1. **Circle one answer to complete the sentence.**

   This map is a _____.

   primary source   secondary source

2. **What events are shown on this map?**

   _____

   _____

3. **How did the early explorers travel? Why?**

   _____

   _____

networks
There's More Online!
- Skill Builders
- Resource Library

A Changing World

Essential Question

Why do people take risks? What do you think?

_____

_____

_____

_____

_____

_____

_____

_____

Words To Know

Find the definition for each word and write a synonym on the line. A synonym is a word that has the same or almost the same meaning.

merchant _____

navigation _____

***chart** _____

A small number of people have traveled into space. Some have even walked on the moon. But for most people, space is the "great unknown."

THINK · PAIR · SHARE

Imagine you are going to travel into space. Discuss with a partner what you know about space travel. What dangers might you face? What skills, knowledge, and supplies would you need for the trip?

List three items you would need in space and explain the importance of each.

Item you would bring	Reason for bringing it along

Just as space is unknown to you, the oceans were the "great unknown" to Europeans in the 1400s. The idea of traveling too far in any direction scared them. Sailors told tales of mermaids, pirates, sea monsters, and ships sailing right off the edge of the world! Soon, though, Europeans would travel farther than they ever had by sea. Using tools new to them would make Europeans able to explore the unknown.

New Trade Routes

European **merchants** were willing to risk everything for the chance to make money. Merchants are people who make their living buying and selling goods. Chinese traders brought goods to western Asia along a trade route called the Silk Road. Here they met European merchants who purchased these goods and then sold them in Europe.

The Silk Road was protected by the Mongolian Empire. In the 1400s, this empire collapsed. Suddenly traveling on the Silk Road became dangerous, and Asian goods became expensive.

Europeans tried new trade routes through the Middle East and in Africa. But Arab merchants controlled these areas and charged high prices for their goods. Europeans found themselves in a tough position. If only there was an easier, faster, and less expensive way to get the goods they wanted!

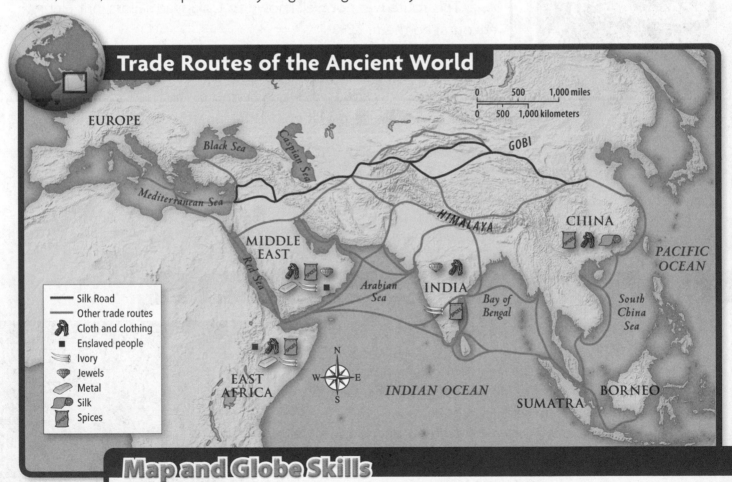

Trade Routes of the Ancient World

Legend:
— Silk Road
— Other trade routes
🐎 Cloth and clothing
■ Enslaved people
Ivory
♦ Jewels
Metal
Silk
Spices

Map and Globe Skills

1. What waterway connected Asian trade routes with Europe?

_____

2. (Circle) the area on the map from which Europeans received silk.

Exploring the Oceans

Europeans still wanted goods from Asia. But they had to find another way to get them. In the 1400s, they turned to the seas. One man did much to encourage travelers to try new routes.

▲ **Prince Henry of Portugal**

Portugal Sails South

Portugal is a small country on Europe's Atlantic coast. It is close to Africa. In the 1400s, Portugal's enemies controlled land routes to Asia. Portugal's traders had no easy way to get there.

Portugal's leaders and merchants wanted to grow their country's wealth through trade. Prince Henry of Portugal didn't believe the legends about monsters and other dangers lurking in the ocean. He wanted Portuguese ships to sail south along Africa to get to Asia. This route was not well known to European sailors, but Henry encouraged them.

Portuguese sailors were successful in sailing the coasts of Africa, and Portugal grew into a major power. It wasn't alone it its desire to explore. Other European powers wanted to find new routes to Asia as well. The age of exploration had begun.

Primary and Secondary Sources

For centuries, people told tales of Prince Henry's "school for sailors." They did this to explain Portugal's sudden success. Recently, historians have shown that no such school existed. Yet we have paintings of it! How can this be? The paintings, like the one shown, were secondary sources.

How does this story show why it's important to use more than one source when studying history?

_____

_____

_____

Improving Navigation

People don't just trade goods. They also trade knowledge, tools, and ideas. **Navigation** tools from other cultures made European exploration possible. Navigation is the science of getting ships from place to place. To navigate, sailors first had to know where they were. Then they had to know which direction to go.

Underline what the astrolabe does and ⦿circle⦿ what the compass does.

The Astrolabe

In the 1100s, Europeans learned about the astrolabe from Arab traders. This tool measures the height of the stars in the sky. The measurement from the astrolabe was used with a **chart** of the stars. With these two items, sailors could find the ship's latitude. Remember, latitude is a location north or south of the Equator.

An astrolabe ▼

Orienteering Compass

To find where they were going, Europeans used an ancient Chinese invention. The orienteering compass shows the direction of travel. It helps sailors orient, or position, their ships.

Compasses have a magnetic arrow that aligns itself with Earth's magnetic poles. The compass allowed sailors to easily find north and south, so they could turn their ship in the direction they wanted to go.

The Sextant

The astrolabe and compass were important navigation tools for about 300 years. With them, sailors could find direction and latitude. But measuring longitude, or the distance east or west of the Prime Meridian, was still impossible.

That changed in 1759 when John Bird invented the sextant. This tool uses two mirrors and a movable arm to precisely measure the angles of stars in the sky. This was an important piece to the puzzle of how to measure longitude. With the help of the sextant, navigation and mapmaking became more accurate. In fact, sextants are still used today!

▲ **The sextant allowed sailors to find their exact longitude.**

How did new tools improve navigation?

_____

_____

_____

Seaworthy Ships

Sailors now had better tools with which to navigate, but they also needed better ships. They wanted ships to be faster, safer, and easier to control. Sailors also needed more space to store supplies and goods to trade.

Stern Rudder

Navigation tools helped sailors identify their location and the direction they were traveling. But European sailors also needed to be able to steer their ships. The Chinese used an oar that hung off the stern, or back of the boat, to control the direction of a ship. Eventually these "rudders" became a common part of ships. This addition made steering much easier.

The Caravel

The stern rudder helped control a ship, but sailing still wasn't perfect. Sailors needed to be able to catch more wind so they could travel faster. In the late 1400s, the Portuguese developed the caravel. This type of ship had rectangular sails on the front and middle masts. The sail in the middle of the ship was largest and captured a lot of wind, propelling the ship forward. A triangular sail on the stern worked with the rudder to help steer the ship.

Caravels were better in other ways too. They had more room for cargo than earlier ships. They also had flatter bottoms and could float in shallow water. Sailors now could get closer to land to repair ships and make more accurate maps of coastlines.

A stern rudder ▲

Reading Skill

Explain Relationships

Explain how the stern rudder and larger sails made ships more seaworthy.

_____

_____

_____

_____

_____

_____

Reading Skill

Key Details

<u>Underline</u> the details in the text which describe the sails and rudder on the caravel. Use these details to draw the sails and(circle) the rudder on the ship.

DID YOU KNOW?

One more Chinese invention made European exploration possible: gunpowder. Ship's cannons and explorer's guns were used to protect sailors and conquer peoples. When lit, gunpowder made these weapons fire.

Lesson 1

? Essential Question   Why do people take risks?

_____

_____

_____

_____

_____

Go back to *Show As You Go!* on pages 72–73. «

 networks

There's More Online!
⊙ Games ⊙ Assessment

Spanish Exploration and Conquest

? Essential Question

What happens when different cultures meet? What do you think?

_____

_____

_____

_____

_____

_____

_____

_____

_____

_____

_____

_____

_____

Words To Know

Write another form of each word.

enslaved _____

*claim _____

missionary _____

86

Sailing South and West

Recall that sailors from Portugal were looking for southern water routes to Asia. In 1488 Bartolomeu Dias sailed around Africa's southern tip! He was the first European to do this. Vasco de Gama was another Portuguese explorer. He sailed around Africa all the way to India 10 years later. The voyage south around Africa to Asia took about a year.

Christopher Columbus

An Italian named Christopher Columbus thought sailing west would save time. In August 1492, the king and queen of Spain agreed to pay for the voyage. Two months later, Columbus and his crew sighted land. He believed they had reached the Indies islands in Asia. But they had not. They had landed on an island in North America.

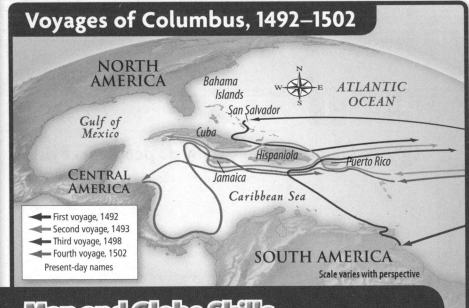

Voyages of Columbus, 1492–1502

NORTH AMERICA
Bahama Islands
San Salvador
ATLANTIC OCEAN
Gulf of Mexico
Cuba
Hispaniola
Puerto Rico
CENTRAL AMERICA
Jamaica
Caribbean Sea
SOUTH AMERICA
Scale varies with perspective

First voyage, 1492
Second voyage, 1493
Third voyage, 1498
Fourth voyage, 1502
Present-day names

Map and Globe Skills

1. Circle the island where Columbus first landed.

2. On which voyage did Columbus sail along the coast

   of Central America? _____

   _____

The Columbian Exchange

Columbus called the people who lived on the island "Indios." This is the Spanish word for "Indians." However, the people already had a name—the Taíno.

The Taíno and Columbus offered gifts to each other. Columbus's men explored the island and found plants that they had never seen before. Columbus took the gifts from the Taíno and many plants with him back to Spain. These items excited the king and queen, who sent him back for more. This was the beginning of the Columbian Exchange, or the movement of people, plants, animals, and diseases across the Atlantic Ocean.

New foods from the Americas, such as corn, tomatoes, and potatoes, made European diets healthier. The exchange also introduced European foods and animals to the Americas. Horses changed the way Native Americans hunted. Sheep's wool brought changes to the clothing worn by some people. Unfortunately, Europeans and their animals also brought germs and diseases that were unknown in the Americas. Smallpox, measles, and other diseases from Europe spread quickly. By 1600, millions of native peoples across the Americas had died from those diseases.

DID YOU KNOW?
The Columbian Exchange included a trade in people. Africans and Native Americans were captured and **enslaved**. To be enslaved means to be forced to work for no pay. Traders brought enslaved people to Europe and the Americas.

Chart and Graph Skills

The lists below show items that crossed the Atlantic Ocean. Circle the items that were used for travel. Underline items that were used for food. Put a dot next to items that were used for clothing.

To the Americas:		To Europe:
wheat	goats	tomatoes
bananas	colonists	pineapples
oranges	enslaved Africans	sweet potatoes
horses	onions	hummingbirds
cattle	melons	squirrels
wheels	peaches	enslaved people
honey bees	pigs	potatoes
rice	plows	corn
sugar	diseases	turkeys
coffee	sheep	diseases

The Aztec Empire

Other Spanish explorers came to the Americas after Columbus. If you asked these explorers in 1520 to name the greatest city in the world, chances are that many of them would have said Tenochtitlán. This large city was the capital of the Aztec Empire. Many millions of people lived in the Aztec Empire. Its territory included much of what is now Mexico.

Hernán Cortés was one of these explorers. In 1519 he landed in Central America with more than 500 conquistadors, or Spanish conquerors. The Spanish explorers were very impressed with the city's size, its huge population, riches, and architecture. Native Americans had never seen white skin. They had never heard guns fire. They had never seen horses.

Montezuma II, the Aztec ruler, welcomed the Spanish explorers. But then, Cortés took Montezuma prisoner and demanded gold for the king's freedom. The Aztec refused and drove the Spanish away. Unfortunately, Montezuma was killed in the violence. Later, smallpox killed tens of thousands of Aztec. Cortés came back to destroy Tenochtitlán.

> Draw your own graphic novel of the interaction explained above between the Spanish and the Aztec. Make sure to include a title.

The Inca Empire

The Spaniards wanted more gold, so they headed south. They didn't know that the Inca Empire ruled much of South America. It extended more than 2,500 miles along the Pacific coast.

Inca leaders didn't worry when they heard about the Spaniards' arrival. They were busy with their own problems. The Inca Empire was collapsing. It was being torn apart by civil war. Diseases from Central America hurt the empire as well. These diseases spread quickly along a system of stone roads that connected cities within the empire.

In 1532, Francisco Pizzaro landed on South America's west coast. He had 168 men and 30 horses with him. They attacked a large Inca city, killing thousands. Pizzaro and his men also captured the Inca ruler Atahualpa.

The Inca offered Pizarro a room filled with treasure in exchange for Atahualpa's life. For months gold and silver objects arrived from all over the empire. When the room was filled, Pizzaro killed Atahualpa. Then the conquistadors melted the gold and silver items into coins or bars and sent them to Spain.

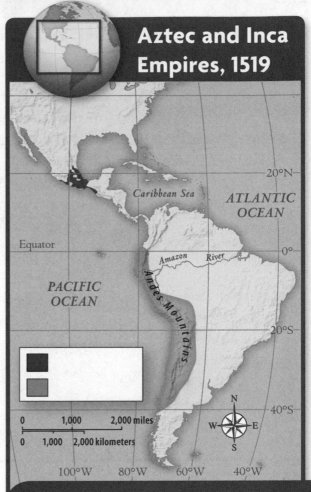

Aztec and Inca Empires, 1519

Map and Globe Skills

1. Label the Aztec and Inca empires and fill in the map key.

2. Which empire covers these coordinates? 20°S, 70°W

_____

Reading Skill

Summarize

In the Headlines Write a short description of each event from the point of view of the Spanish, the Aztec, and the Inca.

Fall of the Aztec	Fall of the Inca
Spanish Description:	Spanish Description:
Aztec Description:	Inca Description:

Letters from New Spain

The Spanish didn't just explore South America. They were also interested in North America. As they traveled, they **claimed** land for Spain. Conquistadors and missionaries traveled through what is now Florida, the rest of the Southeast, and the Southwest region of the United States. A missionary is a person who tries to persuade people to accept new religious beliefs. These ficitionalized letters tell about the journeys and settlements of the Spanish in North America.

Key Details
As you read, underline the key details of each letter.

1513

Hi Mom,
I made it to the new world. It only took two months to get here! Traveling with Juan Ponce de León is so exciting. We are always searching for silver and gold. De León has named this place La Florida, or "place of flowers."

Your son,
Marcos

1542

Isabel,
We are far west of the mighty river that divides this vast land. Francisco Coronado has us marching south at a steady pace. A missionary told us of seven cities of gold. We have searched for nearly two years. Yet, all we have found is a cluster of seven villages. None was made of gold. I was hoping to come home a rich man. I fear I will be disappointed.

Until we meet again,
Yago

1541

Dear Maria,
We are traveling north of Florida in search of gold. Hernando de Soto has us moving west toward a mighty river. The Native Americans say it divides the land. They say there are villages full of treasure on the other side. When we find the villages, I'm going to be a very rich man.

Sincerely,
Jorge

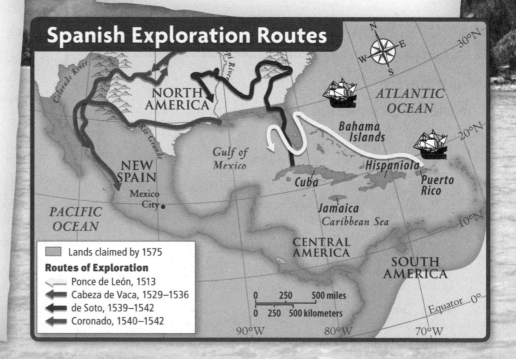

Spanish Exploration Routes

NORTH AMERICA
ATLANTIC OCEAN
Bahama Islands
Hispaniola
Cuba
Puerto Rico
Gulf of Mexico
NEW SPAIN
Mexico City
PACIFIC OCEAN
Jamaica
Caribbean Sea
CENTRAL AMERICA
SOUTH AMERICA
Equator 0°
Colorado River
Rio Grande
30°N
20°N
10°N
90°W
80°W
70°W

Lands claimed by 1575
Routes of Exploration
Ponce de León, 1513
Cabeza de Vaca, 1529–1536
de Soto, 1539–1542
Coronado, 1540–1542

0   250   500 miles
0   250   500 kilometers

1554

Alvaro,
I have decided to stay in New Spain. In exchange I received an encomienda, or large area of land. Encomiendas are given to loyal Spaniards willing to settle in the Americas. I am not sure how I will take care of my land. There are many Native Americans living on it. Other encomienda owners have driven them off or enslaved them. There are also some enslaved Africans on encomiendas nearby. Can you come to help me manage the property?

Sincerely,
Miguel

1563

Brother,
You would not believe the terrible way the conquistadors treat the Native Americans. Native American cultures are developed and sophisticated. The people have roles and responsibilities. They have great cities with buildings and roadways that are as nice as Europe's. How can they not treat the Native Americans as people? I fear my missionary work is the least of my worries.

Humbly,
Father Bartolomé de Las Casas

Lesson 2

 Essential Question   What happens when different cultures meet?

_____

_____

_____

_____

Go back to *Show As You Go!* on pages 72–73.

 networks   **There's More Online!**
   Games   Assessment

French and Dutch Exploration

Essential Question

What happens when different cultures meet? What do you think?

_____

_____

_____

_____

_____

_____

Words To Know

Write the definition of each word in your own words.

*intent

_____

_____

ally

_____

_____

Searching for the Northwest Passage

Have you ever used a shortcut to get somewhere fast? Christopher Columbus's **intent** was to find a shortcut to Asia. Instead, he found two large continents! Still, many people believed there must be a shortcut through North America to the Pacific Ocean. They called this waterway the Northwest Passage. Locating and controlling this shortcut would lead to huge profits. The race was on!

English Exploration

John Cabot, an Italian, was one of the first to search for the Northwest Passage. He sailed for England in 1497 and landed on what is now Newfoundland, an island off the coast of Canada. Cabot searched for the passage as he sailed south along the coast.

▲ John Cabot

He didn't find a shortcut. Instead he found an area of the Atlantic Ocean crowded with fish! Sailors scooped them into baskets dropped from the sides of their ships. Colonists who moved to the area built a fishing industry that exported, or sent, dried fish to Europe. Fishing is still important to the economy of this area today.

After Cabot's voyage, England became more concerned with wars at home. Their exploration of North America ended for a long time. When English sailors returned to the continent, they focused on building settlements.

Reading Skill

Key Details Underline the nationalities, dates of travel, and sponsoring country for each explorer.

French Exploration

Another Italian, Giovanni da Verrazano, sailed for the French in 1525. He went from what is now North Carolina north to the mouth of the Hudson River.

Frenchman Jacques Cartier set out in 1535 as well. He traveled around Newfoundland and the Gulf of St. Lawrence. During two other trips he traveled down the St. Lawrence River.

Dutch Exploration

Englishman Henry Hudson sailed south from what is now Maine along the coast of North America in 1609. The Dutch East India Company paid for his voyage. This group of merchants worked together to pay the costs of the voyage in hopes of making money from it.

A second trip in 1610 took Hudson farther north. As winter set in, the ship froze in ice. It was stuck! When spring came, Hudson tried to continue exploring. Tired, hungry, and ready to go home, the crew took over the ship. Hudson, his son, and eight loyal crew were placed on a boat, left behind, and were never seen again.

◀ Giovanni da Verrazano (top), Jacques Cartier (middle), Henry Hudson (bottom)

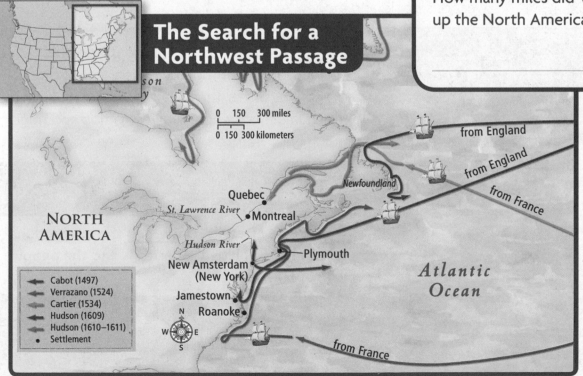

The Search for a Northwest Passage

0 150 300 miles
0 150 300 kilometers

from England
from England
from France

Newfoundland

Quebec
St. Lawrence River
Montreal

NORTH AMERICA

Hudson River
Plymouth

New Amsterdam (New York)

Jamestown
Roanoke

Atlantic Ocean

from France

Cabot (1497)
Verrazano (1524)
Cartier (1534)
Hudson (1609)
Hudson (1610–1611)
● Settlement

N W E S

Map and Globe Skills

How many miles did Verrazano sail up the North American coast?

_____

New France

Jacques Cartier claimed the land near the St. Lawrence River for France in 1534. For more than 60 years, France paid little attention to the colony. Then, in 1608, King Henry IV sent Samuel de Champlain to New France as its governor. Champlain built a permanent settlement and fur-trading post called Quebec.

Fur coats and hats were very popular in Europe. Champlain knew that if he managed the colony well, he would make a lot of money. To make it work, he became an **ally**, or political and military partner, with Native Americans in the area. The French provided guns to these allies in exchange for fur, crops, and other goods.

> **Write a caption for the picture of Champlain in New France.**
>
> _____

Career Opportunities

With the fur trade booming, people rushed to New France with hopes of making a fortune as hunters and trappers. They lived with Native Americans, learned their languages and hunting techniques, and earned their friendship. In exchange, Native Americans received weapons, tools, and money.

French officials feared there were too many hunters exporting fur to Europe. This would lower the price of fur and cause a loss of profit. To control prices, the French government limited the number of people allowed to trap and trade fur in New France.

People who trapped for fur without a permit in New France were known as coureurs de bois, or "runners of the woods." ▼

> **Reading Skill**
> Key Details <u>Underline</u> the interactions between Native Americans and the people of New France.

Slow Growth

The French king expanded the colony. He encouraged more people to settle there. He wanted New France to be a Catholic colony. But many people leaving France weren't Catholic and were fleeing religious persecution. They settled in England's colonies, instead.

New France grew slowly because of this. So slowly, in fact, that Native Americans and French colonists didn't compete for land for many years. This helped the French and native peoples build strong alliances at the time.

French Missionaries

French missionaries traveled deep into Native American lands. French missionaries had come to convert the Native Americans, but they didn't try to change native customs. Instead, missionaries lived among Native Americans, learned their languages, and respected their ways.

The Great Lakes

While their fur trade grew, French explorers continued to look for the Northwest Passage. Étienne Brûlé searched for it in 1610. He didn't find the Northwest Passage. But did he became the first European to see Lakes Ontario, Erie, Huron, and Superior.

Seven years later, Jean Nicolet pushed farther west than Brûlé. He became the first European to reach Lake Michigan. Both Brûlé and Nicolet lived with and learned from Native Americans while exploring.

The Great Lakes

Compare and contrast the interactions of the Spanish and French with Native Americans using the diagram below. Hint: You will have to flip back to pages 86–91 to find information about Spain.

Spanish Interactions   **In Common**   **French Interactions**

New Netherland

While the French settled along the St. Lawrence River, the Dutch settled along the Hudson River. Captain Henry Hudson explored this area for the Netherlands. The newspaper clipping tells about the colony.

Reading Skill

Summarize
Read the newspaper article. Then, write a headline that summarizes the main idea.

FUN FACTS
At this time, 60 Dutch guilders were equal to about $24 today.

DID YOU KNOW?
New Netherland's diverse population included people who were:
- Catholic
- Protestant
- Jewish
- Enslaved Africans
- Native American

Key Details
<u>Underline</u> the benefits of being a patroon in New Netherland.

New Netherland Gazette

Issue 36   September 1653

New Netherland was founded 30 years ago today. In honor of this event, we remember the history of our colony.

Captain Henry Hudson first sailed to North America in 1609. His travels led to the creation of our colony in 1623. We soon built Fort Nassau and Fort Orange along the Hudson River to protect our colonists.

Three years later, Governor Peter Minuit bought the large island in the Hudson River. The Manhattes people sold the land in exchange for goods worth 60 guilders. These goods included cloth and tools.

We named the island New Amsterdam. It soon became the colony's center of trade. This flourishing seaport has allowed all of New Netherland to grow.

As trade increased, so did the number of New Netherland's settlers. Today our colonists are of many backgrounds. They include Dutch, Germans, Swedes, and South Americans.

▲ **New Amsterdam**

Live Like a King

The Dutch West India Company is offering large estates to anyone bringing at least 50 people to the colony. Come to an informational meeting to hear more. Patroons are people who have received these lands. They will speak about their success. Here is some of what we will discussed:

- The largest estates have their own courts and laws.
- Patroons rule their lands like kings.
- People live and work on the land in exchange for a share of their crops.
- This opportunity is open to all colonists regardless of nationality or religion.

Map and Globe Skills

Use clues from the text to finish the map key. Identify the European country that claimed each shaded area of land.

Lake Superior

Quebec

Montreal

Lake Michigan

Lake Huron

Lake Ontario

St. Lawrence

Lake Erie

Fort Orange

Ohio R.

New Amsterdam

ATLANTIC OCEAN

N W E S

0	250	500 miles
0	250	500 kilometers

Explain how the interactions of the French and Dutch with Native Americans were similar.

_____

_____

_____

_____

_____

Lesson 3

? Essential Question What happens when different cultures meet?

_____

_____

_____

_____

_____

Go back to *Show As You Go!* on pages 72–73.

networks There's More Online!
• Games • Assessment

Who and What in Exploration

As the European colonies in North America grew, they changed the lives of Europeans, Africans, and Native Americans. Circle the name of the correct person, group, place, or term described in each riddle below.

1. I named the land I explored *La Florida,* or "place of flowers."

   Juan Ponce de León   **Francisco Pizarro**   **Henry Hudson**

2. This city was the center of trade in New Netherland.

   Mexico City   **Quebec**   **New Amsterdam**

3. The Spaniards enslaved us on our own land.

   conquistadors   **Native Americans**   **missionaries**

4. This man encouraged explorers from Portugal to sail south around Africa.

   John Bird   **Prince Henry**   **Christopher Columbus**

5. The French and Native Americans are best described as which of the following?

   allies   **enemies**   **missionaries**

6. Bartolomé de Las Casas spoke out against bad treatment of Native Americans. Which word best describes him?

   missionary   **merchant**   **conquistador**

7. New France mainly exported which good to Europe?

   gold   **fur**   **spices**

8. This is the word for a Spanish soldier who explored the Americas.

   ally   **missionary**   **conquistador**

Unit Project

Your team will design a deck of Trading Cards for one group of European explorers. Your deck must include facts, images, and a consistent design. Look back at pages 72–73 to review your notes and brainstorm ideas. You may need to do additional research at the library or on the Internet. Read the list below to see what should be included in your deck. Check off the tasks you have completed.

Vasco Nunez de Balboa

Your deck should include: **Yes, it does!**

Explorer's name and nationality ☐

Explorer's sponsor, goal, and date(s) of travel ☐

Location and results of exploration ☐

Issues faced during travels ☐

One or more images ☐

One consistent design and layout for all cards in your deck ☐

Think about the Big Idea

BIG IDEA People's actions affect others.

What did you learn in this unit that helps you understand the BIG IDEA?

_____

_____

_____

_____

_____

Read the story "Enslaved Labor in New Spain" before answering Numbers 1 through 8.

Enslaved Labor in New Spain

By Carly Alemu

Life became very harsh for the Native Americans of New Spain. Spain began to settle its new colonies by granting encomiendas to new colonists. An encomienda was an area of land that included Native American towns. The Native Americans on the land had to work for the new owner, and the colonial holder of the encomienda agreed to house and feed them. The system was like slavery, but there were differences. The colonists had to promise to teach the Native Americans new skills and to tell them about Christianity.

Native Americans worked from dawn to dusk. Sometimes they were treated harshly and could even be whipped. Often, they were hungry. When the Spanish found silver in what is now southern Bolivia and central Mexico, they forced Native Americans to work in these mines. The silver helped to make Spain one of the richest and most powerful countries in Europe.

The Native American population suffered under the ecomienda system. Many died from being overworked and from the diseases that came with the Europeans. Soon, the Spanish ecomienda owners needed to find other sources of labor. Their solution was to enslave large numbers of captive Africans.

Not everyone agreed with the ecomienda system. Bartolomé de Las Casas was a Catholic priest who had come to the island of Hispaniola to run an ecomienda. Once he saw the Native Americans dying of disease and overwork, he decided to try to end the system. Eventually, Spanish laws were changed to better govern the ecomiendas. These laws were ineffective, though. Spain was too far away and could not make the landowners obey. Native Americans continued to be mistreated.

1 What is this article mostly about?

Ⓐ life in New Spain

Ⓑ Native Americans in New Spain

Ⓒ encomiendas in New Spain

Ⓓ Spanish exploration in New Spain

2 Read the sentence from the story.

These laws were ineffective, though.

What does the word ineffective mean in this story?

Ⓕ forceful

Ⓖ organized

Ⓗ weak

Ⓘ courageous

3 According to the article, which of the following statements is true?

Ⓐ Colonists had to house and feed Native Americans living and working on their land.

Ⓑ Native Americans were forced to leave all encomiendas.

Ⓒ Native Americans were given encomiendas.

Ⓓ Colonists accepted the religious beliefs of Native Americans.

4 Which sentence best describes Bartolomé de Las Casas?

Ⓕ He was a missionary who worked against the encomienda system.

Ⓖ He was a missionary who ran a successful encomienda.

Ⓗ He was a missionary who started the encomienda system.

Ⓘ He was a missionary who finally ended the encomienda system.

5 What helped Spain become one of the richest and most powerful countries in Europe?

Ⓐ encomiendas

Ⓑ learning new skills

Ⓒ new colonists

Ⓓ silver mines

6 Why did the encomienda owners enslave captive Africans?

Ⓕ because captive Africans lived far away

Ⓖ because captive Africans lived nearby

Ⓗ because the Native American population had greatly declined

Ⓘ because the Native American population had increased too much

7 What key detail supports the author's statement that "life became very harsh for Native Americans"?

Ⓐ Encomiendas included Native American towns.

Ⓑ Colonists agreed to house and feed Native Americans.

Ⓒ Native Americans were sometimes whipped.

Ⓓ Colonists promised to teach Native Americans new skills.

8 The article says Native Americans worked "from dawn to dusk." What does this mean?

Ⓕ They only worked in the morning.

Ⓖ They only worked in the evening.

Ⓗ They didn't each lunch or dinner.

Ⓘ They worked all day long.

UNIT 4 Colonial America

 BIG IDEA Location affects how people live.

About 400 years ago, the English set up their first settlements in North America. Over time, a few humble settlements grew into 13 busy colonies. Who built these colonies? Why did these colonists come? How did they live? In this unit, you will read about the founding of each of the thirteen colonies and how people there went about their lives. As you read, think about how the location of each colony affected life within it.

networks
connected.mcgraw-hill.com
● Skill Builders
● Vocabulary Flashcards

After Lesson 1
⬜ Add a title above the map.
⬜ Locate and label the early settlements of Roanoke, Jamestown, and Plymouth. Label the Atlantic Ocean and North America.

After Lessons 2, 3 and 4
⬜ Label the location of at least one Native American group that lived in the region you studied.
⬜ Choose a color for the colonial regions you studied in these lessons. Use a different color for each region. Shade the region in that color, and then shade that region's box on the map legend.

After Lesson 5
⬜ Label the compass rose with the cardinal and intermediate directions.
⬜ Label each colonial city on the map.
⬜ Choose one good that colonists might have exported from each region. Create a symbol for each export, and draw it on its correct region on the map. Add your symbols to the map legend.

After Lesson 6
⬜ Draw one arrow pointing toward the colonies. Label it "Goods In." Draw another arrow pointing away from the colonies. Label it "Goods Out." Add an arrow symbol to the map legend. Label it "Triangular Trade Routes."
⬜ Draw a red outline around all the colonial regions that took part in slavery. Add this line to the map legend, and label it.

Show as You Go! After you read each lesson in this unit, complete the activities on page 102. You will use your finished map to help you complete a project at the end of the unit.

Fold page here

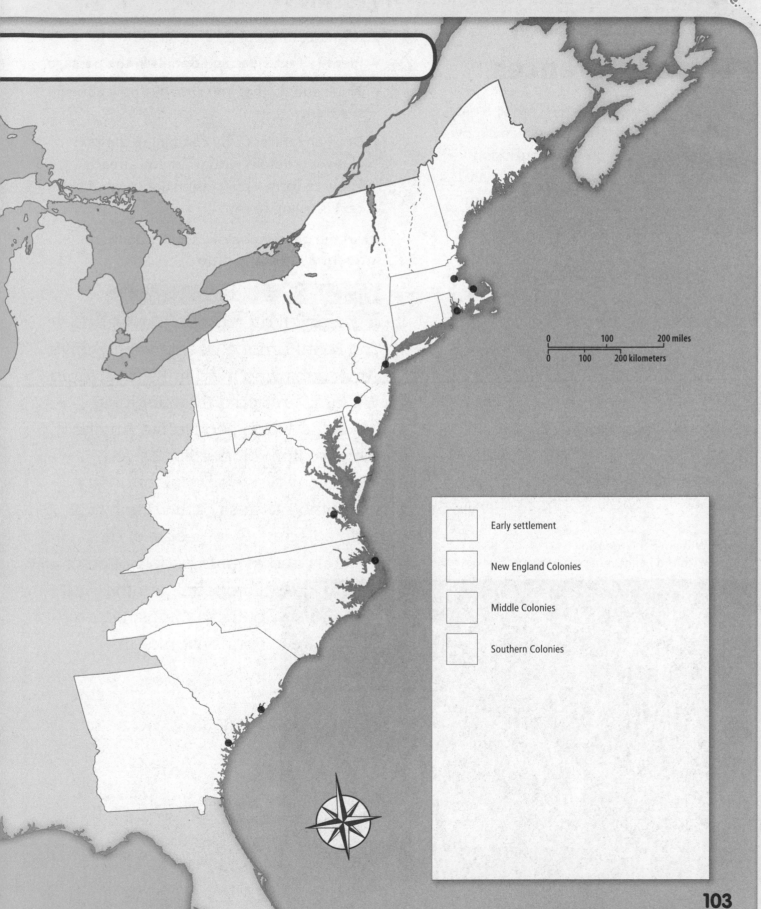

	Early settlement
	New England Colonies
	Middle Colonies
	Southern Colonies

0   100   200 miles
0   100   200 kilometers

Reading Skill

Common Core Standards
RI.1: Quote accurately from a text when explaining what the text says explicitly and when drawing inferences from the text.

Draw Inferences

When you read, you often combine new information with what you already know to draw a conclusion. This conclusion is also called an inference. To make an inference, combine the facts you learn from reading with what you already know.

LEARN IT

To draw an inference:

- **Identify text clues and details in the passage.**

- **Think about what you already know about the topic.**

- **Draw an inference by combining the text clues and details with what you already know to form a conclusion about what the text is trying to say.**

Read the passage below. Think about an inference you could draw.

Text Clue

Details

William Penn did things a little differently than most English settlers. The Lenni Lenape people were Native Americans who lived in Pennsylvania. William Penn paid them for their lands. He welcomed Native American refugees from other colonies, too. The colony was peaceful for a very long time because of this. Penn also granted equality to people of all religions and even to people of other European countries. All of these things helped Pennsylvania grow.

▼ **William Penn meeting with the Lenni Lenape.**

© Corbis

 **TRY IT**

Fill in the chart below in order to draw inferences about good ways to work with people. Use the paragraph on page 104.

Text Clues and Details	What You Know	Inference(s)

APPLY IT

Review the steps for drawing inferences in Learn It. Then, read the passage below. Circle text clues and details that you could use to draw an inference. Draw an inference and explain it on the lines, using details from the text.

The first Jamestown colonists struggled. They didn't want to work, even though they needed to in order to survive. Captain Smith proclaimed, "Those who don't work, don't eat!" He forced them all to work, and things began to look up. But then, Smith was injured in an accident. He had to return to England for treatment. Without his leadership, the colonists quit working. The harsh winter that followed was called the "starving time" because many colonists died.

_____
_____
_____
_____
_____
_____
_____
_____

Words to Know

Common Core Standards
RI.4: Determine the meaning of general academic and domain-specific words and phrases in a text relevant to a grade 5 topic or subject area.

The list below shows some important words you will learn in this unit. Their definitions can be found on the next page. Read the words.

pilgrim (PIHL • gruhm)

covenant (KUH • vuh • nuhnt)

tolerate (TAH • luh • rayt)

proprietor (pruh • PRY • uh • tuhr)

act (AKT)

assembly (uh • SEHM • blee)

occupation (ah • kyuh • PAY • shuhn)

indentured servant (ihn • DEHN • shuhrd SUHR • vuhnt)

The Foldable on the next page will help you learn Foldable these important words. Follow the steps below to make your Foldable.

Step 1 Fold along the solid red line.

Step 2 Cut along the dotted lines.

Step 3 Read the words and their definitions.

Step 4 Complete the activities on each tab.

Step 5 Look at the back of your Foldable. Choose ONE of these activities for each word to help you remember its meaning:

- Draw a picture of the word.
- Write a description of the word.
- Write how the word is related to something you know.

The Pilgrims made a religious journey to find new land in North America. ▼

Library of Congress

A **pilgrim** is a person who makes a journey for religious reasons.	**Circle the three words that belong with the word *pilgrim*.** land journey stay beliefs travel gold
A **covenant** is a contract or agreement between people.	**Circle two key words in the definition of *covenant*. Write the words here:** _____ _____
To **tolerate** is to accept differences among people.	**Write an antonym for the word *tolerate*.**
A **proprietor** is someone who owns a business.	**A proprietor owns a business. What do you think it means to own a business?**
Act is another word for law.	**What do you think the purpose of an act is?**
An **assembly** is a group of people who make laws.	**Cross out the two words that do not belong with the word *assembly*.** one town government rules order animal
An **occupation** is work that a person does in order to make a living.	**Circle two key words in the definition of occupation. Write the words here:** _____ _____
An **indentured servant** is someone who agrees to work for a number of years in exchange for travel to a colony.	**Write a sentence using the words *indentured servant*.**

FOLD

pilgrim	pilgrim
covenant	covenant
tolerate	tolerate
proprietor	proprietor
act	act
assembly	assembly
occupation	occupation
indentured servant	indentured servant

CUT HERE

Primary Sources

Letters

Letters are a type of primary source. People send many different types of information through letters. Letters can reveal what it was like to live in a time and place long ago. Without primary sources, such as letters, some of the rich details of history might have been forgotten.

In this unit, you will learn about how settlers from England and other parts of Europe came to North America and made their homes here. A man named John Dickenson lived during this time. On the right is a letter he wrote to his friends and neighbors in England. As you read it, think about the place it describes, and the details that tell you about the writer's life.

 Document-Based Questions

Read the letter. As you read, complete the following activities.

1. **Underline details that describe where John Dickenson lived.**

2. **Circle details that describe his daily life.**

3. **Put a box around the new vocabulary words in the account.**

Primary Source

My Dear Countrymen,

I . . . settled . . . near the banks of the River Delaware in the **province** of Pennsylvania. . . . My farm is small; my servants are few and good; I have a little money. . . .

I spend a good deal of [my time] in [my] library. . . . I have acquired, I believe, a greater share of knowledge . . . than is generally **attained** by men of my class.

province: a part of a country or settled area

attain: to gain something

---

networks
There's More Online!
● Skill Builders
● Resource Library

Early Settlements

**Why do people move?
What do you think?**

_____

_____

_____

_____

_____

_____

_____

_____

Words To Know

Have you heard these words before? Make a guess about what each word means and write it on the lines. Then find it in the lesson.

*assume

_____

persecution

Have you ever moved to a new home or had a friend who has moved away? In Lesson 1, you'll learn about English colonists who left their homes to move to North America.

> **Think about how you might feel if you had to move to a new place. Use your thoughts to complete the short story below.**
>
> When I was _____ years old, my family moved to
>
> _____. We moved because _____.
>
> I felt _____,
>
> because _____.

In the 1500s, Europeans were excited about new lands in North America. Countries eagerly gobbled up land there, expanding their territories. People **assumed** they would find vast amounts of gold and other riches in North America.

In 1585 Queen Elizabeth I issued a **charter** to settle land in North America. A charter is an official document that gives special rights to its holder. This charter said a man named Sir Walter Raleigh could claim land for England. In this lesson, you will learn about three early English settlements.

> **What continent is on this side of the illustration?**
>
> _____
>
> **Who are these people?**
>
> _____

Roanoke

Founding date: 1585
Location: present-day North Carolina
Founder: Sir Walter Raleigh
Motivations: Expand England's territory;
   search for gold and other riches
Settlement Attempts: Two

Life was rough in Roanoke. The land was bad for farming, and those who traveled there were businessmen, not farmers or woodsmen. They weren't fully prepared, and supply ships were few and far between. The first group of settlers survived a long, hungry winter and returned to England in the spring. They had found no riches in Roanoke.

In 1587 John White led a second group to Roanoke. This time women and children came along, too. They had similar troubles as the first group. White returned to England for supplies and help, but he was held up in Europe by a war. When he finally made it back to Roanoke in 1590, all the colonists were gone. No one knows for sure what happened to them. Roanoke became known as the Lost Colony.

▲ In 1585 Queen Elizabeth I gave Sir Walter Raleigh his charter.

What body of water is this?

_____

_____

In the empty space of the illustration, draw a ship leaving the port.

Think about the illustration and what you already know about European explorers. Make a prediction about how English settlers and Native Americans will interact.

_____

_____

Early English Settlements

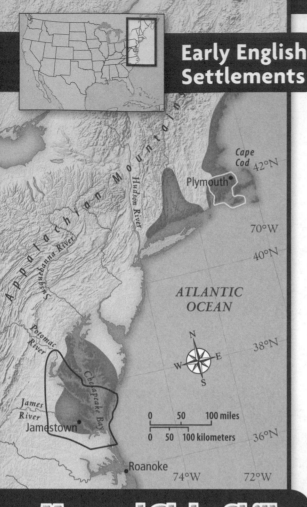

Jamestown

Founding date: 1607
Location: Inside the Chesapeake Bay, on the James River
Founders: The Virginia Company
Motivations: Expand England's territory; search for gold and other riches; grow cash crops
Folk Hero: John Smith

Jamestown's founders were a group of business owners called the Virginia Company. The first Jamestown colonists struggled just like those at Roanoke. Captain John Smith forced settlers to work hard. He proclaimed, "Those who don't work, don't eat!" Unfortunately, Smith was badly injured and had to return to England. Without his leadership, the colonists quit working. The harsh winter that followed was called the "starving time." Many colonists died.

Besides hunger, disease and injury also threatened colonists' lives. During the early years, only 20 percent of the colonists survived. Eventually, they adjusted. John Rolfe planted the first successful tobacco crop in Jamestown in 1612. The money he made inspired others. Tobacco brought stability and wealth, and as a result, Jamestown began to prosper! It became the first permanent English settlement in North America.

Map and Globe Skills

1. Measure the distance between Plymouth and Jamestown.

   Plymouth was about _____

   miles _____ of Jamestown.

2. What line of latitude is closest to Plymouth?_____

 Underline the harsh conditions settlers of Jamestown had to face.

This is what archaeologists think Jamestown may have looked like. ▼

© Corbis

Plymouth

Founding date: 1620
Location: Cape Cod
Founders: The Pilgrims
Motivations: Religious freedom

In England in the 1600s, it was illegal to belong to any church except the Church of England. Those who spoke out against the Church faced **persecution**, or harsh treatment for their religious beliefs. One group who wanted to break away from the Church were the **Pilgrims**. A pilgrim is someone who makes a journey for religious reasons. The Pilgrims thought that the Church would never make the changes they wanted. They decided to head to North America.

A ship called the *Mayflower* left England in September 1620. The 102 men, women, and children aboard faced rough seas, hunger, and disease during their journey across the Atlantic.

When they arrived two months later, a harsh winter was right around the corner. By spring, only half remained—the rest died of disease or starvation. Those who survived set about building a settlement called Plymouth.

▲ In 1620 the first Pilgrims landed in Plymouth.

Native Americans

Native Americans and the settlers at Roanoke and Jamestown competed for food and other resources. Differing languages and cultures made understanding each other very difficult at times. Conflict between the two groups soon became a part of life.

At Plymouth, the Pilgrims found a village abandoned by the Pawtuxet, who had died of European diseases years earlier. One remaining Pawtuxet man lived nearby with the Wampanoag. His name was Squanto, and he spoke some English. The Wampanoag and Squanto helped the Pilgrims survive their first year at Plymouth.

Lesson 1

 Essential Question **Why do people move?**

_____

_____

_____

Go back to *Show As You Go!* on pages 102–103.

 networks **There's More Online!**
● Games ● Assessment

Library of Congress

Settling New England

? Essential Question

How do societies develop? What do you think?

_____

_____

_____

_____

_____

_____

_____

_____

Words To Know

Write a word that sounds like or looks like these words.

covenant _____

tyrant _____

*appropriate

_____

THINK · PAIR · SHARE _Imagine you are the leader of a club, and you want your club to be the best one in school. Work with a partner to come up with rules for your club. What happens if someone breaks a rule?_

Other groups who disagreed with the Church of England wanted to reform the Church. They were called the Puritans. Like the Pilgrims, the Puritans were persecuted for their religious beliefs. Many faced jail, threats, and other difficulties.

In 1625 the new king, Charles I, did not like that the Puritans were calling for change in the Church. The Puritans were treated even worse under Charles I. A group of wealthy Puritans formed the Massachusetts Bay Company. In 1629 they got a charter from the king and sailed west across the Atlantic.

On the next few pages, you will read what happened next, from the points of view of important people who were there.

Mill   Blacksmith's Shop   Stables

As you read, circle the different characteristics of Puritan settlements.

Puritan Villages

John Winthrop

We Puritans arrived in Massachusetts in 1630 and named our first settlement Boston. The year before that, the good men had already elected me, John Winthrop, as their governor.

Next, we set about constructing our villages. Most villages had at least a school and a large common building that served as both a meeting house and church. We arrived in the summer, which gave us enough time to get settled before winter. Puritan parents often treated their children like grown-ups, so kids helped in a big way. Our villages began to do very well.

Our new settlements were to be like "a city upon a hill" that would show all people how God wanted them to live. Each family made a **covenant**, or contract, with the church. Families promised to follow Puritan rules. If they didn't, we would make them leave the community.

Library of Congress

What were the Puritans' motivations for settling in North America?

_____

_____

What do you think "a city upon a hill" means?

_____

_____

Homes

Stocks

Meeting House

School

Common Area

New England Expands

Puritan rules were strict, and people soon disagreed with them. Leaders worried about losing control. They tried to silence new ideas. Some people left to form new settlements. As they left, New England grew. You will read what three of these settlers have to say on page 117. But first, you need to know some new words. A **tyrant** is someone who uses power cruelly or dictates the rules. To **tolerate** means to allow something to be or be done without trying to stop it.

Chart and Graph Skills

Read a Time Line

Once you are done reading page 117, fill in the time line. Write the name of each founder and each settlement under the correct years on the time line.

Winthrop Fleet

John Winthrop 1st Massachusetts governor

Anne Hutchinson arrives at Massachusetts

Rhode Island founded

Parliament reconvened

1630   1640

1630

1636

1638

Founding Rhode Island

Roger Williams

I, Roger Williams, was the first to leave those Puritan tyrants behind. I believed that the government should tolerate people of other religious views. Puritan leaders wanted to throw me in prison for this, so I fled in January 1636.

I am grateful to the Native Americans I met. They were the Narragansett, and they helped me survive the winter. I bought land from them and founded Providence. When the colony of Rhode Island was formed, my dear Providence became its capital. Rhode Island was the first English colony to allow freedom of religion.

Anne Hutchinson

*I am Anne Hutchinson. I had 14 children to care for, but I found time to hold meetings in my house. At those meetings, I boldly questioned the teachings of the Puritan ministers. The Massachusetts government did not think my actions were **appropriate**. They put me on trial and banished me from the colony. In 1638 my followers and I formed Portsmouth, another Rhode Island settlement.*

Founding Connecticut

My name is Thomas Hooker. I wanted Puritan churches to be independent from each other. This idea was less explosive than good man Williams' idea, but Puritan leaders still weren't happy with me. I did not want to wait for a trial, and I wanted new farmland anyway. So, I left on my own. In 1636 I led my followers west and south to the rich soil of the Connecticut River valley. We received a charter from England and called our new settlement Hartford.

Thomas Hooker

Reading Skill

Draw Inferences Underline the reasons each person on page 117 left their Puritan settlements. What can you infer about Puritan leadership?

_____

_____

New Englanders and Native Americans

FUN FACT

Maine and Vermont were never separate colonies. Settlers did live in those areas, but Maine was part of Massachusetts. And England and France fought over Vermont. Even some nearby colonies wanted it! Maine and Vermont became states much later.

Do you remember reading about how Native Americans helped the Pilgrims survive? This kindness led to a long peace between them. Not all New Englanders got along with all Native American tribes, though. Many experienced conflict, especially as settlements continued to expand.

The Pequot War

As Puritan towns grew, settlers needed more land and resources. This increased competition for resources with Native Americans nearby, especially with the Pequot. Tensions exploded into warfare. In 1637 Connecticut settlers attacked the Pequot. The settlers killed or captured hundreds of Pequot, and by 1638, they had defeated them. Pequot survivors joined other Native American villages nearby. English settlers then moved north into what became the colony of New Hampshire.

Underline positive and circle negative interactions between New Englanders and Native Americans.

The New England Colonies

MAINE
(PART OF MASSACHUSETTS)

Kennebec River

VERMONT
(CLAIMED BY
NEW HAMPSHIRE
AND NEW YORK)

ATLANTIC
OCEAN

N
W   E
S

Hudson River

Connecticut River

Boston

Pequot   Plymouth

Providence   *Wampanoag*

Hartford

Narragansett   Portsmouth

Long Island Sound

•	Settlement
Pequot	Native American group
▨	New England Colonies

0   50   100 miles

0   50   100 kilometers

Map and Globe Skills

1. Identify and locate the four New England colonies on the map. Label each one. Use your reference atlas if you need help.

2. **Circle** the name of the Native American group that helped Roger Williams.

3. **Underline** the Native American group that fought with the settlers in 1637.

118

King Philip's War

Even colonists and Native Americans who had been friends, such as the Pilgrims and the Wampanoag, soon viewed each other as enemies. Read what happened next from the point of view of one Native American leader.

Metacomet

I am Metacomet. I was called King Philip by the colonists. My father was Massasoit, the Wampanoag leader who helped the Pilgrims. He had kept peace with the Pilgrims for 40 years. After my father died in 1661, I became the new leader of our people. And soon, the colonists began taking our lands. I was angry that these people, who had been our friends, now had so little respect for us.

Protecting our lands was my duty. Over the years I made plans and convinced other Native American groups to fight with us. In 1675 our warriors attacked more than 50 settlements and killed hundreds of colonists. They fought back, attacking and burning many of our towns.

King Philip's War lasted more than a year, until Metacomet was trapped and killed by rival Native American forces that helped the English settlers. His death ended the war and marked the end of Native American power in the region.

DID YOU KNOW?

Why did the colonists call Metacomet "king"? The colonists often misunderstood the governing systems of Native Americans. To the colonists "leader," "elder," "chief," and "sachem" were the same as "king."

Why did colonists call Metacomet "Philip"? Massasoit had asked the governor of the Pilgrims to give his sons English names. Metacomet received the name Philip.

Lesson **2**

? **Essential Question** **How do societies develop?**

_____

_____

_____

_____

Go back to *Show As You Go!* on pages 102–103.

Settling the Middle Colonies

? Essential Question

How do societies develop?
What do you think?

_____

_____

_____

_____

_____

_____

Words To Know

Find the definition for each word and write a synonym on the line. A synonym is a word that has the same or almost the same meaning.

proprietor _____

*primary _____

When you were little, you probably played with blocks or other building toys. You may have had to defend your creations against others.

> **Think about a time when you had a conflict like this. Write about it on the lines below.**
>
> _____
>
> _____
>
> _____

A group of settlers in North America had to defend their settlement in 1664. They worked very hard building their colony, only to have someone declare that he was taking over! The settlers didn't have anyone nearby to go to for help. Think about this as you read their story.

Traders arrive in New Amsterdam. ▼

England Takes New Netherland

Here's how the story began. Remember that the Dutch had settled New Netherland in 1621. Its largest and most important settlement was New Amsterdam. Settlers to New Netherland came for the opportunity to own land and make a better life. As the colony flourished, England took notice.

> Read the story panels below, then complete the activity.

New Amsterdam, 1664

Meanwhile in England, King Charles II is feeling greedy.

I want to increase our colonies.

There is New Netherland …

Taking it over would make trade easier.

To my brother, the Duke of York, I give a gift. All the land between the Charles and Delaware Rivers!

"You'll have to take it by force."

We hereby claim this land for England. Surrender at once!

The English ships came armed and ready to fight. The Dutch colonists knew they couldn't win. They convinced their governor to surrender to the English. New Netherland became the English colony of New York. The settlement of New Amsterdam became New York City.

The Duke of York shared a small part of the land with his friends. They named their share New Jersey. Like Virginia, New York and New Jersey were run by **proprietors**, another word for business owners. The proprietors' main goal was to make money. They promised settlers land, religious freedom, and a voice in government. In return, settlers paid a tax.

What would you do? Draw yourself as a member of the crowd in the last scene. Then, explain what you would do on the lines below.

_____

_____

_____

_____

A Patron for Pennsylvania

The rest of the Middle Colonies were founded by a man named William Penn. He came from a wealthy and powerful English family. They belonged to the Church of England. Penn, however, joined another religious group called the Quakers. The Quakers were tolerant of other religions. They believed that everyone was equal. Like other religious groups, the Quakers were persecuted in England.

Penn's father had loaned money to the king. When his father died, William asked King Charles II to pay this debt with land in North America. The king gave William a large piece, west of New Jersey and southwest of New York. William named this land Pennsylvania, which means "Penn's Woods." He founded a colony where Quakers—and everyone else—could worship freely.

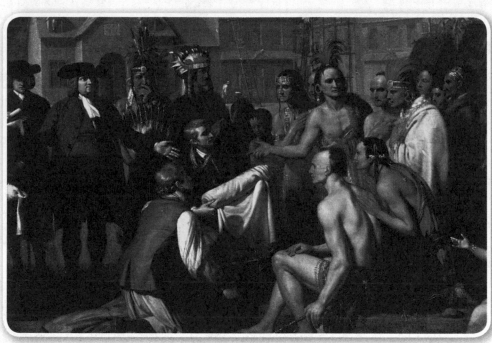

THINK • PAIR • SHARE
Underline the religious beliefs of the Quakers. Work with a partner to discuss how these beliefs differed from those of the Puritans.

This painting shows William Penn (second from the left) meeting with the Lenni Lenape to pay for their lands and negotiate peace. ▶

Describe how William Penn interacted with the Lenni Lenape.

_____

_____

_____

_____

_____

Peace and Diversity

William Penn interacted with Native Americans differently than most English settlers. He signed a peace treaty with the Lenni Lenape and paid them for their lands. Penn welcomed Native American refugees from other colonies, too. The colony was peaceful for a very long time because of this.

Penn also granted equality to people of all religions and even to people of other European countries. Pennsylvania soon had as much ethnic and religious **diversity** as New York and New Jersey. Diversity is the condition of having people who are different in some way living or working together in the same place.

Philadelphia

William Penn's **primary** motivation for founding Pennsylvania was religious freedom. He also wanted to make money, just like the proprietors of New York and New Jersey! He picked the location for the first capital of Pennsylvania and carefully planned it out himself. He called it Philadelphia, which means "city of brotherly love." Philadelphia grew to become the busiest city in the colonies.

Delaware

Pennsylvania was mostly shaped like a box, but it had a little piece of land hanging off its southeastern corner. This piece of land was called the Three Lower Counties. Before the English and the Dutch came, this region had been colonized by people from Sweden.

In 1704 they asked William Penn for the right to make their own laws. He granted their request. The land was still part of Pennsylvania, but the people who lived there called it Delaware. Over time, Delaware came to be thought of as its own colony.

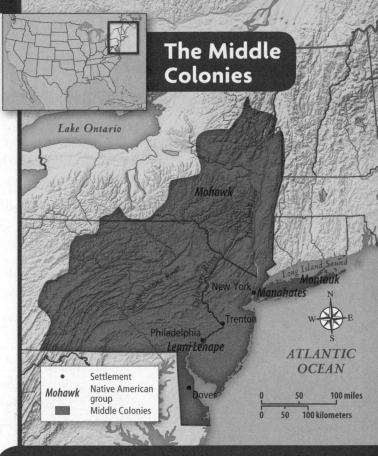

The Middle Colonies

Map and Globe Skills

1. **Identify and locate** the four Middle Colonies on the map. Label each one. Use your reference atlas if you need help.
2. **Circle** the city that used to be called New Amsterdam.
3. **Underline** the "city of brotherly love."

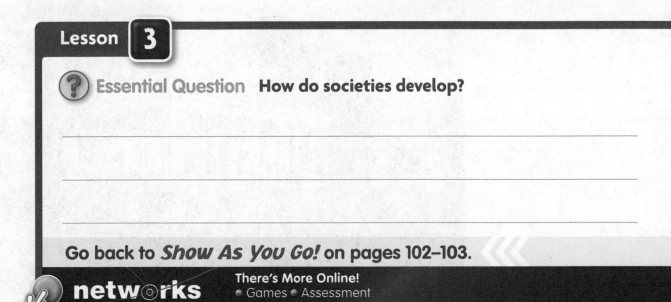

Lesson 3

? Essential Question How do societies develop?

_____

_____

_____

Go back to *Show As You Go!* on pages 102–103. ◀◀◀

Settling the Southern Colonies

? Essential Question

**How do societies develop?
What do you think?**

_____

_____

_____

_____

_____

Words To Know

Look at the words below. Discuss with a partner what you think they mean.

frontier

act

profit

*common

Imagine that you are looking for a new house. Make a short list of some things you want.

_____

_____

_____

Is a big back yard or nearby playground on your list? If so, you have something in common with many who came to the Southern Colonies! You both want land.

You remember reading about Jamestown's first successful tobacco crop, right? Virginia's climate was perfect for growing it. Tobacco was grown on plantations, or large farms that often grow just one crop. Each new harvest earned a lot of money. People flooded Virginia to either start their own farms or work on existing plantations. This caused Virginia to grow and expand each year. Soon, the colonists needed more room.

▼ **A painting of a Virginia plantation**

© Bridgeman Art Library

Virginia and Maryland

As Virginia grew, settlers pushed west, north, and south into new lands. At the same time, English leaders issued new colonial charters. The Southern colonies began to take shape.

George Calvert

Cecilius Calvert

The Algonquians

By now you know that Native Americans already lived on the land that Virginians wanted. Relations between the Jamestown settlers and the Algonquians had never been easy. As colonists claimed more land, conflict became more frequent.

The colonists had advantages, including guns and resistance to the diseases that came with them from Europe. These and other factors wore the Algonquians down year by year. In 1646 a Jamestown settler killed the leader of the Algonquians. This ended most of the major fighting, but smaller conflicts continued on the **frontier**. This is the edge of land settled by colonists. Virginia's growth was unstoppable, however.

1. **Underline** the motivations for founding Maryland.

2. **How was this similar to the reasons for founding colonies in New England?**

_____

_____

Founding Maryland

As you read in Lesson 1, in England in the 1600s it was illegal to belong to any church except the Church of England. Even so, at that time King Charles I was friends with a man named George Calvert, a Catholic.

Calvert hatched a plan to found a colony where Catholics could have religious freedom. King Charles agreed and in 1632 wrote up a colonial charter that founded Maryland. Unfortunately, Calvert died before the first settlers arrived. His son Cecilius took over.

Most of the settlers who came to Maryland from England were Catholic. However, many of Maryland's settlers came from Virginia and were members of the Church of England. Soon, Catholics were outnumbered. They might have faced persecution, but Maryland's charter protected them. In 1649 the Toleration **Act** made religious freedom the law for Christians in Maryland. Act is another word for law.

The Carolinas, North and South

Underline who settled Carolina. Circle their motivations.

England kept adding to its colonies. A new king, Charles II, set his sights on land south of Virginia. In 1663 he gave a charter for the colony of Carolina to eight proprietors. Seven years later, they founded their first settlement, the port city of Charles Towne.

Carolina's settlers established large plantations. They grew crops, such as tobacco and rice, for **profit**. Profit is the money left over after a business has paid all of its bills. They also sold forest products such as timber and tar. Soon Charles Towne prospered.

New settlers continued to arrive, lured by promises of religious freedom and land. Before long, farms and small settlements dotted Carolina's coast.

Carolina was a large piece of land—so large that its northern and southern parts developed differently. The northern part grew slowly because it didn't have a good port. The southern part grew rapidly because of Charles Towne. In 1729 the colonists decided to split their colony in two—North Carolina and South Carolina.

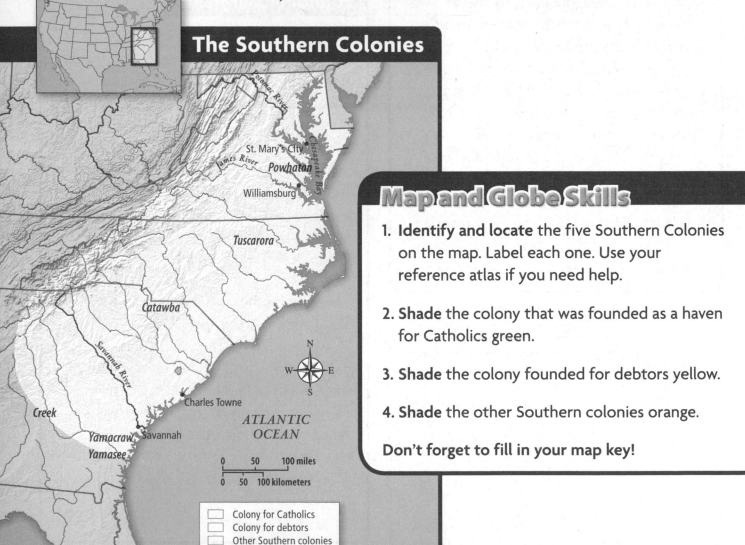

The Southern Colonies

Potomac River
St. Mary's City
James River
Powhatan
Chesapeake Bay
Williamsburg
Tuscarora
Catawba
Savannah River
Creek
Yamacraw
Savannah
Yamasee
Charles Towne

N
W E
S

ATLANTIC
OCEAN

0   50   100 miles
0   50   100 kilometers

Colony for Catholics
Colony for debtors
Other Southern colonies

Map and Globe Skills

1. **Identify and locate** the five Southern Colonies on the map. Label each one. Use your reference atlas if you need help.

2. **Shade** the colony that was founded as a haven for Catholics green.

3. **Shade** the colony founded for debtors yellow.

4. **Shade** the other Southern colonies orange.

Don't forget to fill in your map key!

Founding Georgia

As the colonies continued to bloom in the early 1700s, life back in Great Britain was pretty bad. Many families were poor and in **debt**, which means they owed money to others. It was **common** for debtors to be thrown in prison if they failed to pay. The British needed a solution to the misery.

A Colony for Debtors

James Oglethorpe had an idea. Why not create a new colony and send debtors there? They could work off their debt and make the colony rich! King George II liked the idea. He named the new colony after himself. In 1733 the first families sailed for Georgia.

Hundreds of poor came to Georgia. But in the end, Georgia didn't attract as many debtors as Oglethorpe had hoped. Other groups filled the gap. People from Germany and Switzerland came to Georgia. Promises of religious freedom and land lured them there. Once in the colonies, they fell under British rule. The founding of Georgia made Britain's set of thirteen colonies complete.

Native Americans and Georgia

Oglethorpe worked with Native Americans. Before building a settlement, he met with Tomochichi, the leader of the Yamacraw. The Yamacraw lived in the area where the settlers wanted to build. Oglethorpe obtained land for the settlement of Savannah, and Tomochichi became a friend to the settlers. He helped the settlers keep peace with Creek tribes nearby.

© Bridgeman Art Library

James Oglethorpe

Draw or describe James Oglethorpe's plan in the thought bubble.

Lesson 4

? Essential Question How do societies develop?

_____

_____

_____

Go back to *Show As You Go!* on pages 102–103. 《

networks There's More Online!
• Games • Assessment

127

5 Life in the Colonies

? Essential Question

How do societies develop?
What do you think?

_____

_____

_____

_____

_____

_____

Words To Know

Write the plural form of each word on the lines.

assembly _____

barter _____

occupation _____

*employ _____

In 300 years, your community may look very different from today. Pretend that someone from the future is describing your community. What facts would they need to know?

_____

_____

_____

In Lesson 5 we'll explore what communities looked like in the thirteen colonies. As you will see, communities 300 years ago were very different from those we live in today.

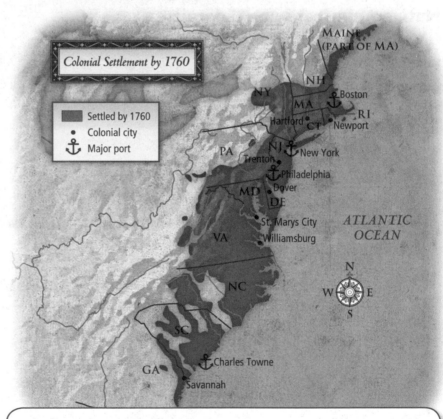

Colonial Settlement by 1760

- Settled by 1760
- Colonial city
- ⚓ Major port

MAINE (PART OF MA)
NH
NY
MA
Boston
Hartford
CT
RI
Newport
PA
NJ
New York
Trenton
Philadelphia
MD
Dover
DE
St. Marys City
VA
Williamsburg
ATLANTIC OCEAN
NC
SC
GA
Charles Towne
Savannah

What can you infer about the colonies based on this map?

_____

_____

How Did Colonists Live?

By the mid-1700s, English colonists had settled the East Coast from Massachusetts to Georgia. They had set up new communities with governments, economies, and ways of life. While each colonial region had similarities, they also had characteristics that set them apart.

As you read this lesson, come back to this page and fill the chart below with the different characteristics of the colonies.

	New England Colonies	Middle Colonies	Southern Colonies
Government			
Economy			
Social Aspects			

Governing the Thirteen Colonies

THINK · PAIR · SHARE

With a partner, compare the characteristics of colonial governments. Discuss the differences in each region. Then, identify similarities.

Settlers typically formed their own governments soon after they arrived. Many colonial charters guaranteed the colonists' right to form an **assembly**, or lawmaking body. The assembly represented the people of its colony. Members gathered to discuss important issues and to make laws based on the needs and wants of their colonists. Each colony also had a governor, who represented the needs and wants of Great Britain. While many things about government in the colonies were the same, there were also some differences. The chart shows ways colonial governments were similar and different.

Characteristics of Colonial Governments

All Colonial Governments

- Each colony had an assembly, a governor, and judges.
- Only white males could vote or hold office.
- Britain's government could reject any law proposed by the colonies.
- Governors and assemblies appointed judges to answer questions about laws and settle disputes.
- The king or colonial proprietors appointed colonial governors.
    - Except in Rhode Island and Connecticut! There colonists could choose their own governors.

Local Governments in New England and the Middle Colonies

- Local government was based around cities and towns.
- Colonists held town-hall meetings where they:
    - discussed important issues.
    - elected local officials.
    - elected their representatives.
    - settled disputes.

County Governments in the Southern Colonies

- Local government was county-wide, instead of city-wide.
- County officials were appointed by the colonial governor.
- People met at the county court house once a month to do business, discuss issues, and hear speeches.

▲ Reenactors recreate Virginia's colonial assembly every year in Williamsburg.

Participating in Colonial Politics

Colonial governments were the early beginnings of our government today, but they were far different from what we're used to. One difference is that there was no national government! Each colony was separate from the others. Everyone was subject to the will of Great Britain.

Another difference is that only a few colonists were allowed to participate. Only white males were allowed to vote. And there were other restrictions. In some colonies, people had to own land or belong to a certain church. If you didn't meet all of an area's requirements, you couldn't vote or hold office.

Colonists often made their needs and wants known to their assembly members and governors. They did this through writing and speaking about political ideas. You'll learn more about these actions in the coming units. For now, just remember this: through their actions, colonists set up the political traditions that we carry on today.

Turn back to page 129. Fill in the "Government" row of your chart.

Reading Skill

Draw Inferences

Using the picture above and the chart on page 130, make an inference about who was NOT allowed to participate in government.

_____

_____

DID YOU KNOW?

Writing down all the rules of government is a time-honored tradition! Here's a short list of some of the government documents written during the colonial period.

- Mayflower Compact
- Fundamental Orders of Connecticut
- Frame of Government of Pennsylvania

Colonial Market Economies

Setting up governments was one step to forming the thirteen colonies. Another step was creating economies. As the colonies grew, they developed **market economies**. In a market economy, people decide what goods to make and for how much to sell their goods. People base these decisions on their needs and what goods are available. They use money to buy and sell goods. Read the paragraphs below to learn about the parts of a market economy.

Supply

Supply is the amount of a good that is available. Resources that exist in an area decide supply. Imagine that an area has a lot of trees and many carpenters. Trees are a natural resource. Carpenters are a labor resource. In this area, furniture would be easy to supply.

Demand

People don't just make things because they can, though. There has to be demand, or a need for a product, too. If the area is growing, then more people are building houses. They'll demand lots of furniture! But if an area is not growing, then the demand for furniture will be low.

Price

Supply and demand affect the price of a good. When supply is high and demand is low, the price of a good drops. But when supply is low and demand is high, the price of a good rises.

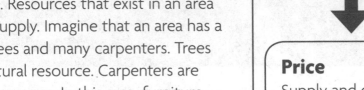

I have need of a new rocking chair.

Identify the parts of a market economy in this picture. Fill in each box with *supply*, *demand*, or *price*.

(bkgd) Siede Preis/Getty Images; (tl) Steven P. Lynch; (cl) Digital Vision/PunchStock; (r)Ingram Publishing

As you read the paragraphs below, (circle) examples of supply and underline examples of demand in the colonial economies. Then, draw a symbol in the boxes at the right for one product that came from each region.

In each region, colonists took advantage of the natural resources around them. As they made and sold goods made from these resources, market economies developed.

In New England

New England's land was rocky and bad for farming, but forested land and fish were both plentiful there. Colonists cut down trees and shaped them into lumber. In the 1700s, Europe needed a lot of this good. People around the world used lumber to construct ships and buildings. New Englanders also made excellent fishing boats. Fishing became profitable. Shipbuilding, lumber, and cod exporting became big industries.

In the Middle Colonies

Land in the Middle Colonies was good for farming. Colonists there grew wheat and raised livestock, such as dairy cows. People in New York City and Philadelphia needed products made from wheat and milk. With the countryside able to support their needs, people in cities made other goods. Printers, shoemakers, carpenters, and other craft workers opened shops in those cities. New York and Philadelphia both had excellent inland ports. Traders shipped goods from the Middle Colonies to other colonies and the rest of the world.

In the Southern Colonies

Both the climate and soil in the Southern Colonies were great for growing cash crops. In Lesson 4, you read about how tobacco and rice made many plantation owners wealthy. Some planters also grew indigo, a plant that is used to make dark blue dye. Planters from the Southern Colonies shipped their crops all over the world.

Describe a market economy in your own words.

_____

Give an example of how the colonies showed characteristics of a market economy.

_____

Turn back to page 129. Fill in the "Economy" row of your chart.

133

Trade With Native Americans

Settlers in the thirteen colonies also traded with Native Americans. Think back to what you learned about trade between Native Americans and European explorers.

> **Use what you know to finish this sentence.**
>
> **Native Americans traded** _____ **for** _____
>
> **with explorers from** _____ .

As you read the paragraphs on page 134, show that you recognize the positive and negative effects of this trade. Highlight positive effects of trade. Underline negative effects of trade.

Native Americans and British colonists traded for many years as well. Native Americans usually didn't use British money, so traders would often **barter**, or exchange goods for other goods. Bartering was also a common practice among European colonists.

This trade affected how colonists and Native Americans interacted with each other. Native Americans and British traders made important business connections and friendships. Sometimes they even married into each other's families.

Trade changed Native American ways of life. They began to hunt for profit, instead of just for what they needed. Trade made them more dependent on British goods, such as clothing and tools.

Settlers benefited by selling furs and other North American goods in Europe for a high price. This brought money into the colonies and created growth, which the colonial proprietors welcomed. But land disputes and arguments over trading practices often turned violent between colonists and Native Americans. The animal populations suffered, as well. For example, beavers became almost extinct in parts of the colonies.

Colonists traded many things with Native Americans. ▶

Stock Montage/Getty Images

Daily Life

In the 1700s, shipping goods over water was the easiest way to transport them. So colonists typically landed, stayed, and built settlements where there were good, deep harbors. Over time, many of these settlements grew into bustling port cities.

In Colonial Cities

Men in the cities had many different **occupations**, or jobs. Many worked at a trade or craft, such as brick laying or shoe making. Others were **employed** as doctors, lawyers, and ministers. They performed services for people in the cities and countryside.

Women in the cities mostly took care of the home and children. Children helped out as soon as they were old enough. There were many chores to do, like cooking, cleaning, washing laundry, and sewing.

In the Countryside

Many settlers came to the colonies for the chance to own land. As a result, most colonial families lived in the countryside on farms. New England farms were typically small and only supported one family. Farms in the Middle Colonies were a little larger. Plantations in the Southern Colonies were the largest of the colonial farms.

Farm life was full of hard work. Men planted crops and hunted. Women did household chores such as cooking, cleaning, and weaving cloth. Children helped take care of farm animals.

Families could often make or grow much of what they needed to survive. They would also sell crops for money to buy other goods.

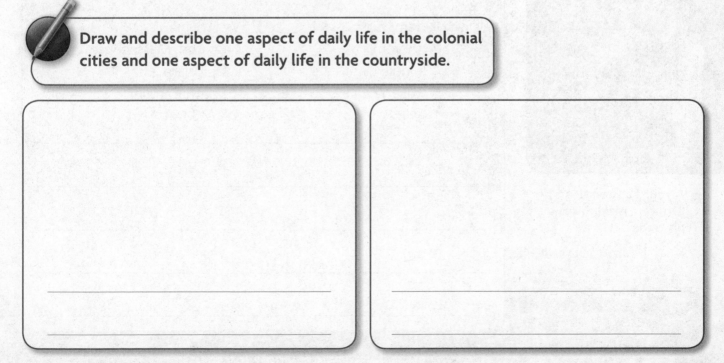

Draw and describe one aspect of daily life in the colonial cities and one aspect of daily life in the countryside.

Education in the Colonies

Schools in the thirteen colonies were very different from what you're used to! The first schools began in New England towns. Children learned in private homes or in small "writing schools." Students learned to read, write, and do basic math. Around the age of eight, though, formal education ended for most girls and many boys. At this age, children were expected to learn how to do things around the home. They also helped with the family farm or business.

In the Middle and Southern Colonies, most children didn't go to school. Most families taught their children at home. Only the largest cities had public schools, anyway.

Throughout the colonies, wealthy families sent their children to private schools, or had them tutored at home. Eventually, wealthy students could go on to colleges in New England or Great Britain.

Children of middle class families had another option. They could become apprentices and learn a trade. An apprentice learns a trade or craft from someone who is already skilled at it. After studying and practicing, an apprentice might become a silversmith or carpenter. At first, only boys were allowed to be apprentices. Later, girls began to learn some trades too. This system offered poorer children a way to move up in society.

FUN FACTS

Benjamin Franklin started out as an apprentice printer. He later became a famous inventor! Two of his inventions were the Franklin stove and bifocals. The Franklin stove was a metal fireplace that used less wood and provided more heat than other stoves at that time. Bifocals are glasses that help people see things both up close and far away.

▲ A young apprentice furniture maker learns his trade.

Imagine you are part of a colonial family. Choose a role by circling one word from each column. Then describe how you might get an education.

My family is:
poor
middle class
wealthy

We live in:
Boston, Massachusetts
Delaware
South Carolina

_____

_____

_____

_____

_____

Colonial Recreation

Of course colonial children and adults alike wanted to have some fun too! When they were not helping at home or studying, children played with wooden toys, marbles, hoops, and dolls. Women gathered in small groups to sew, knit, cross-stitch, and quilt. Board games, such as chess and checkers, were common. Colonists also liked ninepin, a game similar to bowling.

Events, such as feasts and dances, drew community members out to sing, dance, tell stories, and eat. Colonists sometimes staged competitions based on who could do ordinary tasks the fastest or with the most skill. Activities varied from colony to colony and reflected the cultures of the people who settled there.

The Colonial Williamsburg Foundation

▲ Colonial children played many games.

Make a list of some social aspects of daily colonial life. (Hint: These are ways colonists interacted with each other.) Then, ⟨circle⟩ an item on your list that you do today or an item that you'd like to try.

_____

_____

Turn back to page 129. Fill in the "Social Aspects" row of your chart.

Lesson 5

 Essential Question How do societies develop?

_____

_____

_____

_____

Go back to *Show As You Go!* on pages 102–103.

networks **There's More Online!** ● Games ● Assessment

Slavery and the Triangular Trade

How do cultures change? What do you think?

_____

_____

_____

_____

_____

Words To Know

Write the definition of each word in your own words.

indentured servant

_____

_____

*code

_____

_____

When something interesting, exciting, or sad happens to you, what do you do? Do you often tell others about your experience? If you do, you're not alone. Most people tell stories! Sometimes stories are just for fun, but other times stories are serious. In this lesson, you'll learn about someone who had a very important story to tell.

Olaudah Equiano

My name is Olaudah Equiano. I lived at a very interesting and very sad time in history. I was born in Africa in the 1740s, and I traveled the world. Look for me as you read. I'll tell you what I saw.

In 1619 these enslaved Africans arrived in Jamestown, Virginia aboard a Dutch ship. ▼

Hulton Archive/Getty Images

How Slavery Was Introduced

Growing cash crops requires a lot of labor—more labor than colonial planters could do themselves. Planters needed workers. At first, the planters hired **indentured servants** to do the work. An indentured servant agreed to work for a number of years in exchange for travel to a colony. Not enough indentured servants came, though. Planters looked for other sources of labor.

To meet the demand for labor, traders began purchasing captives (people!) in West Africa. Most captives were taken from their homes and families.

This is what happened to me, Olaudah. I was around your age when I was kidnapped and taken from my home. I never saw my mother again.

Traders shipped the captives across the Atlantic Ocean to colonies that needed labor. Tobacco planters brought the first African captives to Jamestown in 1619. As the colonies grew, a system of slavery developed. Recall that slavery is the practice of treating people as property and forcing them to work. By 1750, all thirteen colonies had made slavery legal.

> ### DID YOU KNOW?
> Some of the first Africans in the colonies were treated more like indentured servants than enslaved people. After years of labor, they gained their freedom. Later, colonial assemblies passed laws against setting captive Africans free. This meant that most were enslaved for life.

Reading Skill

Sequencing

Put these events in the correct order to describe the introduction of slavery to the colonies.

_____ Proprietors hire indentured servants.

_____ Colonists settle Jamestown.

_____ Africans are captured and shipped to the colonies.

_____ Jamestown settlers begin growing tobacco.

_____ Captive Africans are sold in the colonies.

_____ Planters look for other people to help grow cash crops.

_____ Slavery is made legal.

The Triangular Trade

During the 1700s, a system of shipping routes developed as trade grew across the Atlantic Ocean. The routes linked Europe and Africa with the West Indies and the thirteen British colonies. Traders exchanged goods and resources. They also brought enslaved Africans to the colonies. This system became known as the Triangular Trade. The groups were each responsible for something different. This is called specialization.

Follow my journey on the map. I was born in Africa. When I was kidnapped, I was put on a ship bound for the West Indies. Later, I was sold to a man in Virginia. Can you imagine being a whole ocean away from your home?

A Very Important Trade

As the Triangular Trade developed, it promoted economic growth in the colonies. In fact, some colonists grew very rich from it, especially in New England.

At this time, British rulers wanted the colonists to trade only with Great Britain. The British government, called Parliament, passed laws to try to control colonial trade. Parliament couldn't control the colonists, though. British taxes cut into merchants' profits. Merchants began secretly importing and exporting goods with traders from other countries. This was an early step on the long road to independence.

The Triangular Trade had another effect. It quickly increased the number of enslaved Africans in the colonies. Traders and planters became dependent on slavery to do business. They were interdependent, or relied on each other to meet needs and wants.

Explain the importance of the Triangular Trade.

_____

_____

_____

_____

Triangular Trade Routes

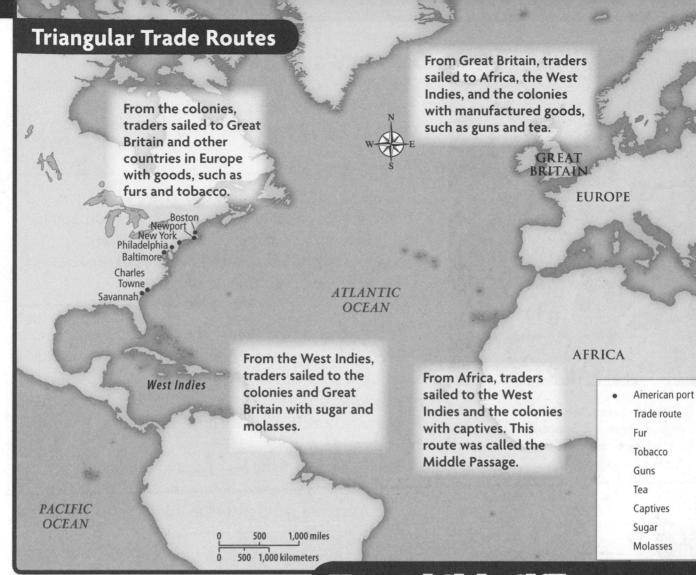

From the colonies, traders sailed to Great Britain and other countries in Europe with goods, such as furs and tobacco.

From Great Britain, traders sailed to Africa, the West Indies, and the colonies with manufactured goods, such as guns and tea.

Boston
Newport
New York
Philadelphia
Baltimore
Charles Towne
Savannah

GREAT BRITAIN

EUROPE

ATLANTIC OCEAN

AFRICA

West Indies

From the West Indies, traders sailed to the colonies and Great Britain with sugar and molasses.

From Africa, traders sailed to the West Indies and the colonies with captives. This route was called the Middle Passage.

PACIFIC OCEAN

0   500   1,000 miles
0   500   1,000 kilometers

- American port
  Trade route
  Fur
  Tobacco
  Guns
  Tea
  Captives
  Sugar
  Molasses

Map and Globe Skills

Read the descriptions of trade routes. Then draw arrows showing how the trade linked each location. Next, draw symbols for the goods shipped from each area next to the routes they were traded on, and add these symbols to the key.

© Art Archive

◄ Captive Africans crowded into the hold of a slave ship.

Slavery's Role

You just learned that slavery started in North America because planters needed laborers to plant and harvest cash crops.

▲ This is a reenactment of a young enslaved apprentice learning to weave a basket.

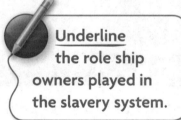

Underline the role ship owners played in the slavery system.

That's not all we did though. There were many different jobs to do, and they varied by region. Some of us were skilled laborers, such as carpenters, blacksmiths, and cooks. Others worked in the homes of slaveholders. I was a sailor on a ship.

In New England and the Middle Colonies, many enslaved Africans worked as servants in wealthy households, in shipyards, on small farms, or at a trade. New York had a large enslaved population. In New York City, some enslaved people were brick layers. They built the wall that gave Wall Street its name.

Some colonists in the New England and Middle Colonies owned slave ships. Before the 1770s, many ships full of African captives sailed to Rhode Island. From there, the captives were sold throughout the colonies. Ship owners, traders, and merchants grew rich from the capture and sale of enslaved people. The New England and Middle Colonies benefitted from slavery. The Southern colonies, however, benefitted a great deal more.

Describe the roles of enslaved people in the New England and Middle Colonies.

_____

_____

_____

_____

_____

This image shows a reenactment of enslaved field work.

Slavery on Plantations

Recall that many farms in the Southern Colonies grew cash crops. Both rice and tobacco plants required many workers to plant, tend, and harvest them. Enslaved Africans did most of this labor. Most farms were small and had just a few enslaved Africans. However, the Southern Colonies became known for their large, stately plantations. These plantations sometimes used hundreds of workers. In fact, many plantations in the Southern Colonies couldn't operate without enslaved workers.

Owners of these plantations hired poor whites, or forced enslaved Africans, to act as overseers. Overseers watched the workers in the fields. They made sure that work continued, dawn to dusk. Plantation owners grew rich from the crops grown by enslaved people. As a result, they enjoyed comfortable lives, free of hard work.

The owners also enriched the economies of their colonies, which benefited traders and other merchants. From Maryland to Georgia, settlers in the Southern Colonies viewed slavery as very important to their way of life.

Highlight the ways plantations relied on slavery.

Describe the roles of enslaved people in the Southern Colonies.

_____

_____

_____

_____

143

After you read, write a sentence about the impact of slavery for each topic below.

Enslaved Africans

_____

_____

_____

Colonists

_____

_____

_____

American Culture

_____

_____

_____

Slavery's Impact

Enslaved people suffered greatly, starting with our kidnapping in Africa. Captains of slave ships chained hundreds of us together in the ship's cargo area. Conditions were terrible, and many died along the way. Once in the colonies, traders sold us at auction.

Laws called slave **codes** set the rules of slavery. Under these laws, slave holders had total power over enslaved workers, whom they often treated brutally. Enslaved people could be beaten, sometimes without reason.

Slave holders only barely provided for workers' needs. Most enslaved people lived in simple cottages with dirt floors. They were cold in the winter and hot in the summer. Children of enslaved mothers were often taken away and sold to another slave holder. An enslaved person who tried to run away could be killed. This almost happened to Olaudah Equiano.

Slavery and Colonists

By the mid-1700s, slavery was a part of daily life. Whole economies required slave labor to keep them running.

Slavery also had other negative affects on colonists. Colonists developed false ideas about the intelligence and value of enslaved people in order to justify their actions. Today we call these ideas racism.

Colonists constantly feared violent revolts as well. Revolts were rare, but they sometimes happened as people struggled to be free. The false ideas and fears they held encouraged whites to reinforce slavery. As time passed, slave codes became harsher.

◀ At slave auctions, people were traded and sold like livestock.

Slavery and American Culture

Despite facing brutal hardships, enslaved Africans kept their cultures alive in the colonies. They contributed words from their native languages, such as *banjo* and *gumbo*, to American English. Enslaved people were not allowed to read or write, so they told stories to teach their children about their culture and life. Spirituals, the religious songs of enslaved Africans, have influenced American music.

▲ The influence of songs of enslaved Africans can be heard in gospel songs today.

Slavery was a miserable system and most enslaved people never escaped it. Despite all that I endured, I was able to save enough money to buy my freedom. This was a rare event, indeed. Very few enslaved people could earn money, much less save it up. After I bought my freedom, I sailed for Great Britain, where I wrote a book about my experiences.

Olaudah Equiano spoke out against slavery. People who came after him spoke out against it, too. Over time, movements against slavery grew in Great Britain and America. Even so, slavery would not end for a long time. It left lasting effects on our country.

Lesson 6

? Essential Question   How do cultures change?

_____

_____

_____

_____

_____

Go back to *Show As You Go!* on pages 102–103.

networks   There's More Online!
● Games ● Assessment

UNIT 4

Wrap Up

networks There's More Online!
• Games • Assessment

1600
1610
1620
1630
1640
1650
1660
1670
1680
1690
1700
1710
1720
1730
1740

Draw a line from each date in the list to its correct spot on the time line. Then, fill in each blank with the correct answer about the founding of the 13 colonies.

- **1607:** The Virginia Company founds ______________, Virginia.
- **1619:** The first enslaved ______________ arrived this year.
- **1620:** The ______________ found Plymouth, Massachusetts.
- **1632:** King Charles I gives a charter to Cecilius ______________.
- **1636:** Thomas Hooker leaves the Puritans and founds ______________.
- **1664:** England takes over New Netherland and renames it ______________ and ______________.
- **1681:** William Penn founds ______________, a colony where Quakers and others could worship freely.
- **1729:** The colony of ______________ splits into North and South.
- **1733:** James Oglethorpe founds the colony of ______________ for debtors.

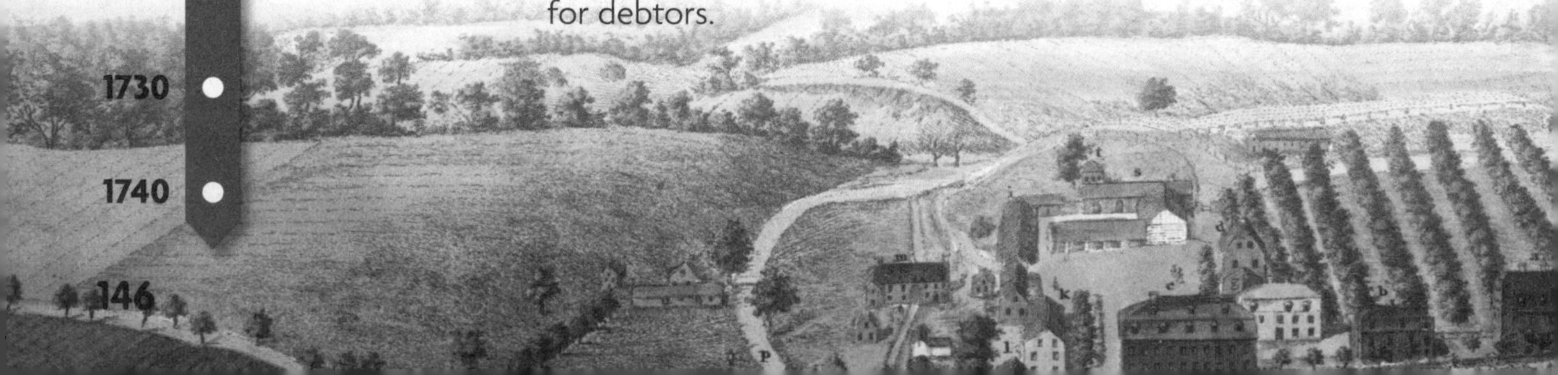

© New York Public Library Picture Collection

Unit Project

Choose a colonial region you learned about in this unit. Imagine that you are a sales person, and you are trying to convince Europeans to move to your colonial region. Create a sales pitch and a pamphlet to promote your region. Before you begin, turn back to pages 102 and 103 to review your map. Read the list below to see what you need to include in your sales pitch and pamphlet. As you work, check off each task.

Your sales pitch and pamphlet should include . . .   Yes, it does

facts about the founding of the colonies in your region   ☐

facts about the government in your colonial region   ☐

facts about the economy of your colonial region   ☐

facts about trade in your colonial region   ☐

facts about daily life in your colonial region   ☐

facts about slavery in your colonial region   ☐

ideas about what your region can offer Europeans who settle there   ☐

at least two illustrations   ☐

Think about the Big Idea

BIG IDEA Location affects how people live.

What did you learn in this unit that helps you understand the BIG IDEA?

_____

_____

_____

Read the passage "Free African Americans in the Colonies" before answering Numbers 1 through 8.

Free African Americans in the Colonies

by James B. Clark

Not all African Americans in the colonies were enslaved. About 5 percent were free. Some had been indentured servants or were the children of indentured servants. They never had been enslaved. Some free African Americans had been emancipated by their slave holders. Others risked their lives by escaping. Still others had bought their freedom by working paid jobs.

Free African Americans lived in both cities and towns in the New England, Middle, and Southern colonies. There were also small communities of free African Americans on the frontier. Many of them lived in friendship with Native Americans in the eastern foothills of the Appalachian Mountains.

Few laws protected free African Americans. Even though they had freedom, they remained in danger of being forced into slavery. Some formed organizations to help protect free African Americans. One was the Brown Fellowship Society of South Carolina. It was founded in 1790. Churches were also among the earliest and most important organizations to help free African Americans. By 1787 there were African American Baptist, Methodist, Presbyterian, and Episcopalian churches in the colonies.

1 What is the author's MAIN purpose for writing "Free African Americans in the Colonies"?

Ⓐ to tell how enslaved people escaped

Ⓑ to tell about African Americans in Florida

Ⓒ to tell when the Brown Fellowship Society was founded

Ⓓ to tell about African Americans who were not enslaved

2 Where did free African Americans live in the colonies?

Ⓕ only in the New England Colonies

Ⓖ only on the frontier

Ⓗ throughout the colonies, in the cities and countryside

Ⓘ only in the foothills of the Appalachian Mountains

3 How many African Americans lived in the colonies as free men and women?

Ⓐ about 5 percent of all African Americans in the colonies

Ⓑ about 5 percent of all people in the colonies

Ⓒ about 5 percent of enslaved African Americans

Ⓓ none

4 What happened in 1790?

Ⓕ The Brown Fellowship Society was founded.

Ⓖ The first African American churches were founded.

Ⓗ Laws began to protect free African Americans.

Ⓘ A small African American community was founded on the frontier.

5 Read the sentence from the passage.

Some free African Americans had been emancipated by their slave holders.

What does the word *emancipated* mean in this passage?

Ⓐ enslaved

Ⓑ given freedom

Ⓒ held captive

Ⓓ allowed to travel

6 Which two words from the passage have nearly OPPOSITE meanings?

Ⓕ enslaved, emancipated

Ⓖ cities, towns

Ⓗ foothill, mountain

Ⓘ friendship, freedom

7 Read the sentences from the passage.

Few laws protected free African Americans. Even though they had freedom, they remained in danger of being forced into slavery. Some formed organizations to help protect free African Americans.

Why did free African Americans turn to churches and other organizations for help?

Ⓐ because they needed money

Ⓑ because they needed food

Ⓒ because they needed work

Ⓓ because they needed protection

8 What was the purpose of the Brown Fellowship Society of South Carolina?

Ⓕ It protected enslaved people.

Ⓖ It protected free African Americans.

Ⓗ It set up African American churches.

Ⓘ It helped build friendships with Native Americans.

UNIT 5

The American Revolution

 BIG IDEA Conflict causes change.

In 1765 Great Britain began passing unpopular tax laws. This sparked a rebellion among the colonists. They organized protests and boycotts. Great Britain's responses further angered the colonists and fighting broke out. Fed up, the colonists declared themselves independent in 1776. The United States of America was born! In this unit, you will learn about the causes, events, and results of American Revolution. As you read, think about how these events affected the lives of everyone involved.

networks

connected.mcgraw-hill.com
- Skill Builders
- Resource Library

▲ Independence Hall in Philadelphia is where the Founders signed the Declaration of Independence.

Show As You Go! After you read each lesson in this unit, record important details about one important event of the American Revolution. You will use your notes to help you complete a project at the end of the unit.

Fold page here.

Lesson 1

_____

_____

_____

_____

Lesson 2

_____

_____

_____

_____

Lesson 3

_____

_____

_____

_____

Lesson 4

_____

_____

_____

Reading Skill

Common Core Standards
RI.8 Explain how an author uses reasons and evidence to support particular points in a text, identifying which reasons and evidence support which point(s).

Explain Author's Purpose

Everything you read has a purpose. An author may try to persuade, or convince the reader to think a certain way about a topic. Authors also try to inform, or teach the reader about a topic by providing information. Authors might simply wish to entertain the reader by telling a good story. Whatever the author's purpose for writing may be, his or her points are always supported with reasons and evidence. Recognizing the purpose of what you read helps you understand what you read.

Main Idea

Supporting Evidence

LEARN IT

To find and explain the author's purpose:

- Begin by identifying the main idea of the passage. This offers clues to the author's purpose.

- Identify the evidence the author provides to support the purpose of the writing.

- Explain the author's purpose by using evidence from the writing to support your conclusions.

While most colonists wanted to end what they saw as British bullying, not all colonists wanted to end their ties to Great Britain. They hoped that the British government would compromise to end the fighting. Some of these colonists worked for the British government. Others feared that they might lose their property during the fighting. Still others simply did not want to separate from Great Britain; they hoped for compromise.

© Historical Art Prints

Complete the chart by stating the author's purpose and supporting evidence from the paragraph.

Author's Purpose	Supporting Evidence

APPLY IT

Read the paragraph below. Explain the author's purpose. Underline or highlight the evidence that supports your conclusion.

Most colonists understood that a compromise would not be reached. They knew that once British soldiers were killed, the British government would not back down. The events around Boston made colonists see themselves in a new way. They were no longer British citizens living in colonies. They were citizens of a new country that was fighting to free itself from British rule. They were Americans.

_____

_____

_____

_____

_____

_____

153

Words to Know

The list below shows some important words you will learn in this unit. Their definitions can be found on the next page. Read the words.

rivalry (REYE • vuhl • ree)

boycott (BOY • kaht)

militia (muh • LIH • shuh)

Patriot (PAY • tree • uht)

Loyalist (LOY • uh • lihst)

profiteering (prah • fuh • TIHR • ihng)

desert (DEH • zuhrt)

blockade (blah • KAYD)

FOLDABLES®

The **Foldable** on the next page will help you learn these important words. Follow the steps below to make your Foldable.

Step 1 Fold along the solid red line.

Step 2 Cut along the dotted lines. ✂

Step 3 Read the words and their definitions.

Step 4 Complete the activities on each tab.

Step 5 Look at the back of your Foldable. Choose ONE of these activities for each word to help you remember its meaning:

- Draw a picture of the word.
- Write a description of the word.
- Write how the word is related to something you know.

© Art Archive

The Boston Tea Party took place in 1773. Similar events happened in other American cities, too. ▶

	FOLD
A **rivalry** is when two or more people or groups compete to become the best at or have the most of something.	**Write the plural form of *rivalry*.**
To **boycott** means to refuse to do business or have contact with a person, group, company, country, or product.	**Write the definition of *boycott* in your own words.**
A **militia** is a group of volunteers who fight in times of emergency.	**Write two words that are related to the word *militia*.**
A **Patriot** was a colonist who supported the fight for independence.	**Write a synonym for the word *Patriot*.**
A **Loyalist** was a colonist who supported Great Britain in the American Revolution.	**Describe the opposite of a *Loyalist*.**
Profiteering means making excess profits from goods that are in short supply.	**Write the root word of *profiteering*.**
To **desert** means to go away and leave a person or thing that should not be left.	**Circle words that mean the same as *desert*.** leave wet dry join quit stay
A **blockade** is a barrier that prevents the movement of troops and supplies.	**Explain how the root word of *blockade* helps you remember the definition.**

rivalry	rivalry
boycott	boycott
militia	militia
Patriot	Patriot
Loyalist	Loyalist
profiteering	profiteering
desert	desert
blockade	blockade

CUT HERE

Primary Sources

Paintings and Speeches

The first photographs weren't taken until the mid-1800s. As a result, we sometimes rely on paintings to help us understand events from the past. Paintings created around the time of an event are primary sources. Those created after the event are secondary sources.

Sometimes paintings are paired with other primary sources to help you analyze an event. Speeches are primary sources if they are recorded at the same time they are actually given.

In this unit you will learn about the American Revolution. Patrick Henry was a powerful speaker who convinced many colonists to join the fight for independence. Examine the painting of Henry giving his famous speech to the Virginia House of Burgesses. Then, as you read parts of this speech, look back at the painting and think about the story the two sources tell together.

 Document-Based Questions

1. (Circle) clues the image gives about how the speech was interpreted by the people listening to Henry.

2. Underline all of the examples Henry gives to show that Great Britain has declared war on the colonies.

THINK • PAIR • SHARE

Discuss how the image and the speech work together to help you understand the importance of Henry's speech.

Primary Source

. . . Has Great Britain any enemy, in this quarter of the world, to call for all this [build up] of navies and armies? No, sir, [Britain] has none. They are meant for us; they can be meant for no other. . . . Gentlemen may cry, Peace, Peace, but there is no peace. The war is actually begun! . . . I know not what course others may take; but as for me, give me liberty or give me death!

networks
There's More Online!
● Skill Builders
● Resource Library

The Road to Revolution

**What is worth
fighting for?
What do you think?**

_____

_____

_____

_____

_____

_____

Words To Know

Write a number on each line
to show how much you know
about each word.

1 = I have no idea!
2 = I know a little.
3 = I know a lot.

____ **treaty**

____ **proclamation**

____ **repeal**

____ ***demand**

New France Expands

You learned in Unit 4 that England built 13 colonies in North
America. The French colonized too, but they also spent over
130 years looking for a shortcut to Asia.

French missionary Jacques Marquette heard Native
Americans speak of a mighty river to the west. He hoped it
was the Northwest Passage. He set out to explore this river,
called Mississippi. Marquette and Louis Jolliet, a fur trader,
traveled south along the river for months. Unfortunately, it
never turned west. They gave up and turned around.

In 1682 Robert de La Salle continued where Marquette
and Jolliet left off. He followed the Mississippi to the Gulf
of Mexico. La Salle claimed the river for France. He claimed
its **tributaries** for France too. A tributary is a river or stream
that flows into a larger river. La Salle named the area Louisiana
after King Louis XIV of France.

At the same time, Britain and France were competing
to be the most powerful nations in Europe. The 13 British
colonies had begun east of the Appalachians. As the colonies
grew, British settlers pushed west into French territory. The
European rivalry spread to the Americas.

THINK • PAIR • SHARE
French land claims in the west limited the growth of the British colonies.
Imagine that a group of kids said you and your friends couldn't use a part of
the playground. Your play area would be limited. How would you feel?

New France and
New England in 1750

Missouri River
St. Ignace
Sault Ste. Marie
Quebec
Montreal
St. Lawrence R.
Detroit
St. Louis
Ohio River
Mississippi River
New Orleans
Gulf of Mexico

N W E S

ATLANTIC OCEAN

0   100   200 miles
0   100 200 kilometers

British lands
French lands
Spanish lands
Disputed lands
Route of Marquette
and Jolliet, 1673
Route of La Salle,
1682

Tensions Grow

By the early 1750s, both Britain and France claimed the Ohio River Valley. The British wanted to farm the land there. They cut down trees to make room to grow crops and build houses. French fur trappers feared that cutting down the forests would drive away the animals, hurting their trade. This conflict over land led to fighting between the British and the French.

Native Americans were drawn into the conflict. To protect their ways of life, they became allies with either the French or British settlers. They chose sides based on who could best protect their land.

Map and Globe Skills

1. Circle the waterways controlled by the French.

2. Why do you suppose British colonists would have worried about the growth of New France?

_____

_____

Create a sign to warn British colonists that they are nearing the Louisiana Territory.

The French and Indian War

By 1753, the problems between the British and French had worsened. In that year, a young British officer named George Washington delivered a message to the French asking them to leave the valley. The French refused. A few months later, in 1754, Washington returned with a small group of soldiers. They built Fort Necessity nearby and from it attacked Fort Duquesne. The British soldiers were quickly defeated. This was the first battle of the French and Indian War.

A painting of fighting during the French and Indian War ▶

(t) MPI/Getty Images, (b) Getty Images/Getty Images

Complete the time line by following the directions in each box as you read about the French and Indian War.

1750 — 1755

Write a caption for this image. Find clues in the text at the top of the page.

In 1755, British troops tried again to capture Fort Duquesne and were defeated again. More than 1,400 British troops were killed or wounded by the French and their Native American allies, the Wyandot.

Connect this box to the correct place on the time line.

Upset by the losses at Fort Duquesne, colonists urged British leader William Pitt to spend more money on the war. Three years later, and with Pitt's support, the British captured Fort Duquesne.

The fort was renamed Fort Pitt. Explain why.

_____

_____

_____

After capturing Fort Duquesne, the British decided to drive the French out of Canada. In June 1759, British forces attacked Quebec. This city was located on steep cliffs above the St. Lawrence River. To carry out their surprise attack, British troops quietly climbed narrow paths up the cliffs at night. After three months of fighting, the French surrendered Quebec.

Draw the soldiers climbing the cliffs to reach the city.

The war ended in North America with the fall of Montreal. But battles between the two countries continued in Europe for three more years. The war finally ended with the **Treaty** of Paris of 1763. A treaty is a peace agreement. Great Britain claimed all of France's colonies in North America.

Unable to afford protection for settlers in the Ohio Valley, Great Britain issued the **Proclamation** of 1763. This official announcement said settlers could not move past the Appalachian Mountains. It set this land aside for Native American groups. This action angered the colonists.

Underline the results of the Treaty of Paris.

1760

1765

One year after the siege of Quebec, the British captured Montreal. They successfully forced the French from Canada.

Connect the box to the correct place on the time line.

Despite the Proclamation of 1763, British settlers didn't leave the Ohio River Valley. That same year, Ottawa Chief Pontiac united Native Americans in the Ohio River Valley in order to drive out the settlers. They captured and burned several settlements but were defeated by the British Army.

Connect this box to the correct place on the time line.

Colonists Protest New Taxes

Reading Skill

Author's Purpose

Imagine you are a member of the Sons of Liberty and are writing a pamphlet against unfair taxes. <u>Underline</u> details you could use in your writing. What is your purpose as the author?

_____

_____

_____

Wars are expensive! British leaders needed to find a way to pay for the French and Indian War. Many people in Great Britain thought the colonists should have to pay for the war since it was fought to protect them.

The colonists disagreed. Before the 1760s, only the colonial legislatures had taxed the colonists. Colonists accepted those taxes because they had voted for, and were represented by, the members of colonial legislatures. But the colonists couldn't vote for members of Parliament. When Parliament passed taxes on the colonies to pay for the war, many colonists saw this as taxation without representation. They felt their rights as British citizens were being violated.

The Stamp Act

In 1765 Parliament passed the Stamp Act. This tax forced colonists to buy stamps for everything made of paper. This included newspapers, wills, journals, and playing cards. Colonists weren't happy about this tax, passed without their consent, or agreement.

In response, a group of colonists called the Sons of Liberty planned to **boycott** British goods. To boycott means to refuse to buy goods or services. The Sons of Liberty organized protests and threatened tax collectors across the colonies.

Leaders called "Patriots" emerged against the British government. Samuel Adams led the fight against the Stamp Act in Massachusetts. In Virginia, Patrick Henry spoke out about the tax. His many speeches inspired others to protest. The protests worked! In 1766 the British government **repealed**, or canceled, the tax.

Colonists protested in the streets. ▼

© Library of Congress

The Townshend Acts

Parliament raised taxes another way, though. In 1767 it passed the Townshend Acts, which taxed goods such as tea, glass, and paint.

Colonists **demanded** that the British repeal the hated Townshend Acts and organized another boycott. This boycott included taxed goods and any colonial businesses selling or using them too.

Boston Massacre

British leaders worried that the colonists, especially those in Boston, were out of control. They sent troops to the city. But that only made things worse.

The people of Boston weren't happy with all the soldiers. Some residents were even forced to allow soldiers to stay in their homes. On March 5, 1770, a crowd of angry colonists began to tease some British soldiers. When the crowd refused to go home, the soldiers shot into the crowd, killing five colonists. News of the Boston Massacre shocked colonists. How could British soldiers kill their own people?

▲ Silversmith Paul Revere made this engraving of the Boston Massacre.

Boston Tea Party and Coercive Acts

Parliament was desperate to get the colonies under control. It repealed the Townshend Acts in 1773 but added a new tax on tea. British leaders thought this was a good compromise. To the colonists, it was yet another tax passed without their approval.

In November, angry Boston residents protested by refusing to allow three British cargo ships to unload. On the night of December 16, about 50 members of the Sons of Liberty dumped the ships' cargoes of tea overboard.

Parliament punished the colonists by passing the Coercive Acts. These acts closed Boston Harbor, banned town meetings, and sent over more soldiers. Colonists called these actions the "The Intolerable Acts." These acts united many colonists against Great Britain.

> **DID YOU KNOW?**
> Crispus Attucks, killed in the Boston Massacre, was the first African American to die in events leading to the Revolution.

Colonists disguised as Native Americans threw British tea into Boston Harbor. ▶

(t) © North Wind Picture Archives, (b) Art Archive

Lesson 1

? Essential Question **What is worth fighting for?**

_____

_____

_____

Go back to *Show As You Go!* on pages 150–151. «

 networks

There's More Online!
● Games ● Assessment

The Revolution Begins

Why do people take risks? What do you think?

_____

_____

_____

_____

_____

_____

_____

_____

Words To Know

Tell a partner what you know about each word:

militia

Loyalist

Patriot

***discuss**

Lexington and Concord

The British decided that capturing colonial leaders might stop colonial protests. When the Sons of Liberty heard of this plan, they sent two important leaders, Samuel Adams and John Hancock, to Lexington, a town outside Boston. The colonists also hid weapons in Lexington and another town, Concord.

On April 18, 1775, General Thomas Gage sent about 700 soldiers from Boston to seize the weapons stored in Lexington and Concord. The soldiers were also ordered to arrest Adams and Hancock. When colonists learned of Gage's plan, they sent two men, Paul Revere and William Dawes, to warn the people of Lexington and Concord. As a result, the colonists were able to hide most of the weapons, and Adams and Hancock escaped.

THINK · PAIR · SHARE

Revere and Dawes warned the colonists and ruined the "element of surprise" for the British. Why might surprise have made a difference? Why did it help the colonists to know the British were coming?

© Corbis

Minutemen, shown wearing blue jackets, fought off an attack by British soldiers, shown wearing red coats, on the Old North Bridge in Concord, Massachusetts. ▼

Routes to Concord

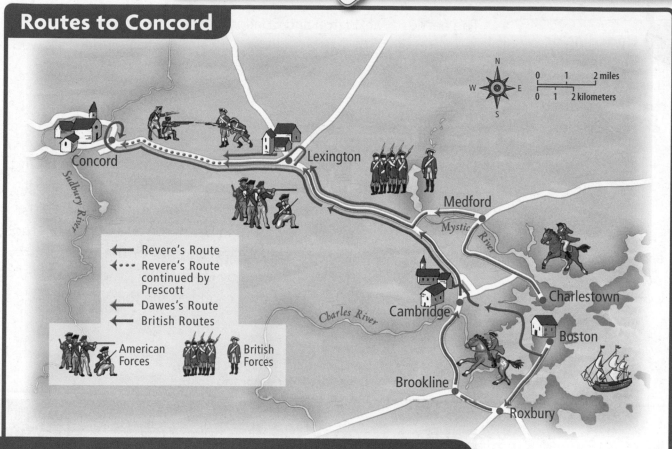

Map legend:
← Revere's Route
◄··· Revere's Route continued by Prescott
← Dawes's Route
← British Routes
American Forces
British Forces

Map labels: Concord, Sudbury River, Lexington, Medford, Mystic River, Charlestown, Cambridge, Charles River, Boston, Brookline, Roxbury

Scale: 0 — 1 — 2 miles; 0 — 1 — 2 kilometers

Map and Globe Skills

1. Which American rode the longest distance to warn colonists that the British were coming?

_____

2. Use the scale to measure the distance from:

Boston to Lexington   Lexington to Concord

_____   _____

DID YOU KNOW?

Paul Revere never completed his famous Midnight Ride. Here's what happened: As Revere and Dawes left Lexington headed for Concord, Dr. Samuel Prescott joined them. Outside Lexington they were stopped by British guards. Prescott and Dawes escaped, but Revere was held for questioning and his horse was taken away. Revere walked back to Lexington. In the meantime, Prescott reached Concord and warned the militia.

In Lexington, a **militia** of 70 men called minutemen were waiting for the British. Militias are groups of volunteers who fight only in an emergency. No one knows who fired first, but many shots rang out. Eight minutemen were killed, and the British marched on to Concord.

A larger militia waited just outside Concord. The British never made it into town and instead retreated toward Boston. The minutemen followed and continued shooting along the way. More than 90 British soldiers were killed. The Revolutionary War had begun.

Early Battles

Underline or highlight the results of each battle described on these pages.

The battles at Lexington and Concord were the beginning of the Revolutionary War. Battles in New York and Boston quickly followed. As militias began to work together, a colonial army took shape.

Fort Ticonderoga

Three weeks after Lexington and Concord, a man from New England named Benedict Arnold led a small militia toward Fort Ticonderoga in New York. News traveled slowly in the 1700s, so the British soldiers there had no idea about the battles in Lexington and Concord. Arnold planned to attack the fort and take its cannons for the colonial army. On May 10, 1775, another militia led by Ethan Allen joined Arnold in the surprise attack. Amazingly, they captured the fort without firing a single shot.

It took teams of oxen nearly eight months to drag the heavy canons from Fort Ticonderoga to Boston. ▼

© SuperStock

DID YOU KNOW?
Benedict Arnold wanted to be a famous war hero. After years of fighting with the colonial army, Arnold felt he wasn't respected by colonial leaders. As a result, he planned to surrender the fort at West Point to the British. His betrayal shocked the colonists. Arnold got his wish: he is remembered but as a traitor. In fact, even today, people who betray others are sometimes called a "Benedict Arnold."

The Battle at Bunker Hill

At the same time, the British were losing control of the Boston area. General Gage decided to attack the hills around Boston. Taking them would give the British a strategic advantage. But the colonists learned of the plan. A colonial militia was sent to protect Bunker Hill across the Charles River from Boston. Instead, the militia decided to protect Breed's Hill, which was closer to the river. The colonists worked all night to build earthen walls for protection.

▲ This painting shows colonists fighting British soldiers at the Battle of Bunker Hill.

On June 17, British soldiers crossed the Charles River by boat and marched up Breed's Hill. The militia waited, hidden behind earthen walls. The Americans didn't have much ammunition, or musket balls and gunpowder. Officers told them not to waste ammunition by firing at soldiers that were too far away. Historians say that either Colonel William Prescott or General Israel Putnam said, "Don't shoot until you see the whites of their eyes."

Twice the British charged up the hill, only to be stopped by the militia. Finally, the Americans ran out of ammunition. After a third try, the British won what became known as the Battle of Bunker Hill. More than 400 colonists were killed or wounded. The victory was costly for the British as well. More than 1,000 soldiers were killed or wounded in the battle.

Reading Skill

Summarize Suppose you are a member of a Committee of Correspondence. You are responsible to report one of these events to another colony. Summarize the information you think needs to be shared.

_____

_____

_____

Choosing Sides

The colonies were divided. Underline details that show what each group wanted.

News of the fighting spread throughout the colonies, and compromise looked less likely with each battle. Many colonists didn't want war and didn't want to pick a side. They feared their property would be damaged in the fighting. They focused on protecting themselves. Many remained undecided throughout the war.

Others easily knew which side was theirs. Colonists called **Loyalists** didn't want to rebel against Great Britain. They thought taxes and restrictions weren't good reasons. Some Loyalists even worked against those who rebelled, helping the British.

For others, the events around Boston changed their point of view. These colonists no longer felt like British citizens living in British colonies. They now saw themselves as Americans, fighting for their rights and freedom. These were the **Patriots**.

The Second Continental Congress

Among the Patriots were many well-respected colonial leaders, such as Thomas Jefferson, Benjamin Franklin, John Adams, and John Hancock. As the war began to rage, these colonial leaders and many others met in Philadelphia's State House. They needed to organize an army and **discuss** what to do next. Their meeting was called the Second Continental Congress. The journal entries on the next page describe key events that took place.

Patrick Henry urged the Continental Congress to declare Independence from Great Britain. ▼

Bettmann / Corbis

May 1775

I'm working as a servant for the Second Continental Congress. Delegates from every colony have arrived in Philadelphia. John Hancock was elected president of the Congress. The delegates are divided and have very different goals.

June 1775

The conversations of the delegates could be seen as treason, or betraying Britain. Sam Adams and John Adams of Massachusetts, and Richard Henry Lee and Thomas Jefferson of Virginia have called for independence. But others, including John Dickinson of Pennsylvania, hope to remain part of Great Britain, with the power to govern ourselves. Neither side seems willing to give in.

The Congress has named George Washington as commander of the Continental Army. His service in the French and Indian War proved his leadership abilities.

July 1775

The delegates have sent what they call an "olive branch petition" to King George III and Parliament. They say the olive branch is a symbol of peace used by the ancient Greeks. They asked the king to repeal his laws and policies for the colonies. I don't think it will work. There is too much at stake—power, money, and pride.

October 1775

The king refused to read the petition. He is angry with the Congress and has sent more troops to enforce his rules. People in the streets are calling for independence.

The delegates sent representatives to France, the Netherlands, and Spain to ask for support. These countries want to help us, but they are afraid to fight Britain—the strongest country in Europe. If we hope to get assistance, we need to win battles, and soon!

Reading Skill

Main Idea and Details These fictional journal entries use real details to help you understand the events of the Second Continental Congress.

1. Read the journal entries and summarize the main topic for each date next to the entry. Underline key details that help you with each summary.

2. Is the person writing the entries a Loyalist or a Patriot? Circle your choice. Then circle the details that helped you decide.

Ideas About Rights

Patriots had ideas about what governments were supposed to do and not do. These ideas were the foundation of their complaints against Great Britain. The colonists' ideas were influenced by John Locke. Locke was an English philosopher, or person who thinks about important ideas. He believed that without governments, humans existed in a "state of nature." In this state, people could deal reasonably with each other. Locke also believed that all people were born free and equal. He also believed that all people had rights given to them by nature. Three of these rights were life, liberty, and the right the own property. Locke wrote that the main duty of government was to protect these rights. When a government violated people's rights, Locke believed the people had the right to overthrow, or change, that government.

Declaring Independence

Many colonists agreed with the idea of natural rights. They saw the king as a tyrant, or a cruel and unfair ruler. In June 1776, the Continental Congress took the next, big step. It appointed a committee to write a Declaration of Independence. The committee decided Thomas Jefferson should write the first draft.

Jefferson included a list of crimes that he accused the king of committing. Some delegates wanted to change this section before sending it to England. Jefferson also attacked the slave trade. Representatives from the Southern colonies, whose economies depended on slavery, removed this part.

The power of Jefferson's words inspired the delegates. But the final statement of his document made the most important point: "The good people of these colonies, solemnly publish and declare, that these United Colonies are, and of right ought to be free and independent states." The Patriots were now Americans.

Benjamin Franklin, John Adams, and Thomas Jefferson writing the Declaration ▼

Each box below describes a complaint listed in the Declaration of Independence. Choose a color for each natural right: life, liberty, and the right to own property. Color each box to show the natural right it addresses.

Tip: If more than one right is addressed in a box, divide the box and color a portion to show each right.

Lack of Representation	Taxes and Trade	Land Issues
The colonists could not govern themselves and were taxed without their consent.	Great Britain limited imports and exports and set high taxes on these goods. Colonists were required to pay taxes on goods.	Britain ignored colonists' land claims west of the Appalachian Mountains, leaving colonists unprotected on the frontier.
Tyranny	**Legal Rights**	**War-like Behaviors**
The government enforced laws the colonists thought were severe and unfair. Colonial charters were taken away. Great Britain refused to make laws necessary to protect the colonists. Colonial legislatures were suspended.	Colonists could be arrested and held without a trial. Some were also taken to Europe to face false charges. New laws prevented immigrants from coming to the colonies. Judges were controlled directly by the king.	Thousands of British soldiers were sent to the colonies. Soldiers took colonial homes to use for shelter. Laws and rules did not apply to soldiers. German soldiers, known as Hessians, were hired to fight the colonists.

Lesson 2

 Essential Question **Why do people take risks?**

_____

_____

_____

Go back to *Show As You Go!* on pages 150–151.

 networks **There's More Online!** ● Games ● Assessment

Fighting the War

Essential Question

**Why do people get involved?
What do you think?**

_____

_____

_____

_____

_____

_____

_____

_____

_____

Words To Know

Add a suffix to each word.

mercenary _____

*technique _____

inflation _____

profiteering _____

Everyone has strengths and weaknesses. Strengths are things you do well, and weaknesses are things that you could improve. What are your strengths and weaknesses?

Strengths	Weaknesses

Ready for War?

Patriot soldiers, now called the Continental Army, were eager to fight. But at first they were no match for the British Army. Many British military leaders believed the war would end quickly. Instead, it would last eight years. The British had not counted on the Americans' strengths. And they didn't recognize their own weaknesses.

The British didn't understand that the Patriots were willing to suffer a great deal to gain their freedom. Many Americans gave everything they had to win their independence.

Reading Skill

Compare and Contrast Use the information on these pages to compare the two armies.

	Strengths	Weaknesses
British		
Americans		

BRITISH ARMY

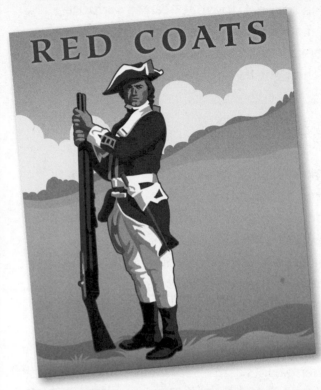

Strengths and Weaknesses

Army Soldiers and military supplies had to be shipped across the Atlantic Ocean. The British had as many as 60,000 soldiers in the American colonies. They included many **mercenaries**, professional soldiers from other countries. Most were Hessians from Germany.

Training British soldiers were well-trained fighters who joined the army for life. Soldiers were only trained to fight in open battlefields.

Equipment Each soldier carried a gun called a musket tip that had a sharp blade, or bayonet, on the front. Uniforms included red coats, which made soldiers easy targets.

Support British soldiers were helped by Loyalists. Many British citizens didn't support the war because it raised taxes.

AMERICAN ARMY

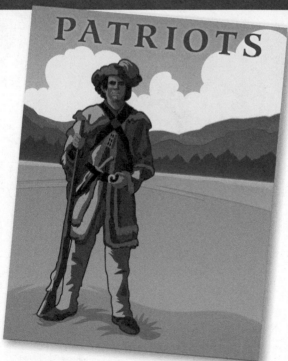

Strengths and Weaknesses

Army Patriots fought to protect their homes, families, and a new nation. General Washington never had more than 19,000 soldiers at any time during the war.

Training Soldiers signed up for six months. This was not enough time to train to fight using traditional military **techniques**. Some Patriots attacked by surprise, firing from well-protected spots.

Equipment Many Patriot soldiers used long rifles, which were more accurate than muskets. A lack of uniforms, especially shoes, was a constant problem.

Support Patriot citizens supported the army by making musket balls or blankets. Farmers gave food to soldiers. Some Americans hid supplies or sold food to the army at high prices.

Supporting the War Effort

My name is Martha. You probably know my husband, General George Washington of the Continental Army. These are turbulent times for us all. We are divided by our ideas and the war. Though I don't fight in battle, I do what I can to support our brave soldiers. I gather supplies such as clothing, food, and blankets for the troops. Read below to see the many ways others at home support the fight for independence.

Support at Home

American women supported the war in many ways. When the men left for war, some women became carpenters, blacksmiths, or shipbuilders. Others took over family farms or businesses.

Some women gave hope to Americans through writing. Mercy Otis Warren recorded the events of the Revolution. This helped everyone know what was happening. Phillis Wheatley, a free African American, wrote poetry which inspired many people.

Other women, like Abigail Adams, greatly influenced the work of their husbands. Abigail and her husband John Adams discussed issues being debated by the Continental Congress. She asked her husband to remember women's rights as the Congress planned the new government.

FUN FACT

Women had already played an important role in the events leading up to the war. Groups called Daughters of Liberty gathered to spin cloth during the boycotts. This allowed Americans to keep the boycotts going.

 Use the information above to complete the captions for each image.

▲ Freed from slavery at the age of 20,

_____

wrote poetry about freedom.

▲ Abigail Adams and her husband John discussed

_____.

▲ Mercy Otis Warren wrote about the events of the

_____.

The snow and bitter winds of winter make battle difficult. This is why troops on both sides remain in camps during the winter months. I spend this time with George. So many men are tired, hungry, injured, and homesick. The other officers' wives and I do what we can to comfort them and keep their spirits high. At night we knit socks and scarves to help keep them covered. I've never seen so many shoeless men! Read below to see other ways our brave soldiers are supported on the battle field.

Support in the Field

Many women helped on the battlefields. Some traveled to military camps to cook or care for wounded soldiers. Sybil Ludington is called the "female Paul Revere" because she warned colonists in Connecticut about a British attack. Deborah Sampson disguised herself as a man to join the army.

At this time, most African Americans were enslaved. As the war continued, many joined the army to support the fight for independence. About 5,000 African Americans served with the Continental Army. The words "all men are created equal" from the Declaration of Independence gave African Americans hope that the new nation would treat all people equally.

In 1777 Rhode Island's African American soldiers formed their own unit called the First Rhode Island Regiment. These soldiers fought in many battles of the Revolution, including the final battle at Yorktown. ▼

© David Wagner

Reading Skill

Make and Explain Inferences

Explain how the roles of women changed during the Revolution. Include the significance of their contributions to the war.

_____

_____

_____

The Problems of War

Funding the Revolution was a major problem. The Continental Congress had no power to raise money through taxes. State treasuries sent some money. Some foreign governements, who wanted to see the British defeated, sent money as well. But it wasn't enough.

Some Americans loaned their own money to the government. Merchants Robert Morris and Hyam Salomon loaned the government money to buy gunpowder, food, and supplies. Other Americans helped by keeping businesses open, while their owners went off to fight.

To pay for the war, the Congress printed paper money called "Continentals." But, the treasury did not have enough gold to back up their value. As more Continentals were printed, their value decreased. Continentals became worthless. The drop in the value of Continentals led to **inflation**, or a rapid rise in prices.

▲ Continental dollars

Chart and Graph Skills

Read a Bar Graph

Bar graphs use bars to show information in a way that is easy to read. Study the graph and answer the questions.

1. In 1779, about how many Continental dollars would you need to by an item worth a one-dollar coin?

2. Describe how the value of Continental dollars changed from 1777 to 1781.

WARTIME SHORTAGES

Paper Dollars Equaling One-Dollar Coin, 1777–1781

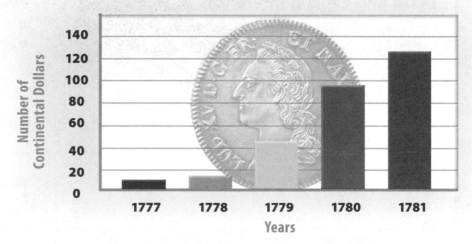

Number of Continental Dollars (y-axis: 0, 20, 40, 60, 80, 100, 120, 140)

Years (x-axis: 1777, 1778, 1779, 1780, 1781)

3. Explain why inflation was a problem.

Wartime Shortages

All trade was cut off at the start of the war. Like Patriot soldiers, most Americans soon faced shortages. Food became scarce, as did items such as cloth, kettles, and tools.

Americans caused shortages as well. Hoarding, or hiding away goods such as flour, molasses, and manufactured items, was a serious problem. Hoarding made these products hard to get—and raised their price. Some farmers and merchants became wealthy by **profiteering**, or charging high prices for goods they hoarded.

The Costs of Loyalty

Loyalists lived in every state. Many Loyalists, however, fled the American colonies during the Revolutionary War. They packed their belongings and sold whatever they could. Some left quickly for England. Others moved to Florida, Canada, or to the frontier beyond the Appalachian Mountains.

Loyalists who stayed in the United States faced many challenges. Their neighbors treated them badly, and some became victims of violence. Loyalist property often was taken or destroyed. Some Loyalists helped the British by spying on the Patriots. If caught, they were arrested by the Continental Army and tried as traitors.

Underline personal hardships faced by Americans during the war.

Lesson **3**

? Essential Question **Why do people get involved?**

_____

_____

_____

_____

_____

_____

Go back to *Show As You Go!* on pages 150–151.

networks There's More Online!
● Games ● Assessment

A Nation is Born

? Essential Question

How do conflicts evolve? What do you think?

_____

_____

_____

_____

_____

_____

_____

Words To Know

Write a synonym for each of the words below.

desert _____

*consequence _____

spy _____

blockade _____

Think about a time when you tried to do something difficult. What happened? Did you give up, or did you keep trying until you succeeded?

Fighting the War

As you read in Lesson 2, the Americans had some early successes. But by October of 1776 they had lost several battles and control of New York City. People began to question George Washington's leadership.

By late December many Patriots had left the army. Some chose to **desert**, or run away. Many who remained had no shoes or supplies. Without a victory to give Americans hope, Washington believed the Revolution would fail. The Americans needed a win, and they needed it fast.

Think back to what you have learned about the problems caused by the war. What personal hardships might have led people to desert the Continental Army? Explain why you agree or disagree with the decision to desert.

_____

_____

_____

_____

_____

_____

_____

_____

Crossing the Delaware

Washington decided that a sneak attack on the Hessian soldiers in Trenton, New Jersey, was the best option. On December 25, an icy storm blew into the area. This made traveling across the Delaware River from Pennsylvania to New Jersey difficult. The Patriots finally reached the shore at 4 A.M. The plan worked! The surprised Hessians quickly surrendered. Washington lost only two men in the battle, and both had frozen to death.

On January 3, 1777, the Patriots defeated the British at Princeton, New Jersey, and captured badly needed supplies. Now Patriot soldiers had food, weapons, shoes—and hope.

▲ Washington led Patriots across the icy Delaware River.

Library of Congress

Main Idea

Key Details

Reading Skill
Main Idea and Key Details
After reading these pages, complete the graphic organizer. Underline information in the text that helps you identify the main idea and key details.

The Turning Point

In June 1777, British General John Burgoyne saw an opportunity to trap Patriot forces. He led thousands of soldiers from Canada into New York. He believed another British force would march North from the Southern colonies, trapping Patriot forces between them.

At first Burgoyne's army was able to push the Americans south. But the British supply wagons got stuck on the muddy forest roads. As a **consequence**, the Americans had time to gather more troops. They decided to stand and fight at Saratoga, New York. Burgoyne finally reached Saratoga on September 16. By then the Patriots had gathered many more soldiers and had built dirt walls for protection.

On September 19, the two armies battled at a farm near Saratoga. The British won control of the farm, but they lost many soldiers. Burgoyne needed help, but none was on the way. On October 7, the two armies fought once more. The British had no chance to win. Burgoyne surrendered 10 days later. The battles at Saratoga were the turning point. The victory boosted American spirits. It also convinced other European countries to become allies with the United States.

DID YOU KNOW?

The first submarine, called the Turtle, was invented and used in 1776. American inventor David Bushnell designed the one-man sub to place bombs on British ships. Unfortunately, the Turtle didn't successfully place a bomb. But another of Bushnell's inventions did work. His floating mines exploded on contact and destroyed many British ships.

▼ Reenactors portray Patriot militia

Reenactors portray the British Red Coats ▲

◀ **Marquis de Lafayette**

Reading Skill

Sequence Events Using pages 178–181, identify four events significant to the Americans' success in the war. In the boxes, describe the events in sequential order. Circle the information from the text that you used.

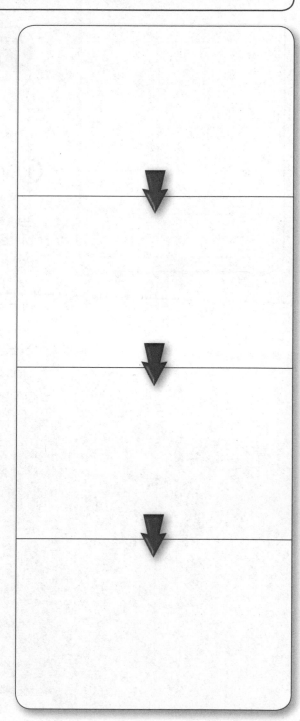

Help from Around the World

News of the American victory convinced France that the Americans could win. As a result, the French and American governments signed a treaty of alliance, or an agreement to work together. Several months later, France sent troops, warships, and supplies.

For years, France had been secretly supporting the Americans with money and supplies shipped through Haiti. At that time, Haiti was a center of French trade and profit. Helping the Americans was a way of protecting their investments from the British.

Individuals helped as well. During the winter of 1777, a military instructor named Baron Friedrich von Steuben arrived from Prussia. He saw that American soldiers needed strict training. Von Steuben taught them to march in rows and fight together instead of separately. By June 1778, the American army had become a well-trained fighting force ready for the open battlefield.

Von Steuben wasn't alone in his desire to help. Thaddeus Kosciuszko was an engineer from Poland. He designed forts, including the dirt walls that protected the Americans at Saratoga. Another Pole, Casimir Pulaski, served in Washington's army and became a general. He died of wounds received in battle while fighting for the young nation.

Finally, there was the Marquis de Lafayette. This 19-year-old from France became a valuable member of the Continental Army. You will learn more about his plans for defeating the British at the Battle of Yorktown later.

Compare and contrast battles in the American Revolution. What was different between battles in the South and the Battle of Yorktown?

_____

_____

_____

_____

_____

The Struggle Ends

Although the Americans now had allies, the war was far from over. The Patriots faced yet another difficult winter. Before the war ended, it expanded to west of the colonies, to the sea, and to the South.

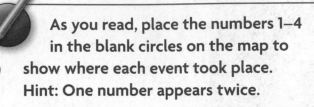

As you read, place the numbers 1–4 in the blank circles on the map to show where each event took place. Hint: One number appears twice.

① Valley Forge

The winter following the victory at Saratoga turned into an extreme hardship for Washington's troops. They faced bitter cold as they huddled around campfires at Valley Forge, Pennsylvania.

For the first two months, soldiers lived in ragged tents. Few had shoes or blankets, and they shared coats and gloves. Food was scarce too. Weak from cold and hunger, many soldiers became sick. Diseases spread quickly because soldiers lived close together. Almost 2,000 soldiers died from illnesses such as typhoid, influenza, and smallpox.

② Outside the Colonies

Not all important Revolutionary battles took place in the colonies. Many key battles occurred in the areas west of the Appalachian Mountains. In February 1779, George Rogers Clark and his men marched for a month before reaching a British fort near Vincennes, Indiana. Here they attacked and defeated the British.

Fighting happened off the coast of Great Britain too. On September 23, 1779, John Paul Jones and his crew defeated a British warship. Today, Jones is known as the "father of the American Navy."

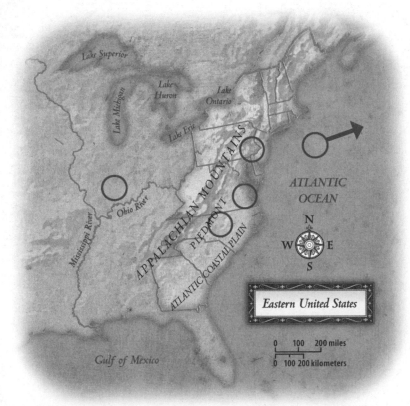

Eastern United States

0   100   200 miles
0   100 200 kilometers

③ In the South

In 1779, Americans gained support from Spain, a French ally. The Spanish loaned money to the Patriots. Bernardo de Gálvez, the governor of Spain's Louisiana Territory, closed the port at New Orleans to Great Britain and opened it to American ships.

Washington sent General Nathanael Greene to lead Patriot forces in the South. In March 1781 Greene's forces fought the British in North Carolina. The British won the battle but lost one-fourth of the soldiers. When one British leader learned of the many troops lost, he said, "Another such victory would destroy the British army."

④ The Battle of Yorktown

In the summer of 1781, General Cornwallis led 8,000 British soldiers to Yorktown, Virginia. One of Cornwallis's servants, James Armistead, was a **spy** for the Marquis de Lafayette. A spy secretly watches people or things to get information. Armistead passed on information that the British were waiting for supplies from New York. This news also was passed to the French navy, which set up a **blockade** to stop British ships. A blockade prevents the passage of people or supplies.

At the same time, Washington's army and a large French force joined Lafayette, who was already near Yorktown. Cornwallis was surrounded. The ensuing battle lasted for weeks, and fresh supplies and troops couldn't get through to the British. On October 19, 1781, Cornwallis finally surrendered to Washington.

Cornwallis surrenders to Washington's troops at Yorktown. ▼

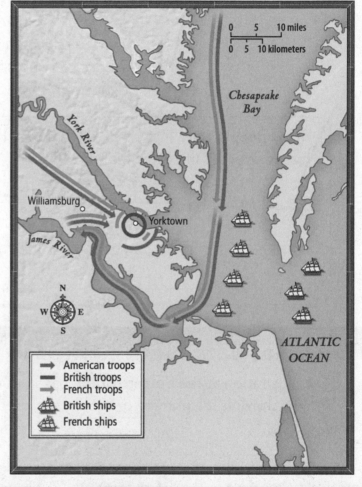

Map and Globe Skills

What do the blue, green and red lines around Yorktown show?

_____

_____

_____

The Results of the War

Fighting continued after Yorktown. But the British recognized they could not afford to continue the war. After Cornwallis's surrender, the British government began peace talks. The Americans, France, and Spain all took part. In 1783 the Treaty of Paris ended the American Revolution.

Under the agreement, Great Britain recognized American independence. The Mississippi River became the country's new western border. The treaty also opened the Mississippi River to ships from France, Spain, Britain, and the United States.

The American Revolution was over. The 13 colonies were now known as the United States. In his farewell orders to the Continental Army, Washington wrote that the determination of the troops "through almost every possible suffering and discouragement for the space of eight long years, was little short of a standing miracle."

Many people were injured or killed during the war. How do you think these casualties and losses affected life after the war?

_____

_____

_____

Primary and Secondary Sources

The illustration at the bottom of the page was drawn in 1906. What does it show? Is it a primary or secondary source? Circle your answer.

_____

_____

© Corbis

Several years after the revolution, John Adams was asked about the war. He said that there had been two revolutions. One was the war itself. The other was "in the minds and hearts of the people." The United States had won independence. But not all of the hearts and minds of the people had been changed. For some groups, this was due to the personal and political hardships they faced long after the end of the war.

Complete the chart by writing the name of the group being described and by describing the result of the hardships.

Group	Personal and Political Hardships	Result
	They lost husbands and sons in the war.	
	The new government needed the support of slave-holding Southern plantation owners.	Slavery continued.
	They were forced to give up their homes and property because they supported Great Britain.	
	They fought alongside the British to protect their homelands.	Americans considered them enemies and took their lands.

Lesson 4

? Essential Question How do conflicts evolve?

_____

_____

_____

Go back to *Show As You Go!* on pages 150–151.

networks There's More Online!
● Games ● Assessment

Complete the crossword puzzle below
with vocabulary words from this unit.

ACROSS

3 to cancel something

7 an official announcement

8 an action to prevent the passage of
people or supplies

11 a river or stream that flows into a
larger river

13 a person who secretly watches people
or things to get information

14 an American colonist who did not
support the fight for independence

DOWN

1 charging high prices for hoarded goods

2 an agreement between two or more
governments

4 a professional soldier from another
country

5 an army of volunteers who fight in an
emergency

6 a rapid rise in prices

9 an American colonist who supported
the fight for independence

10 to run away

12 to refuse to buy goods or services

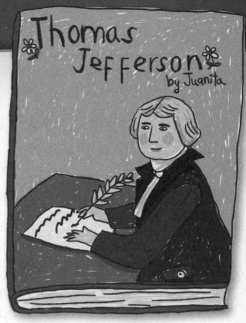

Unit Project

You will write and illustrate a picture book about one person, place, or event from the American Revolution. Your book must include accurate facts and images, and it must be easy to read and understand. Look back through the unit to brainstorm ideas. You may need to do additional research in the library or on the Internet. Read the list below to see what should be included in your picture book. Check off the tasks you have completed.

Your picture book should include	Yes, it does!
Title and dedication pages	☐
Accurate facts about the topic	☐
Pictures or illustrations	☐
Few spelling errors	☐
Few errors in grammar	☐
Few punctuation errors	☐
A reference list on the last page	☐

Think about the Big Idea

BIG IDEA Conflict causes change.

What did you learn in this unit that helps you understand the BIG IDEA?

_____

_____

_____

_____

Read the passage "Thomas Jefferson" before answering Numbers 1 through 8.

Thomas Jefferson

By Lamar Peterson

Thomas Jefferson was one of the most influential men in the history of the United States. He was born in 1743 on his family's plantation in what is now Albemarle County, Virginia. He went to school at the College of William and Mary in Williamsburg, Virginia. Later he practiced law. Jefferson played the violin and studied history, science, and architecture.

Jefferson designed Monticello, his home near Charlottesville, Virginia. He also designed the Virginia Capitol building and the University of Virginia.

In 1775 the Second Continental Congress met in Philadelphia to discuss the recent events in Massachusetts. In June 1776, the Continental Congress named Jefferson, John Adams, Benjamin Franklin, Roger Sherman, and Robert Livingston to a committee to write a statement of independence. Jefferson received the support of John Adams to draft the document. Adams said, "You can write ten times better than I can."

Jefferson was well-prepared to write the Declaration. He had heard Patrick Henry speak against the Stamp Act. He had read Thomas Paine's *Common Sense*. He studied the ideas of John Locke, an English philosopher from the late 1600s. Locke wrote that all people are born with certain rights, including life, liberty, and the right to own property. Locke believed that it was the responsibility of governments to protect these rights.

Using the ideas of these philosophers, the 33-year-old Jefferson wrote his draft in two days and then showed it to Franklin and Adams. They made a few changes and then decided to bring it to the Congress.

Jefferson was a man of many talents, interests, and skills. He served the United States in many ways and at different levels, including his two terms as the third President of the United States.

1 What is the author's purpose?

 Ⓐ to tell about Jefferson as President

 Ⓑ to describe Jefferson's many talents

 Ⓒ to describe Jefferson's designs for Monticello

 Ⓓ to tell about Jefferson writing the Declaration of Independence

2 To whom did Jefferson show the first draft of the Declaration?

 Ⓕ Adams and Paine

 Ⓖ Franklin and Locke

 Ⓗ Sherman and Livingston

 Ⓘ Franklin and Adams

3 Who wrote *Common Sense*?

Ⓐ Thomas Jefferson

Ⓑ Thomas Paine

Ⓒ John Locke

Ⓓ Patrick Henry

4 Read this sentence from the article.

"You can write ten times better than I can."

What did John Adams mean by his statement?

Ⓕ He was a better writer than Jefferson.

Ⓖ Jefferson was good at solving math problems.

Ⓗ Jefferson could write more than Adams.

Ⓘ He trusted Jefferson to write the draft alone.

5 Which information from the article supports the author's statement that Jefferson was well-prepared to write the Declaration?

Ⓐ He had designed both his home and the Virginia Capitol building.

Ⓑ He was a good writer.

Ⓒ He had heard Patrick Henry speak and studied the ideas of John Locke.

Ⓓ He was chosen by the Congress to be on the committee.

6 Which sentence below BEST explains the author's view of Jefferson?

Ⓕ Thomas Jefferson was one of the most influential men in the history of the United States.

Ⓖ Jefferson was well-prepared to write the Declaration.

Ⓗ Jefferson played the violin, and studied history, science, and architecture.

Ⓘ Jefferson designed Monticello, his home near Charlottesville, Virginia.

7 Which two words from the passage have nearly OPPOSITE meanings?

Ⓐ influential, philosopher

Ⓑ talents, interests

Ⓒ support, against

Ⓓ rights, changes

8 Read these sentences from the article.

Locke wrote that all people are born with certain rights, including life, liberty, and the right to own property. Locke believed it was the responsibility of governments to protect these rights.

What is the meaning of *responsibility* as used in the above sentence?

Ⓕ a job or duty

Ⓖ a change

Ⓗ a disagreement

Ⓘ a choice

6 Founding the Nation

BIG IDEA Rules provide order.

Deciding to declare independence was hard for our nation's Founders. More difficult still would be the question of how to govern the new nation. What did the Founders do? And how do their decisions affect us still, more than 200 years later? In this unit, you will read about the development of our nation's system of government and what it means to be an active citizen. As you read, think about how rules affect your everyday life, and how life might be different if rules didn't exist.

The Washington Monument and the Constitution (left)

networks

connected.mcgraw-hill.com
- Skill Builders
- Vocabulary Flashcards

Show As You Go! After you read each lesson in this unit, use this page to record information about the Constitution and how people participate in government. You will use your notes to help you complete a project at the end of the unit.

Fold page here.

Why It Was Created

_____
_____
_____

How It Was Created

_____
_____
_____
_____

Powers and Organization

_____
_____
_____
_____

Rights of Citizens

_____
_____
_____
_____

Civic Participation

_____
_____
_____
_____

Reading Skill

Common Core Standards
RI.3: Explain the relationships or interactions between two or more individuals, events, ideas, or concepts in a historical, scientific, or technical text based on specific information in the text.

Analyze Information

Analyzing information can help you better understand a particular topic. Start by collecting information about the topic. It's important to gather facts from many sources. For example, if you are analyzing information about an event, it's important to have more than one account of the event. Next, look closely at the information you collected to find patterns, relationships, or trends. Patterns are pieces of information that appear more than once. Relationships are the way two or more things interact. Trends are the way things change over time.

It took almost 200 years for African Americans to gain full voting rights. ▼

LEARN IT

To analyze information:

- Identify the topic that the information is about.

- Break the information into smaller pieces, called details.

- Examine each piece of information and look for patterns, relationships, or trends.

Topic

The right to vote used to be limited to a few people. When our country's plan of government was new, only some white men could vote. That changed in 1870, when a new law allowed African American men to vote too. For 50 years, only men could vote. Then, in 1920 women won the right to vote. In the following years, voting rights continued to expand. Today, all U.S. citizens 18 years or older can vote.

Details

AP Images

You can use a graphic organizer like the one below to keep track of the topic and details. Fill in the chart with the topic and details from page 192. Then answer the question below.

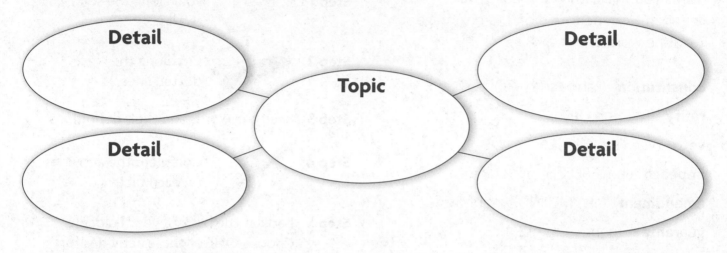

What pattern, relationship, or trend do you notice? _____

APPLY IT

Read the paragraph below. Circle text clues and details that you could use to help you analyze the information. Describe the pattern, relationship, or trend that you notice on the lines.

The Founders were fed up with the powerful British government. They came up with a new plan of government for the United States. The first plan they tried did not make the government powerful. It didn't work well, and over time this caused many problems. The next plan made the government more powerful. But the American people feared it was too powerful! People demanded that the Founders include a list of rights for their protection. Today, our government still works according to this second plan of government created by the Founders. It is powerful, but not too powerful.

_____

_____

_____

_____

Words to Know

Common Core Standards
RI.4: Determine the meaning of general academic and domain-specific words and phrases in a text relevant to a grade 5 topic or subject area.

The list below shows some important words you will learn in this unit. Their definitions can be found on the next page. Read the words.

constitution (kahn • stuh • TOO • shuhn)

ratify (RAT • uh • feye)

veto (VEE • toh)

impeach (ihm • PEECH)

amendment (uh • MEHND • muhnt)

guarantee (gehr • uhn • TEE)

fundamental (fuhn • duh • MEHN • tuhl)

responsibility (rih • spahn • suh • BIH • luh • tee)

FOLDABLES®

The Foldable on the next page will help you learn these important words. Follow the steps below to make your Foldable.

Step 1 Fold along the solid red line.

Step 2 Cut along the dotted lines.

Step 3 Read the words and their definitions.

Step 4 Complete the activities on each tab.

Step 5 Look at the back of your Foldable. Choose ONE of these activities for each word to help you remember its meaning:

- Draw a picture of the word.
- Write a description of the word.
- Write how the word is related to something you know.

◀ **The Constitutional Convention was held in Independence Hall in Philadelphia.**

A **constitution** is a plan for government.

FOLD

Write a sentence using the word *constitution*.

To **ratify** is to approve and adopt an official document.

Circle the three words that belong with the word *ratify*.

accept   reject   document
wrongdoing   adopt   addition

To **veto** is to reject a bill.

Write an antonym for the word *veto*.

To **impeach** is to put an official on trial for wrongdoing.

What do you think is the purpose of impeaching someone?

An **amendment** is a change or addition to an official document.

Circle two key words in the definition of *amendment*. Write the words here:

_____   _____

A **guarantee** is a promise that something will be provided.

What does it mean to give someone a guarantee?

Fundamental is a word that means basic or essential.

Write a sentence using the word *fundamental*.

A **responsibility** is something people do because it is their job or duty.

Write a synonym for the word *responsibility*.

constitution	constitution
CUT HERE	
ratify	ratify
veto	veto
impeach	impeach
amendment	amendment
guarantee	guarantee
fundamental	fundamental
responsibility	responsibility

Primary Sources

Diaries

A diary is one type of primary source. While a diary entry can contain many different types of information, most diary entries are records of a person's day-to-day experiences. Through diaries, we can learn much about what it was like to live long ago. We can even learn more about important events through the eyes of those who lived at that time.

In this unit, you will learn how and why the Founders of our country formed our national government. You will read about how their first plan of government caused many problems. Many people were unhappy, and some people even formed a rebellion. The diary entry on the right was written by someone who lived near the area where a rebellion occurred.

 Document-Based Questions

Read the diary entries. As you read, complete the following activities.

1. **Underline details that describe the writer's environment.**

2. **Circle details that describe the event the writer experienced and who was involved.**

Primary Source

Thursday, the 30th a small snow in the night . . . on Monday last John Bardwell . . . had orders from Shays . . . to have [his company] ready to march. . . .

Monday, the 4th cool towards night snowed . . . John Bardwell marched 40 men with him. . . .

Wednesday, the 6th . . . towards Night orders came . . . for the Militia to be in readiness to march tomorrow to Worcester

Thursday, the 7th . . . Our Militia seemed eager to go . . . I made a speech to them persuading them to be quiet & rest the Matter with [the government]

Friday, the 8th we hear that [General] Shays . . . has took possession of Worcester . . . and has taken [three judges prisoner]

—from the diary of Justus Forward

networks
👆 **There's More Online!**
● Skill Builders
● Resource Library

Struggles of a New Nation

? Essential Question

What is the purpose of government?
What do you think?

_____

_____

_____

_____

Words To Know

Write the definition of each word in your own words.

constitution _____

_____

confederation _____

_____

*conclusion _____

_____

delegate _____

_____

A plan is a set of directions that help people figure out how to do something. There are many reasons to have a plan. Your family probably has an emergency plan, such as how to get out of the house in case of a fire.

Interview a parent or a trusted adult about a plan he or she has. Write his or her answers below.
I interviewed:

_____

Ask: What is your plan for?

_____

Ask: Why do you need your plan?

_____

_____

Ask: What is the most important part of your plan?

_____

_____

Jupiterimages/Comstock Images/Getty Images

Making Plans

Plans are an important part of life. Plans can be simple, such as what to eat for dinner. Or, they can be complicated and very important, especially when there are many things to be done.

Governments have many responsibilities. You already know a little about governments.

Make a list of things governments do.

_____

_____

_____

_____

▲ Our nation's Founders had a lot of work to do to set up our government.

A Plan for Government

Governments serve many purposes. The most important purpose of government is to provide laws. This helps to avoid conflicts and settle disagreements. Governments also provide security for their people. This is why we have police officers and armed forces. Governments must also provide services and supplies that wouldn't be available otherwise. These include building and repairing roads, delivering the mail, and providing money and other aid for those in need. Another function of governments is managing the economy. A government must collect and spend money in order to operate and provide for its people.

Every government in our nation has a plan to help it serve these purposes. This plan consists of a set of laws. There is a special word for a plan for government: **constitution**. Our nation's constitution has an interesting story. In this Lesson, you will learn about that story.

Circle the purposes of a constitution. Rewrite them in your own words.

_____

_____

_____

_____

Northwind Pictures

Creating a New Government

You've already learned about the Declaration of Independence and the Revolutionary War. There's more to the story of forming the United States. To tell it, we have to go back in time a little bit. Think back to the year 1776 and the Second Continental Congress.

At the same time that the Founders were deciding to break away from Great Britain, they were also deciding what to do afterward. How would they govern the thirteen colonies on their own?

It would be a challenge. The Founders wanted to protect the liberties, or freedoms, that Americans were fighting for. And the colonies didn't yet think of themselves as a single country. In fact, some colonies had already written their own constitutions. No one wanted another too-powerful government telling them what to do, as Britain's Parliament and king had.

◀ Painter Archibald MacNeal Willard painted "The Spirit of 1776" more than 100 years after the signing of the Declaration of Independence.

1. **Think back to what you've learned. What else happened at the Second Continental Congress?**

   _____

   _____

2. **Explain why the colonies didn't want a new government to have too much power.**

   _____

   _____

Is this painting a primary or secondary source? Circle your answer.

The Articles of Confederation

Some thought that the new nation would be more like a friendly group of independent states than a single, united country. The Second Continental Congress set about writing a plan of government, called the Articles of Confederation, around this idea. A confederation is a group of separate governments that agree to help one another.

The Articles of Confederation eventually became the first constitution of the United States of America. It took the Congress seven months to complete, and the country started working according to this plan in 1777. However, the thirteen states still had to **ratify**, or approve and adopt it. The Articles were finally ratified by all the states in 1781. From beginning to end, it took more than four years to make the new government final. And the former colonies were fighting the Revolutionary War at the same time. Imagine that!

The Articles of Confederation ▶

Reading Skill

Analyze Information

Using the above image and what you have read in the text, what patterns or relationships do you notice about the loyalties of Americans at the time of the Revolution?

_____

_____

_____

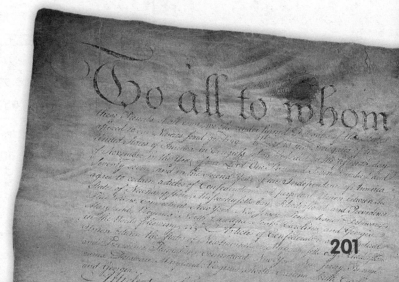

201

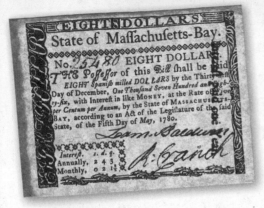

▲ **Paper money from Massachusetts**

A Small Government

The government set up by the Articles of Confederation was very small and limited in its powers. It was made up of one lawmaking body called Congress. Each state sent at least two representatives to Congress, but each state only had one vote on every matter. The individual states kept most of the power. At first, the Articles of Confederation seemed to meet the needs of the young nation. But as time went on, weaknesses emerged. Read the chart below to learn about some of the effects of these weaknesses.

THINK • PAIR • SHARE
With a partner, pick one effect from the chart. Circle it on your page, then brainstorm reasons why this was a problem.

Weaknesses of the Articles of Confederation	
Cause	**Effect**
The national government had no power to raise money through taxes.	The national government could not • pay off high war debts. • pay lawmakers. • pay soldiers for their service.
The national government had no power to support the national currency.	Each state made its own paper money.
	The value of money was different in each state. Some money was worthless.
The national government had no power to manage trade.	Each state made its own trade laws.
	Merchants never knew which laws to follow.
	Trade slowed, as did economic growth.
The national government had no power to force states to follow national laws.	States did whatever they wanted.
The national government had no power to raise an army.	The nation could not defend itself. Britain and Spain both took advantage of this on the frontier by ignoring U.S. claims to land.

Troubles for the New Government

After the Revolutionary War, the new country faced many problems. Congress had borrowed large amounts of money to pay for the war. Now it was unable to collect taxes to repay those debts.

Many state governments also had large debts. To pay off this debt, they increased taxes. Many people and businesses could not afford to pay these taxes and went into debt. Because Congress could not regulate trade, each state made its own trade laws. Some states taxed goods that came from other states or countries. Supplies and goods became more expensive, and people went deeper into debt.

Violence Erupts

When people couldn't pay their debts, they were thrown in jail. Daniel Shays was a military officer in the Revolutionary War. He was now a farmer who was deep in debt. Shays urged others to rebel. He led a group of armed men and across western Massachusetts. They closed courthouses and broke into jails to free debtors. Shays then attacked a federal arsenal, or storage area for weapons.

Shays's Rebellion was quickly stopped by the state militia. However, the rebellion showed many people that the Articles had failed. Wealthy Americans wanted a national government strong enough to protect their property. Farmers wanted a government that could issue paper money that had value.

Shays's Rebellion ▼

1. Why did Daniel Shays rebel?

_____

_____

2. Why did people think they needed a new government after the rebellion?

_____

_____

_____

_____

The Northwest Ordinance

Overall, the Articles were not working. But they did have one lasting success: Congress was able to set up land policies for expanding the country. Many Americans wanted to move west of the Appalachians to search for new land and opportunities. To provide land for these settlers, the Confederation Congress passed the Northwest Ordinance of 1787. This plan created the Northwest Territory out of land north of the Ohio River and east of the Mississippi River.

Settlers poured into the Northwest Territory. They eventually carved out five states under the Northwest Ordinance: Ohio, Indiana, Illinois, Michigan, and Wisconsin.

United States, 1787

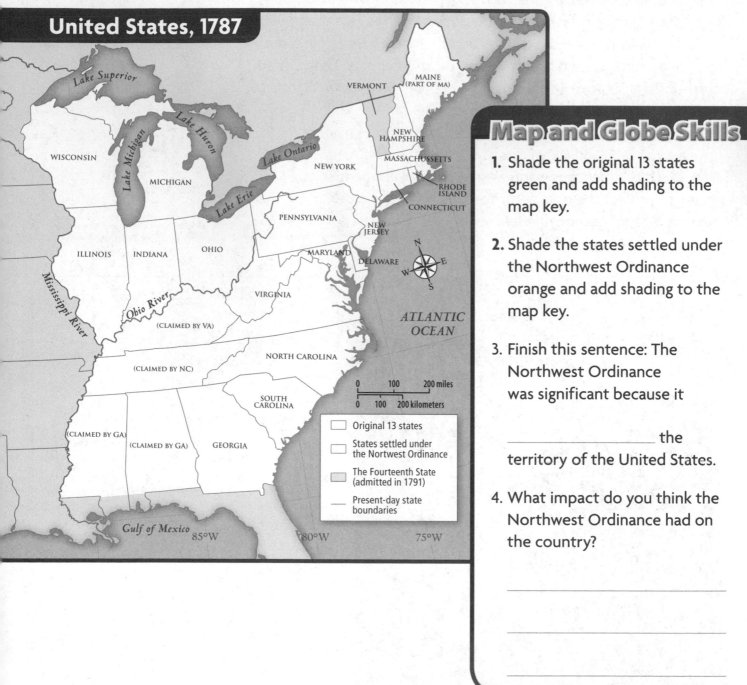

Original 13 states

States settled under the Nortwest Ordinance

The Fourteenth State (admitted in 1791)

Present-day state boundaries

Map and Globe Skills

1. Shade the original 13 states green and add shading to the map key.

2. Shade the states settled under the Northwest Ordinance orange and add shading to the map key.

3. Finish this sentence: The Northwest Ordinance was significant because it

_____ the territory of the United States.

4. What impact do you think the Northwest Ordinance had on the country?

_____

_____

_____

Calls for Change

The Founders came to the **conclusion** that the Articles had failed. But what should they do about that? This was an urgent matter, indeed. Violence had already become a reality, and more violence could be on the way. Many Americans called for the Articles of Confederation to be changed. A few members of Congress called a special meeting to decide what to do.

▲ The Constitutional Convention was held in Pennsylvania's State House in Philadelphia. Today this building is called Independence Hall.

The Constitutional Convention

In May 1787, leaders from 12 states convened, or met, in Philadelphia. There, the **delegates** to the Constitutional Convention had to decide the future of their government. A delegate is a person who represents others at an important meeting. They elected George Washington to lead the convention and began a long, difficult discussion. The delegates decided that the Articles were too broken to be saved. Instead, they decided to start over with a new constitution. The fate of the young nation was in their hands.

DID YOU KNOW?
Rhode Island did not send a delegate to the Constitutional Convention. State leaders didn't want any national government to "interfere" with their state.

© Getty Images

Lesson **1**

(?) Essential Question   What is the purpose of government?

_____

_____

_____

_____

_____

_____

Go back to *Show As You Go!* on pages 190–191. ≪

networks   **There's More Online!**
● Games ● Assessment

Writing the Constitution

(t) Oleksiy Maksymenko/Alamy, (bkgd) © Getty Images.

? Essential Question

What are the functions of government?
What do you think?

_____

_____

_____

_____

_____

_____

Have you ever heard or seen the phrase "We the People"? You can find it at the very beginning of our nation's Constitution—the plan for government written at the Constitutional Convention. "We the People" sums up the idea that the government of the United States is run by its people, for its people. This idea is also called popular sovereignty. Read the rest of the Preamble, or beginning words, of the Constitution below.

We the People of the United States, in Order to form a more perfect Union, establish Justice, insure domestic Tranquility, provide for the common defence, promote the general Welfare, and secure the Blessings of Liberty to ourselves and our Posterity, do ordain and establish this Constitution for the United States of America.

Words To Know

Have you heard these words before? Make a guess about what each word means. Then find it in the Lesson.

*persuade _____

_____

federalism _____

_____

appeal _____

_____

impeach _____

_____

(Circle) one phrase from the Preamble. Then, go to a dictionary to look up any words you don't know. Once you know the meaning of those words, write on the lines what the phrase you circled means.

_____

_____

_____

_____

_____

_____

Key Concepts of the Constitution

You might be wondering what happened at the Constitutional Convention. We'll get to that soon, but first you should know about some key concepts, or ideas, that took shape as the Convention went on. Each of these concepts limits the government's power. You see, even as the framers of our government knew that the Articles of Confederation were too weak, they continued to worry about making our government too powerful.

Key Concept	Origin (Where it Came From)
Popular Sovereignty The government is run by its people. The people choose their own leaders.	This idea is also called democracy. The ancient Greeks invented democracy thousands of years ago.
Rule of Law The Constitution is the highest set of laws. No one is above the Constitution. This is also called "Limited Government."	England's plan of government, called the Magna Carta, limited the power of the king or queen, or monarchies.
Separation of Powers Government is divided into three branches. Each branch has a different job to do.	A French writer named Montesquieu wrote about these ideas in the mid-1700s. The delegates decided to try them out.
Checks and Balances Each branch of government has power over the other two branches.	
Federalism The national government and the states share power.	This concept was invented at the Constitutional Convention. The delegates wanted to give the federal government just enough power, and reserve all other powers to the states.
Individual Rights This is the idea that people have rights, which should be protected by their government.	John Locke and other philosophers said people have "natural rights" that cannot be taken away.

Chart and Graph Skills

1. Circle the concept supported by John Locke.

2. **Highlight** the concept invented by the delegates to the Constitutional Convention.

3. Put a box around the concept that is related to the Magna Carta.

Separating the Powers

Discussions at the Constitutional Convention were serious business. The big problem with the Articles of Confederation was that it didn't give the national government enough power. But no one wanted to give any person or group too much power. The representatives decided to separate the powers of government into three branches. The first three articles, or major parts, of the Constitution describe the branches of our government and their powers.

DID YOU KNOW?

Another big debate at the Constitutional Convention was over how to count enslaved Africans in the population. Under the Three-Fifths Compromise, only three-fifths of a state's enslaved population could be counted toward representation in the House.

Circle for whom Congress works.

the Senate
the President
the People

The Legislative Branch

Find it in: Article I of the Constitution

Name: Congress

Most Known For: Making our nation's laws

The Great Compromise: Delegates suggested two different ways to organize Congress. One plan gave small states more power. Another gave large states more power. The delegates argued for weeks, but were finally **persuaded** into a compromise. They combined parts of the two plans. This solution was called the Great Compromise.

How Congress is Organized: Congress has two houses, or parts. In the House of Representatives, the number of members sent by each state is based on a state's population. In the other house, called the Senate, each state has two senators.

Electing Law Makers: The Constitution created a representative government. This means that the people elect, or choose, people to represent them in government. Members of the House of Representatives serve for two years. In the beginning, the state legislatures chose the senators. Today, the people also elect their senators directly. Senators serve for six years.

Writing Laws: A bill is an idea for a new law. To become law, first a bill has to be approved by both houses of Congress. Then the bill goes to the President. Bills about money must always begin in the House of Representatives.

Other Powers: Congress has many other powers. These include the power to collect taxes, control trade with other countries, manage a national currency, and declare war.

THINK · PAIR · SHARE

Work with a partner and use the Internet or other resource to find both an audio and a video recording of different State of the Union addresses. Discuss what the speech tells you about what was happening in the country at that time.

The Executive Branch

Find it in: Article II of the Constitution

Name: The President of the United States

Most Known For: Carrying out, or enforcing, the laws

The Electoral College: Constitutional Convention delegates worried that the people would choose power-hungry leaders, or leaders who couldn't do the job. The delegates created the Electoral College to choose the President. In this system, each state gets one electoral vote for each of its members of Congress.

Signing Bills Into Law: A bill that has been approved by both houses of Congress goes on to the President. The President then has a choice. He or she can sign the bill, making it a law. Or, the President can **veto**, or reject, the bill. If a bill is vetoed, it goes back to Congress. Congress can still pass the law if two-thirds of the members of both houses approve the bill. This is called overriding the veto.

Other Powers: The President serves for four years. The President also is the commander-in-chief of our nation's military and is responsible for signing treaties and appointing government officials.

Kings vs. Presidents: Kings inherit their power, which means they receive their power from their parents. But U.S. Presidents are chosen by—and get their power from—the people.

▲ George Washington was our first President under the Constitution.

The Constitution requires the President to report to Congress on the "state of the union" each year. In 1947 Harry Truman was the first President to deliver the State of the Union address on television. ▼

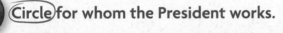

Circle for whom the President works.

Congress   the President   the People

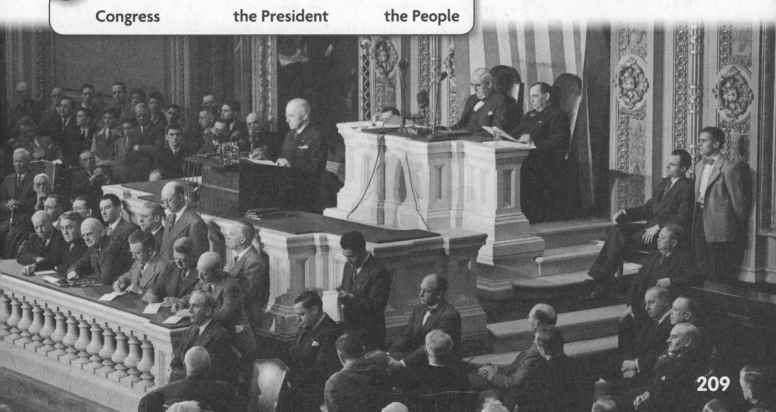

(t) © The Granger Collection, New York, (b) Bettmann/Corbis

The Judicial Branch

Find it in: Article III of the Constitution

Name: The United States Supreme Court

Most Known For: Interpreting the laws and settling conflicts

Our Legal System: The courts are the foundation, or base, of our legal system. All people, including members of government, have to follow what our courts say. This is part of having our government's power limited by the rule of the law.

The Court's Make-up: There are nine justices, or judges, on the United States Supreme Court. Each justice is appointed by the President. Then he or she has to be confirmed by the Senate. They serve for the rest of their lives or until they retire.

How It Works: Conflicts about national laws go to lower national courts first. The side that loses can **appeal**, first to a higher court, and then the Supreme Court. To appeal is to ask for a case to be heard again. The Supreme Court is the highest court in our country. Its decisions are final. The Court only hears about 2 percent of cases that are submitted for its review each year.

Power of Judicial Review: The Supreme Court can declare a law unconstitutional, which means that the law goes against the Constitution. If a law is declared unconstitutional, it is no longer enforced. This power was established in 1803. That year, the Supreme Court, led by Chief Justice John Marshall, ruled that a law passed by one of the states was unconstitutional.

▲ Chief Justice John Marshall

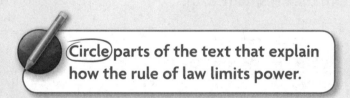

Circle parts of the text that explain how the rule of law limits power.

How a Bill Becomes a Law

A member of Congress introduces the bill.

The members of Congress discuss and debate the bill.

The House and Senate vote to approve the bill.

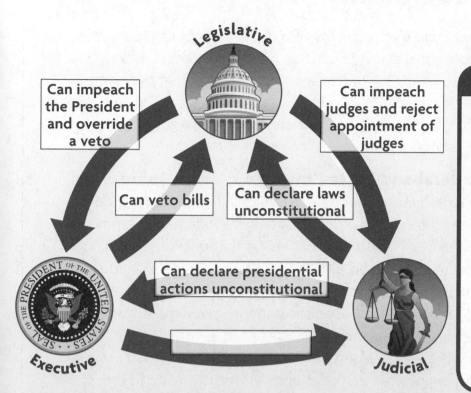

Legislative

Can impeach the President and override a veto

Can impeach judges and reject appointment of judges

Can veto bills

Can declare laws unconstitutional

Can declare presidential actions unconstitutional

Executive

Judicial

Chart and Graph Skills

Read a Flow Chart

Use the chart to answer the following questions.

1. Underline the judicial check on the legislative branch.

2. Highlight the executive check on the judicial branch.

3. Which branch can veto bills?

_____

Checks and Balances

By separating the powers of government, the Constitution places limits on each branch's power. Because one branch can't do everything, each branch has to work with the other branches. In addition, the delegates also gave each branch some authority over the other branches. This principle is called checks and balances, and it makes sure that no one branch of government becomes too powerful.

Study the chart to learn about ways each branch limits the powers of the other branches. You will see that Congress has one power you've not heard of before: the power to **impeach** a member of government. Impeach means to put an official on trial for wrongdoing.

Circle the sentences that explain how the separation of powers and checks and balances limit the powers of government.

The President signs or vetoes the bill.

Congress can override a veto with a two-thirds majority vote.

If a law is challenged, the Supreme Court justices decide if the law is constitutional.

211

Federalism

You know that problems with the Articles of Confederation proved that the young nation needed a stronger national government. But the delegates still worried that they were making the national government too powerful. They needed a way to balance power between the national government and the states.

Underline details that tell how federalism limits the powers of the national government.

Federal and State Powers

The delegates designed a system called **federalism**. Under federalism, power is shared between a national government and states. There are certain things that only the national government can do. Other things only the states can do. By creating this system, the delegates hoped that state governments could keep the national government from becoming too powerful.

The national, or federal, government has certain powers and responsibilities. Federal powers mostly relate to the needs of the whole nation, such as declaring war or coining money. "Coining" money is another way of saying "minting" or "printing" money. Other powers are reserved for the states, such as creating public schools or making traffic laws. Some powers are shared between the federal and state governments.

> **Explain what federalism is.**
>
> _____
>
> _____
>
> _____

▲ A state capitol building

▼ The United States Capitol

The chart below gives examples of how power is divided between the federal and state governments. On the blank lines, fill in two more examples for each set of powers. Try to do this without looking back at page 212.

Division of Powers Under Federalism

Federal Powers

- Make treaties with other countries

- Control trade between the states

- _____

- Run the postal service

- _____

- Settle disputes between the states

A U.S. postal worker ▶

State Powers

- Set up local governments

- Build roads

- _____

- Run elections

- _____

- Make laws that control trade within the state

▲ A public school

Shared Powers

- Set up courts

- Enforce laws

- Collect taxes

- Borrow money

- Maintain parks

- Protect the environment

Why do you think some powers are shared?

_____

_____

Police officers ▶

Amending the Constitution

The delegates to the Constitutional Convention knew their new plan wasn't perfect. They knew the country would grow and that its needs would change over time. So in Article V of the Constitution they laid out the **amendment** process. An amendment is a change or an addition to the Constitution.

There are two parts to the amendment process: proposal and ratification. During the proposal process, supporters of an amendment submit it to the government for review. If the amendment has enough support, it moves on to the ratification, or approval, process. Under the Constitution, there are two ways of proposing an amendment and two ways of ratifying it. Read the flow chart below to learn how it works.

FUN FACTS
There have been 27 constitutional amendments. You will learn more about some of these in Lesson 4.

Amending the Constitution

Chart and Graph Skills

Read a Flow Chart
Imagine that you want to amend the Constitution. Write a set of step-by-step directions that describe the amendment process.

_____

_____

_____

_____

_____

_____

PROPOSAL		PROPOSAL
Vote of two-thirds of members of both houses	OR	National convention called at the request of two-thirds of 50 state legislatures

RATIFICATION		RATIFICATION
Approved by three-fourths of 50 state legislatures	OR	Approved by three-fourths of ratifying conventions held in 50 states

New Amendment to the Constitution

Review the Constitution

Use information you learned in Lesson 2 to review what you know about the Constitution.

Explain how each concept listed places limits on the powers of the federal government.

Popular Sovereignty: _____

Rule of Law: _____

Separation of Powers: _____

Checks and Balances: _____

Federalism: _____

Lesson 2

 Essential Question   What are the functions of government?

_____

_____

_____

_____

_____

_____

Go back to *Show As You Go!* on page 190–191. ⫷⫷⫷

 netw⊙rks   **There's More Online!**
● Games ● Assessment

Convincing the People

? Essential Question

How do people make decisions?
What do you think?

_____

_____

_____

_____

_____

_____

_____

_____

_____

Have you ever had an idea that you thought was great, but your friends disagreed? Did you try to win them over? Think of positive ways you can persuade someone to agree to something you want.

_____

_____

_____

Once the Constitution was finished, the delegates had to convince the nation's people that it was a good plan. In Lesson 3, you will learn about what they had to do to get the Constitution ratified.

Delegates signed the Constitution on September 17, 1787. ▼

Words To Know

Look at the words below. Tell a partner what you think you already know about each word.

*debate
guarantee
submit

Signing the Constitution

The delegates to the Constitutional Convention worked for nearly four months. They had decided to keep their meetings a secret, so they kept the windows and doors to the Philadelphia's state house closed and locked. The summer sun made the building a hot and uncomfortable place to work. Delegates held passionate debates over many points in the Constitution. Some delegates even left in protest. By the time the Constitution was finished, everyone was ready to go home. The 39 remaining delegates finally signed the Constitution on September 17, 1787.

More Work to Do

This was not the end of the Constitution's story, however. The delegates needed the states to agree to it, so that the whole country could work together. They decided that in order to make the Constitution official, at least 9 of the 13 states had to ratify it. A long national **debate**, or careful discussion, was about to begin.

Reading Skill

Summarize

How was the U.S. government created?

_____

_____

_____

The Debate Over Federalism

Many Americans did not immediately accept the Constitution. They had just fought a war for independence from a powerful and tyrannical government. Many people thought the Constitution could lead to more tyranny. People spoke up with concerns, and two sides emerged over the issue. One side argued for the Constitution. The other argued against it. Read the descriptions of each side from the points-of-view of two people who were there.

The Anti-Federalists

I, George Mason, was an Anti-Federalist. We Anti-Federalists did not like the Constitution. We desired strong state governments and a more limited plan for the federal government. Anti-Federalists included people who had been delegates to the Constitutional Convention but refused to sign the final document. I was one such delegate. We didn't want another set of tyrants to rule us, as King George and the British Parliament had. We feared that this Constitution would lead to just that.

*We Anti-Federalists also wanted a bill of rights. This would be a list of rights **guaranteed**, or promised, to individual Americans. We felt that a powerful government could take away the people's rights if they weren't spelled-out. This is what Britain's government had done, and we didn't want to go back to that! I had argued for a bill of rights during the Constitutional Convention, but one was not included. We Anti-Federalists continued to argue for one during the ratification debate.*

Circle two things that the Anti-Federalists wanted in the paragraphs above.

Reading Skill

Draw an Inference

Now that you know what the Anti-Federalists wanted, draw an inference about what the other group wanted. Use text clues and what you already know. Write your inference below.

_____

_____

The Federalists

My name is James Madison, and I was a Federalist. Federalists supported the new Constitution. We felt that making the national government less powerful would lead to problems in the future. And we felt that federalism protected against government tyranny because it reserved powers for the states and divided powers among three government branches. In short, we felt we had spread government powers out among enough people. We were confident that no one could ever become too powerful.

We Federalists also didn't feel the Constitution needed a bill of rights. Many state constitutions already had statements protecting rights. We also thought that listing some rights and not others could allow the government to take away rights that weren't listed. What a mistake that would be!

Federalists worked to preserve the Constitution. Alexander Hamilton, John Jay, and I published several essays. These essays are now called the Federalist Papers. They explained why we felt federalism was a good solution to our nation's problems. Federalism was a new idea, and the Federalist Papers helped many Americans understand how it would work, and why.

PhotoLink/Getty Images

Reading Skill

Compare and Contrast

Fill in the Venn diagram below to compare the Anti-Federalist and Federalist views of government.

Anti-Federalists | **Both** | **Federalists**

Wanted to protect the people from government tyranny

Ratifying the Constitution

The Federalists' arguments won over many people. Between September 1787 and May 1788, eight states ratified the Constitution. In June 1788, New Hampshire became the ninth state to ratify it. The Constitution officially became the law of the United States.

Anti-Federalists Hold Out

Some people worried that 9 of 13 states wouldn't be enough, though. Of the states that remained, two were the largest in the nation—New York and Virginia. These states had strong groups of Anti-Federalists who fought against ratification. These groups demanded that the Constitution clearly spell out the individual rights of the people. A nation that had won independence from a king would never approve a plan that did not guarantee their liberties, said the Anti-Federalists. Federalists, such as Virginia's James Madison and New York's Alexander Hamilton, feared that the Constitution would fail without the support of these states.

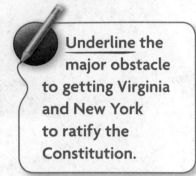

Underline the major obstacle to getting Virginia and New York to ratify the Constitution.

FUN FACTS

Vermont was the first state added to the country under the new plan of government. It became the fourteenth state to ratify the Constitution on January 10, 1791.

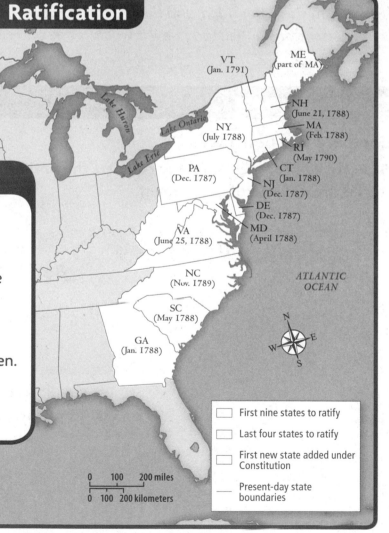

Ratification

VT (Jan. 1791)
ME (part of MA)
NH (June 21, 1788)
NY (July 1788)
MA (Feb. 1788)
RI (May 1790)
PA (Dec. 1787)
CT (Jan. 1788)
NJ (Dec. 1787)
DE (Dec. 1787)
VA (June 25, 1788)
MD (April 1788)
NC (Nov. 1789)
ATLANTIC OCEAN
SC (May 1788)
GA (Jan. 1788)
Lake Huron
Lake Ontario
Lake Erie

First nine states to ratify
Last four states to ratify
First new state added under Constitution
Present-day state boundaries

0   100   200 miles
0   100   200 kilometers

Map and Globe Skills

Use text clues and the dates on the map to help you complete the activity.

1. Shade the first nine states to ratify the Constitution yellow.

2. Shade the last four states to ratify the Constitution pink. Shade Vermont green.

Make sure you remember to fill in your map key!

◄ New York City celebrated the ratification of the Constitution with a parade.

What did Madison agree to do in order to get Virginia and New York to ratify the Constitution?

_____

_____

_____

Adding the Bill of Rights

To win ratification by Virginia and New York, James Madison agreed to **submit**, or offer for approval, a bill of rights to Congress in the form of Constitutional amendments. He promised the Anti-Federalists that he would work to get the bill approved if they voted to ratify the Constitution.

Each side kept its end of the bargain. Virginia and New York both ratified the Constitution in 1788. James Madison submitted a list of amendments to the House of Representatives in June 1789. The final two states to ratify the Constitution were North Carolina and Rhode Island.

Lesson **3**

? **Essential Question** **How do people make decisions?**

_____

_____

_____

Go back to *Show As You Go!* on pages 190–191. ◄◄◄

netw⦿rks **There's More Online!**
● Games ● Assessment

Protecting and Expanding Rights

How do we protect our rights?
What do you think?

_____

_____

_____

_____

Words To Know

Write a number in each box to show how much you know about the meaning of each word.

1 = I have no idea!
2 = I know a little.
3 = I know a lot.

___ **fundamental**

___ **press**

___ **due process**

___ **jury**

___ ***defend**

When people have needs or wants, they sometimes make a list. Your parents might make a list of groceries they need. You might make a list of presents you want for your birthday. Lists don't always have to be about things, though. They can be about ideas or tasks. Make a list of three ways you want to be treated by your friends, and give your list a title.

List title: _____

1. _____

_____

2. _____

_____

3. _____

_____

The Bill of Rights

As part of his agreement with the Anti-Federalists, James Madison submitted a list of amendments to Congress. Of those, Congress agreed on 12 and sent them to the states for approval. The amendments were debated in each state, and eventually 10 were ratified. From beginning to end, the process took about a year and a half. The amendments were finally added to the Constitution in December 1791. These first 10 amendments are called the Bill of Rights.

The Bill of Rights wasn't the first document to define the rights of citizens. For example, the British government had a bill of rights, as did many of the state governments. In writing the amendments to submit to Congress, James Madison looked to the Virginia Declaration of Rights. This document had existed since 1776. And it had been written by George Mason—James Madison's Anti-Federalist rival!

The Bill of Rights is part of the Constitution, but it is also talked about as a separate document. The rights that it defines are central to our lives as Americans. When people speak of protecting our liberties or freedoms, often they are talking about freedoms granted by the Bill of Rights.

Underline words that tell you the origins of the Bill of Rights. **Circle** words that tell you about governments that had similar documents.

Freedom of speech is protected by the Bill of Rights. ▼

The McGraw-Hill Companies - Inc./Christopher Kerrigan - photographer

Protecting Individual Rights

The Bill of Rights begins by protecting **fundamental**, or basic, rights of all U.S. citizens. The First Amendment guarantees five freedoms: freedom of religion, freedom of speech, freedom of the **press**, freedom of assembly, and freedom to petition. *Press* refers to members of the news media, such as reporters and columnists. Many Americans find this to be the most important amendment.

The Second Amendment lists another basic freedom: the right "to keep and bear arms." The Supreme Court has interpreted this to mean two things. First, states have the right to maintain their own militias. And second, governments can pass laws to control, but not prevent, individuals from owning firearms. The Third Amendment prevents the government from forcing people to house soldiers.

Fundamental Rights Under the First Amendment

Freedom of . . .	What it Means	Picture or Symbol
	People are free to choose their own system of beliefs or none at all.	
	People can say what their political ideas are without fear of punishment by the government.	
	Newspapers and other members of the media are free to publish news and opinions, even if they are critical of the government.	
	People are free to hold meetings and gather peacefully in groups.	
	People are free to write to the government about its policies and ask for help without fear of punishment.	

Right to Due Process

Just as important as basic freedoms is the right to "**due process** of the law." Due process of the law means the government must follow the rules established by law. The Fourth through Eighth Amendments protect the right to due process.

Due Process Amendments

Fourth Amendment The government cannot search through or take away any property without a specific reason that is approved by a court.

Fifth Amendment The government needs to prove it has a good reason to put someone on trial. A person cannot be tried twice for the same crime, or be forced to be a witness against him- or herself. Property cannot be taken away unless the government pays for it.

Sixth Amendment People have a right to a speedy and public trial by a **jury**. A jury is a group of citizens who decide a court case. Accused people have the right to be **defended** by a lawyer.

Seventh Amendment In lawsuits, people have the right to a trial by a jury.

Eighth Amendment People are protected from high bail and fines. People are protected from cruel and unusual punishment.

> Tell in your own words how the Bill of Rights limits the power of the federal government.
>
> _____
>
> _____
>
> _____
>
> _____
>
> _____

Limiting the Government

The Bill of Rights puts firm limits on the federal government in the Ninth and Tenth Amendments. The Ninth Amendment says that the rights of the people are not limited to what is listed in the Constitution. The Tenth Amendment says that powers not given to the federal government belong to the states or to the people.

If an accused person can't afford a lawyer, then the government has to provide him or her with one. This is guaranteed by the Sixth Amendment. ▶

Brand X Pictures

Expanding Voting Rights

In addition to the Bill of Rights, 17 other amendments have been added to the Constitution over the years. Many of these amendments expanded the right to vote to more people. When the Constitution was signed, only some white males had the right to vote. Today, most U.S. citizens who are 18 years or older can vote.

1788 *The U.S. Constitution is ratified.*

1780 — 1870 — 1900

1870 *15ᵗʰ Amendment*

Formerly enslaved African American men gain the right to vote.

1920 *19ᵗʰ Amendment*

Women win the right to vote across the country.

Take a Look Back . . .

The 15ᵗʰ Amendment would not have been possible without the following:

13ᵗʰ Amendment: Made slavery illegal throughout the United States in 1875.

14ᵗʰ Amendment: Made African Americans citizens of the United States and guaranteed them the same legal rights as whites in 1868.

The 13ᵗʰ, 14ᵗʰ, and 15ᵗʰ Amendments are often called the Civil War amendments because they grew out of that great conflict.

1971 *26th Amendment*

The voting age is lowered to 18 years. The legal voting age had been 21 in most states. But men and women only had to be 18 to fight in war. Because 18-year-olds could serve our country in the military, people argued that they should be able to vote.

Draw a picture of yourself as an 18-year-old voting for the first time.

(l) Peter Gridley/Photographer's Choice/Getty Images, (r) AP Images

1930	1960	1990

1961 *23rd Amendment*

Residents of Washington, D.C., receive the right to vote for President. Until then, they had not been allowed to vote for any federal office.

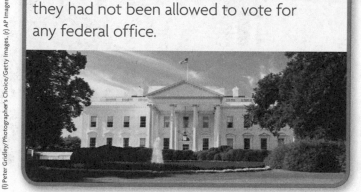

1964 *24th Amendment*

Poll taxes are made illegal. These unfair taxes had taken the right to vote away from many people, especially African Americans in the South.

Lesson 4

(?) Essential Question **How do we protect our rights?**

_____

_____

_____

Go back to *Show As You Go!* on pages 190–191. ≪

netw⊙rks **There's More Online!** • Games • Assessment

Active Citizenship

Essential Question

How do citizens
participate?
What do you think?

_____

_____

_____

_____

Words To Know

Think of a synonym for each
word. A synonym is another
word that means the same
thing.

responsibility _____

_____

politics _____

_____

***inform** _____

_____

Think back to the Constitutional Convention. The delegates had kept their meetings secretive, and no one outside knew what was going on. The citizens of Philadelphia were curious about what was being planned. Benjamin Franklin was a delegate at the convention. As he left the state house on the final day, a woman called out to him. Read their conversation below.

Well Doctor, what have we got: a republic or a monarchy?

A republic, if you can keep it.

Republic is the word for the type of government that we have under the Constitution. It is a government in which the people choose representatives to govern for them. What do you think Franklin meant when he said "if you can keep it"?

_____

_____

_____

_____

Civic Responsibilities

All citizens of the United States have civic **responsibilities**. A responsibility is something that people must do because it is their job or duty. These responsibilities are things good citizens do to help keep their city, state, and national governments working effectively.

For example, respecting and obeying the law is one important civic responsibility. By obeying the law, citizens help each other stay safe and healthy. Paying taxes is another civic responsibility. Taxes pay for services and projects that benefit all Americans. Without money from taxes, we wouldn't be able to keep our roads, public buildings, or schools maintained.

▲ One responsibility of citizenship is to serve on juries.

Jury Duty

One particular duty of citizens is to serve on juries. You read in Lesson 4 that the Bill of Rights guarantees all citizens the right to a trial by a jury. Juries sit in on a court case, listen to the facts, and then make a decision about whether the accused person is guilty or innocent. Without participation by citizens, it would be impossible for us to have this right, or any other rights at all.

> **Evaluate the importance of civic responsibilities to our democracy. Tell why it is important for citizens to participate.**
>
> _____
>
> _____
>
> _____
>
> _____
>
> _____

Tim Pannell/Corbis

229

Political Participation

You've already learned that voting is a right. Did you know it is a civic responsibility too? Good citizens participate in **politics**. Politics is the process of choosing government leaders and running the government. To participate in politics effectively, good citizens stay **informed** about public issues and candidates. Then, through voting, they tell the government who they want to represent them and what actions the government should take. Voting is one way that responsible citizens make their voices heard.

Responsible citizens make their voices heard in other ways too. They write letters or e-mails to their government leaders and representatives. This helps government leaders determine the will of the people. Responsible citizens might also sign a petition about an issue that they agree with. Sometimes, responsible citizens participate in marches or protests in support of or against a political idea.

As you read pages 230 and 231, (circle) ways citizens can participate in the political process. Highlight ways citizens can go beyond their basic responsibilities.

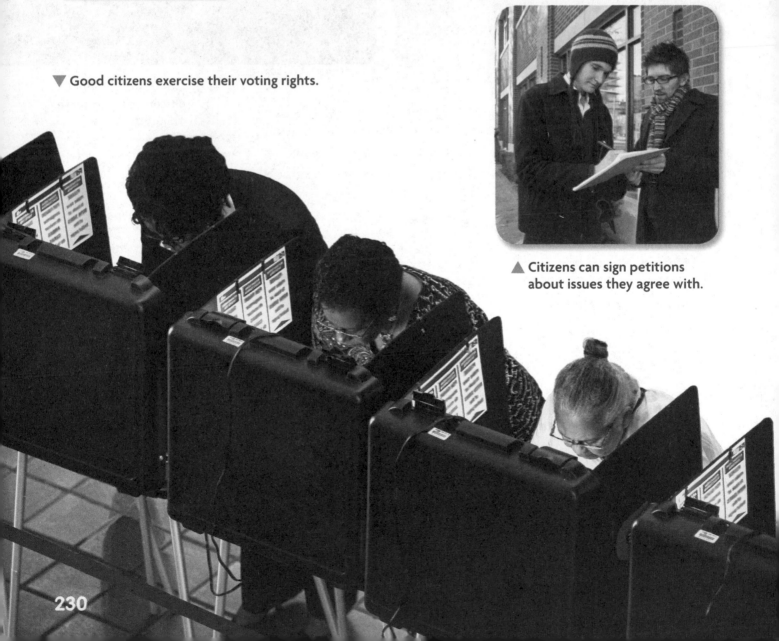

▼ Good citizens exercise their voting rights.

▲ Citizens can sign petitions about issues they agree with.

(t) ML Harris/Iconica/Getty Images, (b) Getty Images

230

Going Above and Beyond

Citizens can go above and beyond their basic civic responsibilities. One way to do this is to become a volunteer. As a volunteer, you might work with others on a civic issue, such as a neighborhood watch or a litter clean-up event. Political campaigns are always looking for volunteers as well. They need workers to help convince voters to choose their candidate.

Another way to go above and beyond is to initiate, or begin, changes in laws or public policy. The simplest way to do this is to write to a lawmaker about a problem that exists in your community and propose a solution. In some cities and towns, citizens can initiate a change themselves through a petition. If citizens gather enough signatures from voters, their issue is put up for a vote. If the issue passes, then it becomes law.

Finally, some citizens go above and beyond by becoming public officials. Any citizen who meets some very basic requirements can run for office. Requirements usually include age and residency, which is the place where a person lives. Becoming a government leader is an excellent way to serve your community.

▲ **Jerrod W. Holton served his community as a member of the city council. He was only 23 years old when elected!**

(t) Courtesy of Jerrod W. Holton, (b) Fuse/Getty Images

▲ **Citizens of all ages can volunteer to help their community.**

Think of a new law for your community. Describe your law and one way you could initiate this change in policy.

_____

_____

_____

_____

_____

231

Participation: Then and Now

In the United States, political participation is important for keeping our democracy running. Our tradition of political participation goes all the way back to our country's colonial period. Since then, it has continued to develop into what it is today.

✎ Underline different ways people participate in politics.

The Colonial Era

From the very beginning, white male settlers were able to vote for their leaders in colonial governments. They also participated by speaking up at local meetings. They let their leaders know their wants and needs by writing letters. Letter writing was the main form of communication back then.

As frustrated colonists grew tired of British policies, more people became involved in politics. Colonists held protests, such as the Boston Tea Party. And before declaring their independence, colonists sent a petition to the British government, asking for help one last time.

▲ Only white males had a voice in colonial governments.

Participation by Non-voters

In the colonial era, African Americans—both enslaved and free—and women weren't allowed to vote. A few still found ways to participate in politics. For example, one group of enslaved Africans sent petitions to colonial leaders in Massachusetts. These petitions tried to bring attention to the living conditions of enslaved people. Political participation by groups who couldn't vote was very rare. For many years, women and non-white individuals who tried to participate were usually ignored, discouraged, or even arrested.

Women fought for the right to vote for many years. ▶

Participation Today

Citizens today participate in their government in many of the same ways the colonists did. We still vote, protest, and petition. We still write letters and have discussions about issues at local meetings. We also use some new ways, too.

One major difference in participation is in the ways people stay informed. Radio, television, and the Internet all make it easier for citizens to learn about issues. And through e-mail, it's easier than ever to contact representatives. Most government leaders have Web pages, where you can read their opinions on the issues of the day.

You might say that the most important difference of all is in who can participate. Male and female citizens of all races can all participate in our democratic process by voting and speaking out on important issues.

▲ Don't forget to vote!

What is different between political participation in the colonial period and participation today?

_____

_____

What is the same?

_____

_____

Lesson 5

 Essential Question **How do citizens participate?**

_____

_____

_____

Go back to *Show As You Go!* on pages 190–191.

  networks **There's More Online!** • Games • Assessment

Yellow Dog Productions/Lifesize/Getty Images

Fill in the flow chart with words from the box to tell
how and why the U.S. government was created.

taxes	**amendments**	**ratified**	**government**
separated	**Articles**	**juries**	**Constitution**
Convention	**responsibilities**	**states**	**Bill of Rights**

After the Revolutionary War, Americans

created a new plan of _____

called the _____ of

Confederation.

The new government failed to meet

citizens' needs. Leaders called a

Constitutional _____

to discuss what to do.

Delegates wrote a new plan called the

_____. This plan

_____ the powers of government

into branches. And it reserved many

powers for the _____.

The states _____ the Constitution.

But many people demanded that a

_____ be added. The first 10

_____ were added in 1791.

Citizens all have rights and

_____,

such as voting, serving on _____,

and paying _____.

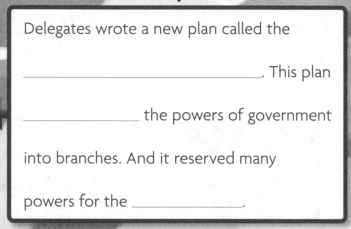

BIG IDEA 💡

Unit Project

Your class will participate in a mock U.S. government. Each student will be assigned to one branch of the federal government. As a class you will write, vote on, sign, and review a new classroom rule. At the end of the experience, you will share your role in the law-making process with the class. You will also evaluate your role in the process. In your evaluation, you will tell what branch you were a part of, what you did, and how well you think you did your job. As you work, keep these tasks and behaviors in mind.

Tasks and behaviors to keep in mind...   Yes, I do!

I know the branches of government and how bills become laws.   ☐

I know what role my assigned branch plays in the law-making process.   ☐

I know how my branch works with the other branches.   ☐

I participate in the law-making process.   ☐

I listen respectfully during debates.   ☐

I share my views and opinions on proposed rules.   ☐

Think about the Big Idea

BIG IDEA 💡 Rules provide order.

What did you learn in this unit that helps you understand the BIG IDEA?

_____

_____

_____

235

Read the passage "How Should the President Be Elected?" before answering Numbers 1 through 6.

How Should the President Be Elected?

by Jennifer Beyer

The United States uses a system called the Electoral College to choose its Presidents. Each state gets one electoral vote for each of its members of Congress. This means that states with more people get more votes.

When voters cast their ballots on Election Day, what they're really doing is choosing for whom all the electors from their state should vote. A presidential candidate who wins a state is supposed to receive all of that state's electoral votes. Because some states get more electoral votes than others, a candidate can sometimes win the Electoral College but lose the popular vote!

Some voters don't think this is fair. When this happened in the year 2000, it started a debate about the Electoral College. Fifth-grade students from across the country were interviewed about this subject. Here's what some of them had to say.

Trevor from Oklahoma

"I think the popular vote should be counted instead of the electoral vote. . . . The Electoral College was developed in the 1700s when the citizens of America were less educated. . . . Americans today have information available . . . from newspapers, magazines, the Internet, TV, and radio. People can make educated decisions about their vote, and we should let them elect their own President."

Matthew from Iowa

"We should keep the Electoral College, but we should change it to make it fairer. We should let the states divide up their electoral vote. For example, if one-fourth of a state's voters pick Candidate A, . . . then Candidate A should get one-fourth of the state's votes. . . . The way it is now, some voters might feel that their vote doesn't count."

Ebony from Florida

"The Electoral College is an easy, simple, organized way to elect the President. The electors . . . are supposed to vote in the Electoral College for the candidate that the majority of people in their state voted for. . . . This system makes sure that the majority of states get the President they want."

What happened in the year 2000?

Ⓐ The Electoral College chose the wrong candidate.

Ⓑ The vote was unfair.

Ⓒ The winning candidate won the Electoral College but lost the popular vote.

Ⓓ The losing candidate won the Electoral College but lost the popular vote.

Which person thinks the Electoral College should NOT be changed?

Ⓕ Ebony

Ⓖ Matthew

Ⓗ Trevor

Ⓘ the author

3 Read the sentences from the passage.

The Electoral College was developed in the 1700s when the citizens of America were less educated. . . . Americans today have information available . . . from newspapers, magazines, the Internet, TV, and radio.

Which statement tells Trevor's feelings about modern Americans?

Ⓐ Americans today are more informed than Americans in the 1700s.

Ⓑ Americans today are less informed than Americans in the 1700s.

Ⓒ Americans today are uninformed.

Ⓓ Americans today have too much information.

4 What is the author's MAIN purpose for writing the passage?

Ⓕ to tell her opinion about the Electoral College

Ⓖ to tell who won the 2000 presidential election

Ⓗ to describe different opinions about the Electoral College

Ⓘ to describe how voting rights have changed over time

5 How does the student from Iowa think the Electoral College should change?

Ⓐ Each vote should count more than it does now.

Ⓑ Each elector should be able to choose whom he or she wants.

Ⓒ Each candidate should get one-fourth of the votes.

Ⓓ Each state should divide up its electoral votes.

6 Read the sentence from the passage.

The electors . . . are supposed to vote in the Electoral College for the candidate that the majority of people in their state voted for.

What does the word *majority* mean in this passage?

Ⓕ an unknown number

Ⓖ the largest number

Ⓗ the least number

Ⓘ an equal number

BIG IDEA Relationships affect choices.

The young nation changed in many ways. The borders of the country grew and expanded. A new war with Great Britain led to a new sense of national pride. New technologies changed the way people lived and the ways the country did business. Internally, the country struggled with conflicts over Native American lands and the issue of slavery. In this unit, you will read about the causes and effects of these changes in the United States.

networks

Add the following to the map:

After Lesson 1:
- ⬭ Louisiana Purchase
- ⬭ Routes of Lewis and Clark

After Lesson 2:
- ⬭ Land gained through the Adams-Onís Treaty

After Lesson 3:
- ⬭ Erie Canal
- ⬭ Major Railways

After Lesson 4:
- ⬭ Missouri Compromise Line
- ⬭ Trail of Tears

After Lesson 5:
- ⬭ Overland Trails
- ⬭ Land gained through the Treaty of Guadalupe Hidalgo
- ⬭ Gadsden Purchase
- ⬭ Complete the Map Key
- ⬭ Give the map a title

Show As You Go! After you read the following lessons, complete the map of the United States. Use the checklist on page 238 for suggestions of what to add to your map and map key.

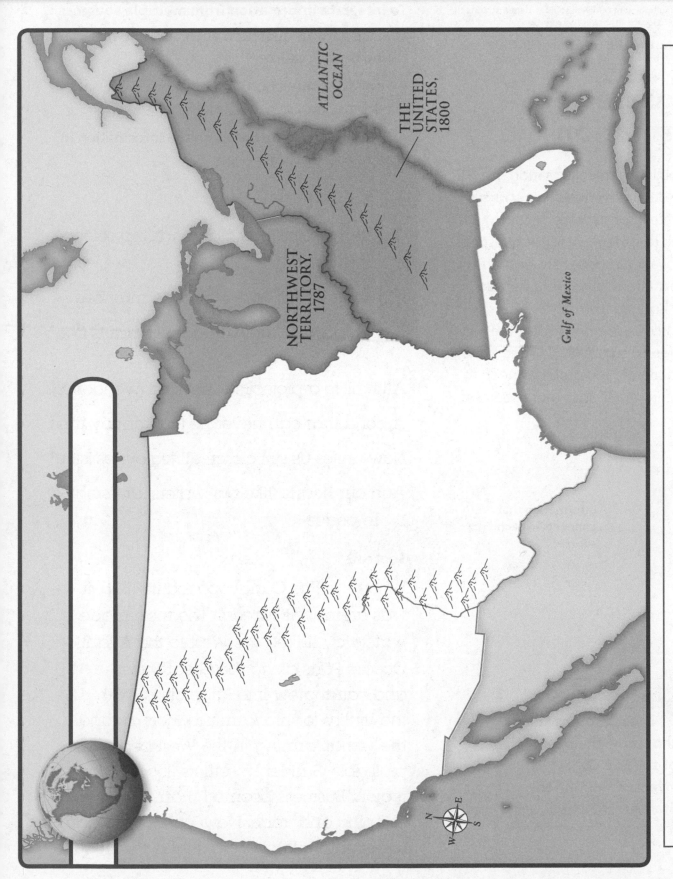

ATLANTIC OCEAN

THE UNITED STATES, 1800

NORTHWEST TERRITORY, 1787

Gulf of Mexico

Map Key

Fold page here.

239

Reading Skill

Common Core Standards

RI.6: Analyze multiple accounts of the same event or topic, noting important similarities and differences in the point of view they represent. **RI.7:** Draw on information from multiple print or digital sources, demonstrating the ability to locate an answer to a question quickly or to solve a problem efficiently. **RI.9:** Integrate information from two texts on the same topic in order to write or speak about the subject knowledgeably.

Integrate Information

When you integrate information, you combine details from multiple sources. To integrate information effectively, it is a good idea to generate a list of questions that you want to answer about the topic. Then chart information from each source that fits those questions.

If the sources agree on an idea, the information is most likely correct. If the sources disagree, you probably need to check the information in more sources.

> Information that connects in each source

> Underline details in each source that show how the opening of the Erie Canal affected the United States.

LEARN IT

To integrate information from multiple sources:

- **Make a list of questions and chart answers you find in each source.**

- **Look for connections between the pieces of information.**

- **Draw a conclusion based on the information in all of the sources.**

Source 1

'Tis, that Genius has triumph'd and science
    prevail's . . .

It is, that the [people] of Europe may see

The progress of mind, in a land that is free

All hail! to a project so vast and [wonderful]!

A bond that can never be [broken] by time

Now unites us still closer, all jealousies [stop]

And our hearts, like our waters, are singled
    in peace

Source 2

When the Erie Canal opened in 1825, it was an instant success. The man-made waterway linked the West to the Atlantic Ocean. Ports along the Great Lakes and canal grew into large cities. With the ability to ship farm products around the world, farming in the West became profitable. Suddenly, settlers flooded the region. Business boomed thanks to shipping and trade. New York City became the country's largest city in the mid-1800s.

Graphic organizers like the one below help you integrate information. Fill in the chart with the information from both texts on page 240.

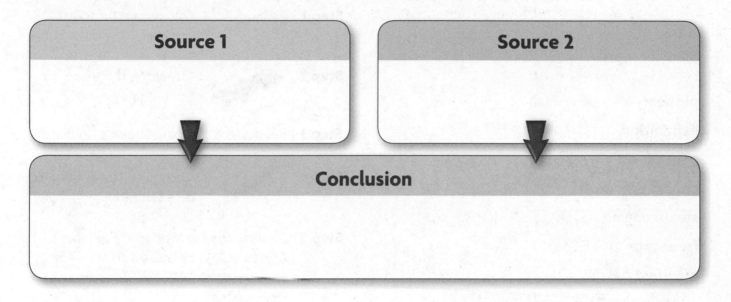

Source 1	Source 2

Conclusion

My Question: How did the opening of the Erie Canal affect the United States?

- Review the steps for integrating information in Learn It.

- Find another source about the opening of the Erie Canal on the Internet.

- Find details in this source that answer the question in Try IT.

- Integrate the information in all three sources to draw a conclusion.

Conclusion:

_____

_____

_____

_____

_____

Words to Know

The list below shows some important words you will learn in this unit. Their definitions can be found on the next page. Read the words.

pioneer (py • uh • NEER)

expedition (ehks • pih • DIHSH • uhn)

neutral (NOO • truhl)

cotton gin (KAHT • uhn jihn)

steam engine (STEEM EHN • jihn)

free state (FREE STAYT)

manifest destiny
(MAN • uh • fehst • DEHS • tuh • nee)

overland wagon
(OH • vuhr • land WA • guhn)

FOLDABLES®

The Foldable on the next page will help you learn these important words. Follow the steps below to make your Foldable.

Step 1 Fold along the solid red line.

Step 2 Cut along the dotted lines.

Step 3 Read the words and their definitions.

Step 4 Complete the activities on each tab.

Step 5 Look at the back of your Foldable. Choose ONE of these activities for each word to help you remember its meaning:

- Draw a picture of the word.

- Write a description of the word.

- Write how the word is related to something you know.

Bettmann/Corbis

	FOLD	
A **pioneer** is a person who settles a new part of the country.		Write another meaning for *pioneer*.
An **expedition** is a journey made for a special purpose.		Write a synonym for *expedition*.
To be **neutral** means to not take sides.		What do you think it means to be *neutral*?
A **cotton gin** is a machine that separates cotton from its seeds.		Circle two key words in the definition of *cotton gin*. Write the words here: _____ _____
A **steam engine** is an engine that is powered by the energy produced by steam.		Explain how steam is created.
A **free state** was a state that did not allow slavery.		Explain the opposite of a *free state*.
Manifest destiny is the belief that the United States had a right to expand its borders and claim new lands.		Write the definition of *manifest destiny* in your own words.
An **overland wagon** was a covered wagon that pioneers used to transport their belongings to the West.		Write a sentence using *overland wagon*.

pioneer

CUT HERE

expedition

neutral

cotton gin

steam engine

free state

manifest destiny

overland wagon

pioneer

expedition

neutral

cotton gin

steam engine

free state

manifest destiny

overland wagon

Newspapers

Newspapers are usually printed daily or weekly. They report on current events, or things that have recently happened, on the local, state, national, or world level. To read a newspaper correctly, you need to understand the parts of newspaper articles. These parts are:

- the headline or title
- the dateline (when and where the story took place)
- the by-line, or author's name
- the article or story.

Each newspaper story answers six questions about the topic: Who was involved? What took place? When did the event happen? Where did it happen? Why did it happen? How did it happen?

Library of Congress Prints & Photographs Division [LC-US262-68175]

 Document-Based Questions

Study the newspaper article, then complete the activities.

1. **Use different colors or symbols to highlight the answers to the following questions: Who? What? When? Where? Why? How?**

2. **What did you learn about what happened to Washington, D.C., during the War of 1812?**

_____

_____

THE AMERICAN NEWSPAPER

Washington, D.C., August 25, 1814

Dolley Saves the Day!
by Jim Smith

Yesterday the British burned down the White House. They did this as payback for the United States burning down Canada's capital. During the chaos and confusion of the British invasion of Washington, D.C., one person certainly kept her cool. First lady Dolley Madison acted quickly to save what she could from the White House.

Mrs. Madison was able to save important documents, silverware, and other items. The most important thing she saved was a portrait of our first President—George Washington. The frame it was in was too large to carry. So Mrs. Madison used a knife to cut the painting from its frame! Now, the painting will hang in the White House for generations to come.

networks
There's More Online!
- Skill Builders
- Vocabulary Flashcards

245

Early Expansion

North Wind/ Nancy Carter/ North Wind Picture Archives

? Essential Question

Why do people take risks? What do you think?

_____

_____

_____

_____

_____

Words To Know

Write a number on each line to show how much you know about each word.

1 = I have no idea!
2 = I know a little.
3 = I know a lot.

_____ **pioneer**

_____ **expedition**

_____ ***interpreter**

THINK • PAIR • SHARE *Imagine you are alone in the woods or wilderness where you've never been before. How would you find your way around? What would you do to survive?*

Expanding the Nation

You learned in Unit 6 that in 1787 Congress issued the Northwest Ordinance. It created the Northwest Territory north of the Ohio River and east of the Mississippi River. The ordinance stated that an area became a territory when its population reached 5,000. Territories could apply for statehood when the population reached 60,000. This led to the addition of Ohio, Indiana, Illinois, Michigan, and Wisconsin. The ordinance also pushed Native Americans off their lands, leading to many conflicts.

One important piece of the Northwest Ordinance was the bill of rights for settlers. It guaranteed freedom of religion, and the right to trial by jury. It also banned slavery. This was the first attempt to prevent slavery in the United States.

This law allowed the country to expand in a slow and specific way. Soon, **pioneers** began making the journey west in search of new lives. A pioneer is a person who settles a new part of a country.

▼ **Early pioneers packed their belongings into Conestoga wagons like this one.**

Let's Go West!

In 1790 only about 200,000 settlers lived west of the Appalachian Mountains. By 1820 that number had exploded to nearly 2 million Americans! One reason people were able to settle that land was because of the work of Daniel Boone.

I'm Daniel Boone. I'm from the Pennsylvania countryside. I've spent my whole life learning how to live off the land. So I know my way around the wilderness. The new territory was wild and confusing for some folks. I was hired to find a route from North Carolina to Kentucky. As I made my way west, I discovered a natural passage that led through the Appalachian Mountains. I called this passage the Cumberland Gap.

In 1775 Boone and 30 men began to fix up the trails between the Carolinas and the Northwest Territory. They cleared a road by cutting down trees and clearing brush. This road became the main way people traveled west.

Circle important contributions made by Daniel Boone during the period of westward expansion.

The Wilderness Road, 1770s

0 50 100 miles
0 50 100 kilometers

Ohio River
Lexington
Boonesborough
Harrod's Town
Kentucky R.
Cumberland River
Cumberland Gap
APPALACHIAN MOUNTAINS
VIRGINIA
NORTH CAROLINA
SOUTH CAROLINA
ATLANTIC OCEAN

— Wilderness Road
)(Gap

Map and Globe Skills

1. Using a dark color, trace the southern edge of the Northwest Territory on the map.

2. The Cumberland Gap passes through which mountain range?

_____

_____

247

Jefferson and Louisiana

While the size of the country was changing, so were the politics. In 1800 the United States elected a new President. He was a famous Patriot who changed the boundaries of the United States. This multi-talented writer, inventor, and statesman was Thomas Jefferson.

I was born in Virginia in 1743. I accomplished so much in my life, it's hard to know where to start. You may remember that I wrote the Declaration of Independence. I also wrote Virginia's state constitution and founded the University of Virginia!

In your opinion, which of Jefferson's accomplishments was most important? Why?

_____

_____

_____

_____

▼ **The Jefferson Memorial in Washington, D.C.**

The Louisiana Purchase

Jefferson believed that expanding the United States was essential to its success. In the South, the French port city of New Orleans was an important center of trade along the Mississippi River. In 1803 American representatives in France offered to buy New Orleans for $10 million. To the surprise of the Americans, the French offered to sell the entire Louisiana Territory for $15 million. The purchase nearly doubled the size of the United States.

I was shocked that we got such a tremendous bargain. I mean, look at these numbers—we received almost 525 million acres of land for about 4 cents an acre! But we had a problem: few Americans knew anything about this huge territory. We needed to find out as much about this land as we could. And I knew just the man for the job.

© Chicago History Museum - USA / The Bridgeman Art Library International

DID YOU KNOW?
The French sold Louisiana to pay for an ongoing war with Great Britain. Napoleon Bonaparte, France's leader, planned to take Louisiana back after they defeated Great Britain. However, France lost the war with Great Britain.

▼ **The city of New Orleans before the sale of Louisiana**

UNDER MY WINGS EVERY THING PROSPERS

The Corps of Discovery

Jefferson asked his personal secretary Meriweather Lewis to lead an expedition into the Louisiana territory. The two-year journey explored the geography and cultures of the region. The expedition opened the door for westward expansion.

DID YOU KNOW?
Jefferson also hired Zebulon Pike to explore new territories in the West. In 1805 Pike looked for the source of the Mississippi River. He never found it, but he did explore the Rocky Mountains. Today a mountain in Colorado is named after him—Pike's Peak.

Meriwether Lewis

I was President Jefferson's personal secretary. He asked me to lead an **expedition**, *or journey, to map out the course of the Missouri River and to find a land route to the Pacific Ocean. I offered to share command with a friend of mine from the army, William Clark.*

President Jefferson also wanted us to gather information about the land, its resources, and the Native Americans who lived in the region. It was a journey that would take us thousands of miles.

William Clark

We called our expedition the Corps of Discovery. Our group included 42 men who were soldiers, trappers, and scouts. I personally brought along an enslaved African soldier named York. In May 1804 we headed west from St. Louis on the Missouri River.

As we traveled, we created detailed and accurate maps. These helped others who came to the area get around.

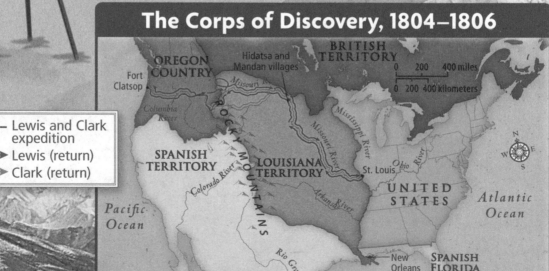

The Corps of Discovery, 1804–1806

Legend:
← Lewis and Clark expedition
→ Lewis (return)
→ Clark (return)

OREGON COUNTRY
Fort Clatsop
Hidatsa and Mandan villages
BRITISH TERRITORY
Columbia River
ROCKY MOUNTAINS
SPANISH TERRITORY
Colorado River
LOUISIANA TERRITORY
Missouri River
Mississippi River
St. Louis
Ohio River
Arkansas River
UNITED STATES
Atlantic Ocean
Pacific Ocean
Rio Grande
New Orleans
SPANISH FLORIDA

0   200   400 miles
0   200   400 kilometers

Sacagawea

I met Lewis and Clark in 1805. They hired my husband, a fur trader, to be part of their expedition. As daughter to a Shoshone chief, I knew several Native American languages. I joined the expedition as an interpreter and guide.

My son, Jean Baptiste Charbonneau, or "Pompy," as Clark called him, was born during the expedition in early 1805. Still, I stayed with Lewis and Clark all the way to the Pacific Ocean and back.

What Came from the Expedition?

Lewis and Clark had an amazing journey. They traveled and mapped out 8,000 miles of land. Finally, they returned to St. Louis in 1806.

The Lewis and Clark expedition paved the way for the country to expand. People soon flooded the Louisiana Territory in search of new opportunities.

THINK · PAIR · SHARE
Work with a partner to create a comic strip that describes the causes and effects of the Louisiana Purchase.

Underline the contributions of Lewis, Clark, and Sacagawea to westward expansion.

Lesson 1

 Essential Question **Why do people take risks?**

_____

_____

_____

Go back to *Show As You Go!* on pages 238–239.

The War of 1812

What do people fight for? What do you think?

_____

_____

_____

_____

Words To Know

Write the definition of each word in your own words.

neutral _____

_____

impressment _____

_____

*response _____

_____

Have you experienced friends or family members having a disagreement? Did you try to stay out of it? Or did you get involved? What happened?

_____

_____

_____

On the Brink of War

While Jefferson expanded the country, he also dealt with the war between France and Great Britain. The United States tried to stay **neutral**, or not take sides in the war. Americans continued to trade with both countries. This angered both the British and the French. Warships from both countries stopped American merchant ships at sea and took their goods. The British also forced American sailors to serve on British ships. This practice, called **impressment**, enraged Americans.

To protect American ships and lives, an angry Congress passed the Embargo Act in 1807. The act closed all American ports. It also prevented trade in American waters. Though it was meant to hurt Great Britain and France, the law actually weakened the American economy. As the United States continued to remain neutral, its relationship with France and England worsened.

Many Americans were forced to serve in the British Navy

North Wind Picture Archives

June 1812   *Networks News*   Special Edition

WAR DECLARED!

A Call to Arms

Conflict seemed to be on the horizon. In 1810 a new group was elected to Congress. They were called "**War Hawks**" because they wanted to go to war with Great Britain.

Many War Hawks were settlers from areas west of the Appalachian Mountains. Native Americans in that area wanted settlers to stop taking their lands. A Shawnee chief named Tecumseh tried to unite all western tribes to fight against these settlers. The British provided support and supplies to Tecumseh and other Native Americans in the area. This angered War Hawks.

▲ As Speaker of the House, Henry Clay led War Hawks in Congress.

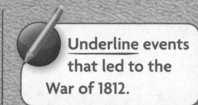

Underline events that led to the War of 1812.

"Mr. Madison's War"

In June 1812 Congress declared war on Great Britain. President James Madison signed the declaration.

Not all Americans supported the war. New England merchants depended on trade with Great Britain. The Embargo Act had damaged their businesses, and they feared the war would cause more problems with trade. Many Americans wanted to settle their problems with Great Britain peacefully. Many New Englanders called the war "Mr. Madison's War." Today, this war is known as the War of 1812, although it lasted several years.

How did the economy contribute to the start of the War of 1812?

_____

_____

_____

_____

The Course of the War

Washington, D.C., Under Siege

During the first two years of the War of 1812, most fighting occurred west of the Appalachian Mountains, in Canada, and on the Atlantic Ocean. In 1814 the British invaded the United States in **response** to the American invasion of the Canadian city York.

By the time British soldiers marched into the nation's capitol, American leaders had fled. This didn't stop the British from leaving a trail of destruction throughout Washington, D.C. Most important government buildings were destroyed, including the White House and the Capitol building. The city was not fully rebuilt until 1819.

The Flag Still Stands

As Washington, D.C., lay in ashes, the British attempted to capture Fort McHenry, near Baltimore, Maryland. Rockets and cannonballs blasted the fort for 25 hours.

Francis Scott Key, an American prisoner on a British ship off the coast of Baltimore, watched the nighttime attack. The next morning, Key saw the American flag flying over Fort McHenry. He expressed his feelings in "The Star-Spangled Banner," a poem that later became our national anthem.

This painting shows the burning of Washington, D.C. On the lines above, write a caption for this image.

Why did Key title his poem "The Star-Spangled Banner"?

The War Ends

The Treaty of Ghent ended the war in December 1814. Neither side won, but both agreed to end the war. News of the treaty traveled slowly, so fighting continued in the far west. In January 1815, American troops led by Andrew Jackson crushed the British at the Battle of New Orleans. As a result, Jackson became a national hero.

Under the treaty, no borders were changed. The United States maintained control of the Northwest and Louisiana territories, as well as the Mississippi River. Native American groups that fought with the British were forced to sign away more of their land. This allowed more settlers to move into these territories.

Britain wanted to protect its goods from foreign competition. They implemented **protectionism** on any U.S. imports, or added many tariffs and restricted trade with U.S. imports. This made Britain the leader in exports to the U.S. This is the opposite of free trade.

Underline the results of the War of 1812 for the British, Americans, and Native Americans.

The War of 1812

Map and Globe Skills

1. Circle all the American victories on the map.

2. Why was control of New Orleans important?

_____

_____

_____

_____

_____

_____

Write your own headline for pages 256–257.

National Pride

The War of 1812 had many effects on the young nation. Before the war, much of the world had considered the United States a trouble-making British colony. The war showed that the United States was a nation willing and able to defend itself.

For the first time since the Revolutionary War, Americans felt a strong sense of national pride. Those who had been against the war lost power in government. The lack of major political divisions created a feeling of unity among Americans. This period became known as the "Era of Good Feelings."

The Adams-Onís Treaty

Along with a sense of pride came a desire to expand the country's borders. In 1818 Andrew Jackson was sent to Georgia to stop a conflict with Native Americans. Instead, Jackson invaded Florida, a Spanish colony. Jackson took over Spanish settlements and removed the Spanish governor from power.

Spain didn't want to start a war with the United States. In 1819 the two countries signed the Adams-Onís Treaty. In the agreement, Spain sold Florida to the United States. In return, the United States gave up its claim to Texas west of the Sabine River.

(bkgd) Nic Taylor/Getty Images

Reading Skill

Cause and Effect

Use the chart to identify the causes and effects of the War of 1812.

Causes	Effects

President Monroe and his cabinet members discuss the Monroe Doctrine.

Underline the ways the War of 1812 changed how the United States dealt with foreign countries.

Dealing with Foreign Countries

The War of 1812 made people in the United States feel like they were as powerful as Great Britain, Spain, and France. This feeling was challenged by issues in Latin America. Many of the former European colonies there had recently declared independence. In response, some European countries formed an alliance and planned to regain control of the area.

President James Monroe did not want European powers so close to the United States.

In 1823 he issued the Monroe Doctrine. It stated that the United States would not allow European powers to start new colonies In the Americas. In return, the United States would not involve itself in existing European colonies or issues in Europe.

The doctrine's authors saw it as a way for the United States to oppose colonial powers. Americans would later use it to expand the borders of the United States even further.

Lesson 2

 Essential Question   **What do people fight for?**

_____

_____

_____

Go back to _Show As You Go!_ on pages 238–239.

 netw⊙rks   There's More Online!
• Assessment • Games

The Industrial Revolution

Essential Question

How do ideas influence choices?

What do you think?

_____

_____

_____

_____

_____

_____

Words To Know

Add a suffix to the end of each word to make it plural.

cotton gin ____

*application ____

reaper ____

interchangeable part ____

stagecoach ____

Think about the different kinds of technology you use everyday. Which item is most important to you? What would life be like if you didn't have that item anymore?

_____

_____

_____

A World of New Technology

Until the early 1800s, most families made the items they needed, such as tools and clothes, by hand. Then came a period of rapid invention, when machines began to do the work people once did. This period of invention is called the Industrial Revolution. During this time, new machines and new ideas changed the way people worked, traveled, and lived.

The Industrial Revolution greatly affected the market economy of the United States. In Unit 4, you learned that in a market economy, people decided what goods to make and how much to sell their goods for. Because of the advancements made during the Industrial Revolution, businesses were able to make more goods and sell them at reduced cost. This also meant that more people could afford to buy goods than ever before.

Eli Whitney: Inventions and Innovations

In 1793 Eli Whitney built a **cotton gin** to remove seeds from cotton. The gin, which is short for "engine," could clean more cotton in a few minutes than a whole team of workers could clean by hand in a day. The cotton gin made cotton the most important cash crop in the South.

A cotton gin ▶

Bettmann/Corbis

In 1801 Whitney had another important idea that would change the way goods were made—**interchangeable parts**. These are pieces made to fit any specific tool or machine. A barrel for one rifle would fit another rifle of the same type, for example. Whitney's idea had many **applications**, and allowed guns, tools, and other products to be made faster and at a lower cost.

Textile Mills

New inventions, such as the double-sided needle, sewing machines, and spinning machines, made it faster and easier to make cloth and clothing. People no longer had to do the whole process by hand. Soon, large factories called textile mills began producing more cloth than ever before. Mills were built near swift rivers. The rushing water turned a large wheel in the factory, which powered the machines. Most mills were built in the North, since that was where the country's known fast-moving rivers were located at that time.

Francis Cabot Lowell was one person who prospered from these inventions. In 1813 he built a textile mill in Waltham, Massachusetts. Lowell's business partners later built several textile mills as well as a town, called Lowell, for the workers. By 1850, Lowell had more than 10,000 workers. Many were young women who left home to work in the town of Lowell.

Explain how the Industrial Revolution affected the market economy of the United States.

_____

_____

_____

_____

_____

_____

_____

Workers weaving cloth in a Lowell textile mill ▼

North Wind / North Wind Picture Archives

259

Farming Improves

The Industrial Revolution was not limited to manufacturing. The reaper and better plows greatly improved farming during the Industrial Revolution.

The Reaper

In 1832 Cyrus McCormick invented the **reaper**. A reaper is a machine with sharp blades to cut grain. The reapers could harvest four times as much grain as people working by hand in the same amount of time.

The Mechanical Plow

Farmers had traditionally used hand tools to plant seeds. The first horse-drawn mechanical plow was invented in 1797 by Charles Newbold. His iron plow made planting seeds much quicker and easier.

John Deere's Plow

In 1837 John Deere improved the mechanical plow by adding a steel blade. This blade was better able to cut through tough soil. The blade was also polished so that mud would not stick to it.

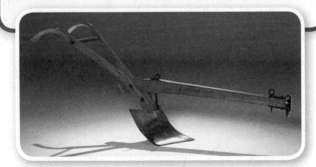

Reading Skill

Draw Conclusions

How did new farming equipment impact farming?

_____

_____

What were the effects of these improvements?

_____

_____

New Forms of Transportation

Farming wasn't the only area where improvements brought changes. Transportation also changed quickly. As more people moved westward, the demand for safer, easier, and faster forms of transportation increased. Suddenly, connecting the West and the East Coast became a priority.

Underline details explaining how improvements to roads impacted the United States.

The Road to Better Travel

In the early 1800s, most people traveled in large, horse-drawn carriages called **stagecoaches**. At the time, the best roads in the United States were paved with rocks or logs. Most others were narrow dirt trails that were full of potholes and tree stumps. When it rained, these roads became muddy, and horses and wagons were slowed down or became stuck. Even on a good day, travel on these roads was slow.

In 1811 the federal government began construction on the National Road. This road stretched from Cumberland, Maryland, to Vandalia, Illinois. The National Road was made of stone and gravel. It connected the East Coast with what was then the West. Businesses could now move more goods and move them faster. The National Road also made it easier for people to settle new lands in the West.

How did improved roads help businesses?

_____

_____

_____

(bkgd) Creatas/PunchStock, (c) North Wind Picture Archives

Rolling on the River

Until the early 1800s, people and goods were also moved on flatboats that traveled on rivers. These boats were pushed downstream by hand with long poles. Traveling upstream was a much tougher job!

River travel improved quickly with the **steam engine**. A steam engine uses compressed steam to power a motor. It produces more power than a team of horses and can pull heavier loads. In 1807 Robert Fulton designed a boat powered by a steam engine. His steamboat traveled 150 miles in 32 hours. Boats without steam engines took 4 days to make the same trip.

These steamboats had one major problem: most rivers don't connect with each other. To solve this problem, people built canals. Canals use a system of locks to raise and lower the water level. In 1825 the Erie Canal was opened. It connected Lake Erie with the Hudson River and the Atlantic Ocean.

The Erie Canal was a huge success. Goods were shipped more quickly between the East and the Midwest. The canal connected Midwest goods with the Atlantic Ocean, making it easier to trade with foreign countries. Trade boomed, and New York City became the country's largest and most important port.

DID YOU KNOW?

The success of the Erie Canal caused a rush of canal-building in the 1820s. These canals helped people move more quickly to the West. It wouldn't be long before the United States would need even more land.

Reading Skill

Use Visuals Examine the diagram of the lock. Then answer the questions.

1. Why were locks necessary? _____

2. How did canals improve transportation and trade?

_____

_____

The Iron Horse

Within a few years, a new steam-powered invention made canals less important. People had traveled by railroad for years, but on early railroads, horses pulled coaches over iron rails. In 1814 British inventor George Stephenson built the first train powered by a steam engine. These new trains were nicknamed "iron horses."

In 1830 Peter Cooper, an American merchant, built a small locomotive he named *Tom Thumb*. At first, few people believed a locomotive could move without horses. A Baltimore stagecoach company challenged Cooper and his locomotive to a race against a horse-drawn carriage. Although this train lost the race, trains won in the end. Railroads soon became the main form of transportation in the United States.

The combination of canals and railroads made shipping goods quicker and cheaper than **previous** methods. As a result, businesses sold goods at lower prices, which meant more people could afford them.

▲ **Tom Thumb racing a horse-drawn carriage**

FUN FACTS

Trains provided Americans with one of their first chances at tourism. Passengers took tours of new lands in the West. Granted, at first only the wealthy could afford to ride trains.

Explain why railways were located near rivers or large ports.

_____

_____

_____

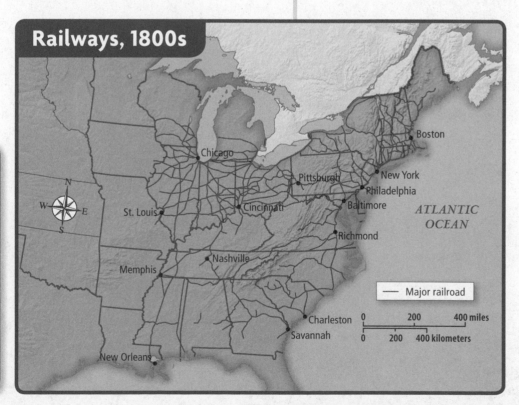

Railways, 1800s

Boston
Chicago
Pittsburgh
New York
Philadelphia
St. Louis
Cincinnati
Baltimore
Richmond
ATLANTIC OCEAN
Nashville
Memphis
Charleston
Savannah
New Orleans

— Major railroad

0   200   400 miles
0   200   400 kilometers

Highlight the effects of the telegraph and the Pony Express.

Better Communication

New inventions also helped people communicate much faster. Samuel Morse began working on an invention called the telegraph in 1832. The telegraph sent messages using electricity. It could send a message in a matter of minutes, compared to waiting weeks for letters to arrive in the mail. Telegraph messages were a series of clicks and sounds that stood for letters and numbers. By 1844, the first telegraph line connected Washington, D.C., to Baltimore, Maryland.

A telegraph machine ▼

DID YOU KNOW?
By 1861, there were over 67,000 miles of telegraph lines across the country.

The Pony Express

It took a while for telegraph lines to reach the western United States. In the meantime, people needed a faster way to send and receive messages. In April 1859 the Leavenworth & Pike's Peak Express Company was created. The company employed mail carriers who traveled on horseback along a trail that was nearly 2,000 miles long. Because carriers rode horses, the service was referred to as the Pony Express. The Pony Express was in operation until late October 1861, when telegraph lines finally reached the West Coast.

A Pony Express rider passes crews installing telegraph poles ▼

(t) Comstock Images/Alamy, (b) North Wind Picture Archives

The Growth of Cities

With better communication, new jobs, and new ways to get from place to place, cities grew quickly during the Industrial Revolution. In 1820 only about 700,000 people lived in all of the cities in the United States. By 1840, urban populations totalled almost 1.8 million people.

You learned earlier that some of this growth happened when people moved from rural areas in search of work. Others came in search of a better life too. **Immigrants**, mostly from Europe, came to find new job opportunities or to seek fortunes. An immigrant is a person who moves to and lives in a country in which he or she was not born. Almost all immigrants entered the nation through port cities like New York City, Boston, and New Orleans. Some immigrants moved westward, but many remained in the cities on the East Coast.

Yet another reason for the growth of cities was the Industrial Revolution itself. Cities sprung up around factories and along rail routes. Roads and railroads connected cities around the country. These routes also made moving to and trading with areas in the West easier. As more and more people moved westward, the boundaries of the United States began to change and take the form they have today.

Reading Skill

Main Idea and Key Details Circle the main idea of this text passage and underline key details that support it.

Lesson 3

? Essential Question   How do ideas influence choices?

_____

_____

_____

_____

_____

Go back to _Show As You Go!_ on pages 238–239.

networks   **There's More Online!**
● Games ● Assessment

Internal Struggles

How do ideas influence choices?

What do you think?

Have you ever had to compromise with someone?
What did you give up? What did you receive?

_____

_____

_____

The Nation Begins to Divide

By the late 1700s, feelings about slavery began to change in the United States. The economies, cultures, and attitudes of the North and South were very different.

Large cities and new factories were growing quickly in the North. Immigrants flooded the United States to fill factory jobs. By 1804 all Northern states had outlawed slavery.

In the South, the economy had not changed much. The plantation system was still the main way of life. On large farms, hundreds of enslaved Africans worked without pay. Most Southerners worked on small farms, and not all had slaves. However, the plantation owners were the wealthiest and had the most political power.

Library of Congress

Enslaved workers use a cotton gin ▼

Words To Know

Tell a partner what you think you know about these words.

slave state

*balance

free state

Union

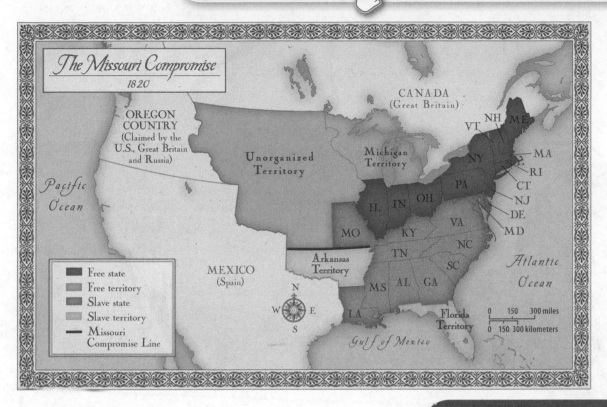

The Missouri Compromise
1820

CANADA
(Great Britain)

OREGON COUNTRY
(Claimed by the
U.S., Great Britain
and Russia)

Pacific Ocean

Unorganized Territory

Michigan Territory

VT NH ME
NY MA
RI
PA CT
IL IN OH NJ
DE
MO KY VA MD
Arkansas Territory NC
TN SC
MEXICO (Spain) MS AL GA
LA
Florida Territory

Atlantic Ocean

Gulf of Mexico

N W E S

0 150 300 miles
0 150 300 kilometers

Legend:
- Free state
- Free territory
- Slave state
- Slave territory
- Missouri Compromise Line

Compromise for Missouri

As the United States expanded west, many wondered if slavery would expand as well. In 1819 Missouri applied for statehood as a **slave state**, a state in which slavery is allowed. At the time, the nation had a **balance** of 11 slave states and 11 **free states**, or states in which slavery was not allowed. Letting Missouri enter the Union as a slave state would give slave states more votes in the Senate.

Congress argued over Missouri for a year. In 1820 Senator Henry Clay from Kentucky came up with the Missouri Compromise. Under this plan, Missouri was added as a slave state. Maine, which had been part of Massachusetts, became a free state. The compromise stated that, in the future, slavery would not be allowed in any states north of Missouri's southern border.

This compromise was only a temporary solution. As the United States continued to expand, new compromises and decisions had to be made.

Map and Globe Skills

1. Was slavery allowed in Alabama?

_____

2. Which state entered the Union as a free state under the Missouri Compromise?

_____

Reading Skill

Cause and Effect Underline the causes and ⌢circle⌣ the effects of the Missouri Compromise.

267

The Age of Jackson

Prior to 1824, only wealthy men were allowed to vote. Then, new laws were passed that allowed all white men age 21 or older to vote. This wave of new voters helped elect a "common man" as President—Andrew Jackson.

Andrew Jackson: Biography

▲ Andrew Jackson

Born: March 15, 1767

Early Life: Jackson was born in rural South Carolina. At age 13, he worked as a courier during the Revolutionary War. He later became a lawyer. Jackson earned fame as a general during the War of 1812.

Crisis in South Carolina: During Jackson's Presidency, lawmakers in South Carolina threatened to leave the **Union** if they were forced to collect a new federal tax on imported goods. A union is a group of states joined together.

Jackson sent troops and warships to South Carolina to enforce collection of the tax. The tax was collected and the crisis passed. People accused Jackson of acting more like a king than a President.

Primary Source

Political Cartoons

Political cartoons express an artist's opinion about people or events. Often, the image exaggerates details in a humorous or ridiculous way. The title, labels, or details will help you identify and understand the opinion being expressed.

Many people were outraged that President Jackson would order military action against his own people over taxes. In fact, it reminded them of events that happened before the Revolutionary War. They felt Jackson had violated their rights and was acting more like a king than President.

Circle the parts of the political cartoon that support this opinion of Jackson.

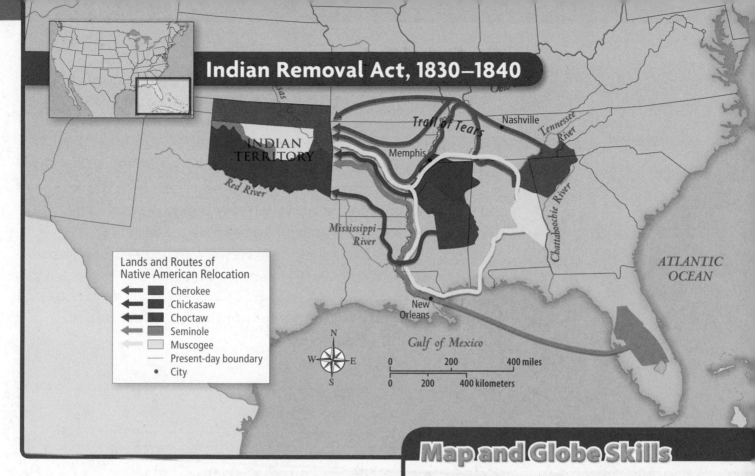

Indian Removal Act, 1830–1840

Trail of Tears
Nashville
Memphis
INDIAN TERRITORY
Red River
Mississippi River
New Orleans
Tennessee River
Chattahoochie River
ATLANTIC OCEAN
Gulf of Mexico

Lands and Routes of Native American Relocation
- Cherokee
- Chickasaw
- Choctaw
- Seminole
- Muscogee
- Present-day boundary
- City

0   200   400 miles
0   200   400 kilometers

Conflicts Over Land

In the early 1800s, many Native Americans in the Southeast, such as the Cherokee, lived peacefully with their white neighbors. Their right to their homeland had been guaranteed by treaties signed with the United States government.

As settlers continued to move to the West and Southeast, the demand for land increased. This sometimes led to conflicts with Native Americans.

The Indian Removal Act

President Jackson and some of his supporters believed that Native Americans should leave their lands in the Southeast and allow settlers to live there. In 1830 Congress passed the Indian Removal Act. This act forced Native Americans to move to an area called the Indian Territory, in parts of present-day Oklahoma.

The Cherokee believed this act was unfair. They sued the state of Georgia to stop the government from forcing them out of their homeland. Eventually, the case went to the United States Supreme Court. The Court ruled in favor of the Cherokee. President Jackson, however, refused to obey the ruling.

Map and Globe Skills

1. In which states did the Cherokee originally live?

_____

_____

2. Describe the route of the Seminole.

_____

_____

_____

DID YOU KNOW?
In 1821 a Cherokee named Sequoyah developed the first written Native American alphabet. It took him 12 years to create this alphabet. It has 86 letters!

The Trail of Tears

In May 1838, General Winfield Scott and 7,000 federal troops arrived at the Cherokee capital. Scott threatened to use force if the Cherokee didn't leave. He told the Cherokee that they were surrounded and escape was impossible. The Cherokee knew that fighting would lead to their destruction.

Filled with sadness and anger, Cherokee leaders gave in, and the 800 mile march to the Indian Territory began. Around 2,000 Cherokee died in camps waiting for the move to begin. About another 2,000 died along the way from starvation, disease, and harsh weather conditions. This journey became known as the Trail of Tears.

> **How did the westward movement of settlers affect Native Americans in the Southeast?**
>
> _____
>
> _____

Primary Source

Quote

This primary source describes what one soldier saw along the trail.

> "[In] May 1838 . . . I saw helpless Cherokee arrested and dragged from their homes. . . . I saw them loaded like cattle or sheep into six hundred and forty-five wagons and starting toward the west. . . . Many of the children rose to their feet and waved their little hands good-by to their mountain homes, knowing they were leaving them forever."

—A section from *Story of the Trail of Tears* by John G. Burnett, published in 1890

How did John Burnett feel about the way Native Americans were relocated? Circle the words and phrases that led to your answer.

_____

_____

SuperStock

The Seminole Fight Back

The United States also tried to relocate the Seminole, who lived in Florida. In 1832 some Seminole leaders signed a treaty with the United States agreeing to relocate. However, others refused and retreated south into the Everglades.

Led by a man named Osceola, the Seminole who decided to stay fought against United States troops. Osceola eventually was captured, but the Seminole continued to fight. The Seminole wars would last nearly 50 years and cost the United States $40 million. A few hundred Seminole survived and remained in the Everglades.

▲ Osceola

Explain how westward expansion affected Native Americans.

_____

_____

_____

Getty Images/Archive Photos/Getty Images

Lesson **4**

 Essential Question   **How do ideas influence choices?**

_____

_____

_____

_____

_____

_____

Go back to *Show As You Go!* on pages 238–239. ≪≪

 networks   **There's More Online!**
● Assessments ● Games

The Overland Trails

? Essential Question

Why do people move? What do you think?

_____

_____

_____

_____

_____

_____

Words To Know

Rank the words (1–5) to show how well you understand each term.

_____ **wagon train**

_____ **manifest destiny**

_____ **overland wagon**

_____ ***conditions**

_____ **forty-niner**

THINK · PAIR · SHARE *Imagine you had to start a new life in a place far away from your home. Would you go alone? What would you take with you? What hardships might you encounter?*

Taming the Wild Trails

As you learned in Lesson 1, people like Daniel Boone helped early pioneers find their way into the Northwest Territory. As the United States continued to expand west, settlers relied on new people to help them find their way. In the 1820s, they were helped by mountain men.

Mountain men were traders and fur trappers who lived along the streams and rivers of the Pacific Northwest and the Rocky Mountains. They trapped along Native American trails and discovered new paths through the Rockies. Mountain men created guidebooks that outlined new trails.

Eventually, **wagon trains** started to make their way across these trails to the West. A wagon train was a line of wagons led west by an experienced guide. As more people moved west, new trails were discovered and used.

As more people headed west, settlers and Native Americans clashed. Many lives were lost in battles over land. Eventually, most Native Americans were driven from their homes.

A wagon train approaches a mountain pass ▼

Bridgeman Art Library · London / SuperStock

Oregon Fever

By the 1840s, Americans were inspired by **manifest destiny**. This was a belief that the United States had the right to claim new lands and expand its borders all the way to the Pacific Ocean. Early settlers in the Oregon Territory sent stories of rich farmland and lush forests. Families began catching "Oregon Fever"—the desire to get a fresh start in the West.

The Mormons Settle Utah

Some people were forced to move west because of their religious beliefs. One example of this is the Church of Jesus Christ of Latter-Day Saints, or the Mormon Church.

The Mormons were forced west from New York where many people disagreed with their beliefs. In 1847 the first Mormons arrived at the Great Salt Lake and settled what is now Salt Lake City, Utah.

How did the concept of manifest destiny contribute to westward expansion?

_____

_____

Map and Globe Skills

1. Circle the end of the Oregon Trail.

2. Which trail traveled the farthest south?

   _____

3. Through which mountain range did most of the trails pass?

   _____

   Label the mountain range.

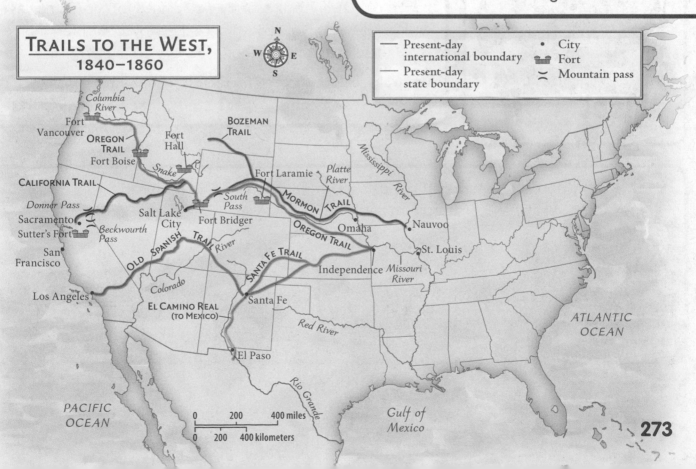

TRAILS TO THE WEST, 1840–1860

Legend:
— Present-day international boundary
— Present-day state boundary
● City
🏛 Fort
≍ Mountain pass

Columbia River
Fort Vancouver
OREGON TRAIL
Fort Hall
Fort Boise
Snake
BOZEMAN TRAIL
CALIFORNIA TRAIL
Donner Pass
Sacramento
Sutter's Fort
Beckwourth Pass
Salt Lake City
South Pass
Fort Bridger
Fort Laramie
Platte River
Mississippi River
MORMON TRAIL
OREGON TRAIL
Omaha
Nauvoo
St. Louis
San Francisco
OLD SPANISH TRAIL
River
SANTA FE TRAIL
Independence
Missouri River
Los Angeles
Colorado
EL CAMINO REAL (TO MEXICO)
Santa Fe
Red River
El Paso
Rio Grande
PACIFIC OCEAN
ATLANTIC OCEAN
Gulf of Mexico

0   200   400 miles
0   200   400 kilometers

273

LIFE ON THE OVERLAND TRAILS

One of the most popular overland trails was the Oregon Trail, which stretched from Independence, Missouri, to western Oregon. It was a long, hard journey of 2,000 miles. It took nearly six months to reach Oregon! Read these pages to find out what the trip was like for a typical family.

Men were responsible for driving the oxen, repairing the wagon, hunting, and protecting their families.

Women cooked, set up camp, and managed supplies. They also cared for and educated their children along the way.

Children helped around camp. They gathered "buffalo chips," dung left by bison. These "chips" were used as fuel for fires.

Settlers used **overland wagons** called prairie schooners. Wagons had to carry everything a family would need for the journey, as well as what they would need once they got to their new home. Label these items on the schooner shown to the left:

weapons	**tools**	**medicine**	**seeds**
books	**meat**	**pans**	**spare wagon parts**

People found strength in numbers on wagon trains. This helped in the event of animal attacks or conflict with Native Americans.

Pioneers often used guidebooks they purchased from mountain men or at one of the many stops or forts along the trail. However, these guidebooks weren't always reliable and didn't accurately describe **conditions** on the trails.

As pioneers headed west, unpredictable weather often greeted them. Sometimes, violent storms popped up with little warning. Pioneers had to scramble to make sure their belongings weren't damaged in the storms. As they approached the Rocky Mountains, pioneers had to deal with freezing temperatures and snow storms.

The trails were not always smooth. As pioneers headed west, they had to deal with rocky terrain and rough trails. Sometimes they would have to repair broken wheels. Pioneers had to deal with plants, vegetation, and wildlife with which they were not familiar. Pioneers had to figure out how to get around or through deep rivers. Some pioneers altered their wagons to float across the river like a boat.

Draw a hardship faced by pioneers on the trails. Underline details in the text that help you.

The War with Mexico

Instead of moving west, some people settled in an area of the Southwest that belonged to Mexico. Eventually, the demands and needs of these settlers led to war with Mexico.

Americans Settle in Texas

In 1821 Mexico won its independence from Spain. At that time, Mexico's northern areas included present-day Texas, New Mexico, and California.

During those years, few people lived in this huge area. To keep the area under Mexican control, Mexico's government offered land and citizenship to Americans who settled in Texas. By 1835, about 25,000 Americans lived in the area. Many of these Americans didn't want to live in Mexico. They complained about Mexican laws. They also wanted slavery, which was illegal in Mexico, to be legal.

Texas Goes to War

Texans went to war with Mexico in December 1835. After a year of fighting, Texans voted to join the United States. They adopted a constitution and made slavery legal.

The U.S. Congress felt that allowing Texas to join the Union might lead to war with Mexico. Instead, Texas became an independent country—the Republic of Texas. It was also known as the Lone Star Republic.

In December 1835, a force of 500 Texans attacked the town of San Antonio. Within days, they had control of the Alamo, a Spanish fort. Three months later, the Mexicans recaptured the Alamo after a two-week battle. ▶

The United States Goes to War

In 1845 Texas joined the Union. However, the United States and Mexico disagreed over the southern border of Texas. Later that year, President James Polk offered to buy the Mexican territories of California and New Mexico for $30 million. When Mexico refused, Polk ordered General Zachary Taylor to march through Texas to the Rio Grande. Fighting broke out with Mexican soldiers in April 1846. As a result, the United States declared war on Mexico.

Fighting continued until 1847, when U.S. troops captured the Mexican capital, Mexico City. The Mexican government signed the Treaty of Guadalupe Hidalgo in February 1848. Under this treaty, Mexico sold Texas to the United States for $15 million. The treaty also included land in much of the Southwest.

Map and Globe Skills

Which present-day states had their borders expanded in 1853?

_____

_____

How did the War with Mexico help the United States achieve the idea of manifest destiny?

_____

_____

_____

_____

DID YOU KNOW?

In 1853 the United States paid Mexico $10 million for the Gadsden Purchase. This strip of land included the southern edge of present-day Arizona and New Mexico. With this purchase, the nation reached its present size (not including Alaska and Hawaii).

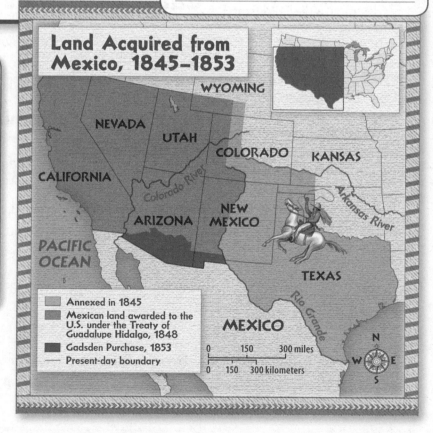

Land Acquired from Mexico, 1845–1853

WYOMING
NEVADA
UTAH
COLORADO
KANSAS
CALIFORNIA
Colorado River
Arkansas River
ARIZONA
NEW MEXICO
PACIFIC OCEAN
TEXAS
MEXICO
Rio Grande

Annexed in 1845
Mexican land awarded to the U.S. under the Treaty of Guadalupe Hidalgo, 1848
Gadsden Purchase, 1853
Present-day boundary

0   150   300 miles
0   150   300 kilometers

N W E S

▲ Miners often searched for gold in rivers, using pans to separate the gold from pebbles and sand.

DID YOU KNOW?

John C. Fremont was a mapmaker who led several expeditions, including ones to Mexican California. He wrote about California's mild climate and vast natural resources. His explorations inspired many American pioneers to move west. Later, Fremont helped organize a rebellion against Mexican California in 1846, creating the Bear Flag Republic.

California Joins the Union

As a result of the War with Mexico, the United States gained possession of California. Soon, a large flood of people would move to California in hopes of making a fortune.

Gold Fever in California

In January 1848, a man named James Marshall saw something glittering in the American River outside the town of Sacramento, California. What he saw was gold. Marshall tried to keep the discovery a secret, but the news quickly spread.

Over the next year, thousands of miners came to search for gold in the area. Prospecting, or exploring for gold, required only a few tools and the willingness to work hard. It was difficult work, and few people struck it rich.

> **How did the discovery of gold in California influence boundary changes in the United States?**
>
> _____
>
> _____

The idea of sudden wealth drew thousands of people to California. So many people came that the period became known as the Gold Rush. By May 1849, more than 10,000 wagons had crossed the continent to reach California. In that year alone, more than 80,000 people arrived in California from around the world. Because these people came to California in 1849, they became known as "**forty-niners**."

The Thirty-First State

By 1850, there were enough people in California to apply for statehood. Settlers wanted courts, land and water laws, mail delivery, and other government services. On September 9, 1850, President Millard Fillmore signed a law that made California the thirty-first state to enter the Union.

▲ Miners used pans such as this one to find gold.

Jules Frazier/Getty Images

> How did California becoming a state fulfill the idea of manifest destiny?
>
> _____
>
> _____
>
> _____

Lesson **5**

? Essential Question   **Why do people move?**

_____

_____

_____

_____

_____

Go back to *Show As You Go!* on pages 238–239. ❮❮

networks   **There's More Online!**
● Assessment ● Games

Follow the steps below to complete the vocabulary activity.

1. Place four related words from this unit in the circle. Write a title for this set of words.

3. Replace one or two words with different words and create a new title for that circle.

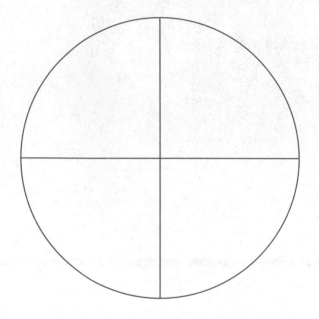

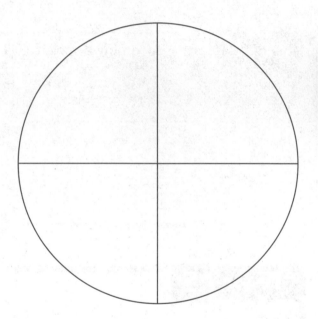

2. How is each word related to your title? Could other words from this unit have been placed in the circle? If so, explain.

4. Explain the connections between words and how this impacted your new title. Be sure to use details in your explanation.

Unit Project

Use the information you learned in this unit to create a board game about a family going west on the overland trails. Your game should focus on the potential hardships that settlers faced. Brainstorm how the elements you want to include in your game will work together. Make a game board and a list of rules for the game.

Your board game should include...   **Yes, it does!**

a game board made of cardboard or thick poster board   ☐

a story that focuses on potential hardships faced
by settlers along the overland trails   ☐

game pieces and a method for moving on the board,
such as dice or a spinner   ☐

clear and easy rules that explain how to play the game   ☐

....

Think about the Big Idea

BIG IDEA Relationships affect choices.

What did you learn in this unit that helps you understand the BIG IDEA?

_____

_____

_____

_____

Read the passage "The City of Lowell" before answering Numbers 1 through 8.

The City of Lowell

by Donnie Tadele

In 1810 Francis Cabot Lowell visited some textile factories in Great Britain. A textile factory is a place where workers turn cotton into cloth. At the time, Britain made it illegal to export machines or machine parts. During his visit, Lowell memorized how the machines in the factory worked.

In 1813 Lowell built a textile factory in Waltham, Massachusetts. All stages of cotton-making—from spinning cotton into thread to weaving thread into cotton—happened under one roof.

Lowell died in 1817. His business partners later built several textile mills along the Merrimack River in Massachusetts. They also built a town, called Lowell, around the factories for workers to live in. Workers used half of their pay to live in the houses owned by the mills. Lowell was the first planned town in the United States.

By 1850, Lowell had more than 10,000 workers. Many of them were young women, sometimes called "Mill Girls." The company hired mainly women and children because they would work for lower wages than men. However, the women still made more money than they could working on farms. They signed one-year contracts agreeing to work 13-hour days, six days a week.

1 What is this passage mostly about?

Ⓐ how the British protected their factory secrets

Ⓑ how the Lowell mill started and functioned

Ⓒ working conditions in Lowell mills

Ⓓ how many hours Mill Girls worked

2 How long were the contracts that mill workers signed?

Ⓕ 13 hours

Ⓖ 6 days

Ⓗ 1 year

Ⓘ 13 years

3 Read the sentence from the passage.

> **At the time, Britain made it illegal to export machines or machine parts.**

What does the word *illegal* mean in this passage?

Ⓐ to be free

Ⓑ to be against the law

Ⓒ to be encouraged

Ⓓ to be expensive to buy

4 Along what river was the city of Lowell built?

Ⓕ the Massachusetts River

Ⓖ the Waltham River

Ⓗ the Lowell River

Ⓘ the Merrimack River

5 In what city did Lowell build his first factory?

Ⓐ Lowell

Ⓑ Great Britain

Ⓒ Waltham

Ⓓ Merrimack

6 Which two words from the passage have the SAME meanings?

Ⓕ factory, workers

Ⓖ cotton, cloth

Ⓗ women, children

Ⓘ wages, pay

7 What happened in 1813?

Ⓐ Lowell built a textile factory in Waltham.

Ⓑ Lowell died.

Ⓒ Lowell had more than 10,000 workers.

Ⓓ Lowell traveled to Great Britain.

8 Which of the following was NOT part of the experience for workers in Lowell, Massachusetts?

Ⓕ 13-hour work days

Ⓖ living in houses owned by the mill

Ⓗ exporting British machine parts

Ⓘ six-day work weeks

Reference Section

Geography and You

Geography is the study of Earth and the people, plants, and animals that live on it. Most people think of geography as learning about cities, states, and countries, but geography is far more. Geography includes learning about land, such as mountains and plains, and bodies of water, such as oceans, lakes, and rivers.

Geography includes the study of how people adapt to living in a new place. Geography is also about how people move around, how they move goods, and how ideas travel from place to place.

Dictionary of Geographic Terms

1 **BAY** Body of water partly surrounded by land

2 **BEACH** Land covered with sand or pebbles next to an ocean or lake

3 **CANAL** Waterway dug across the land to connect two bodies of water

4 **CANYON** Deep river valley with steep sides

5 **CLIFF** High steep face of rock

6 **COAST** Land next to an ocean

7 **DESERT** A dry environment with few plants and animals

8 **GULF** Body of water partly surrounded by land; larger than a bay

9 **HARBOR** Protected place by an ocean or river where ships can safely stay

10 **HILL** Rounded, raised landform; not as high as a mountain

11 **ISLAND** Land that is surrounded on all sides by water

12	**LAKE** Body of water completely surrounded by land		**17**	**PLAIN** Large area of flat land
13	**MESA** Landform that looks like a high, flat table		**18**	**PLATEAU** High flat area that rises steeply above the surrounding land
14	**MOUNTAIN** High landform with steep sides; higher than a hill		**19**	**PORT** Place where ships load and unload goods
15	**OCEAN** Large body of salt water		**20**	**RIVER** Long stream of water that empties into another body of water
16	**PENINSULA** Land that has water on all sides but one		**21**	**VALLEY** Area of low land between hills or mountains

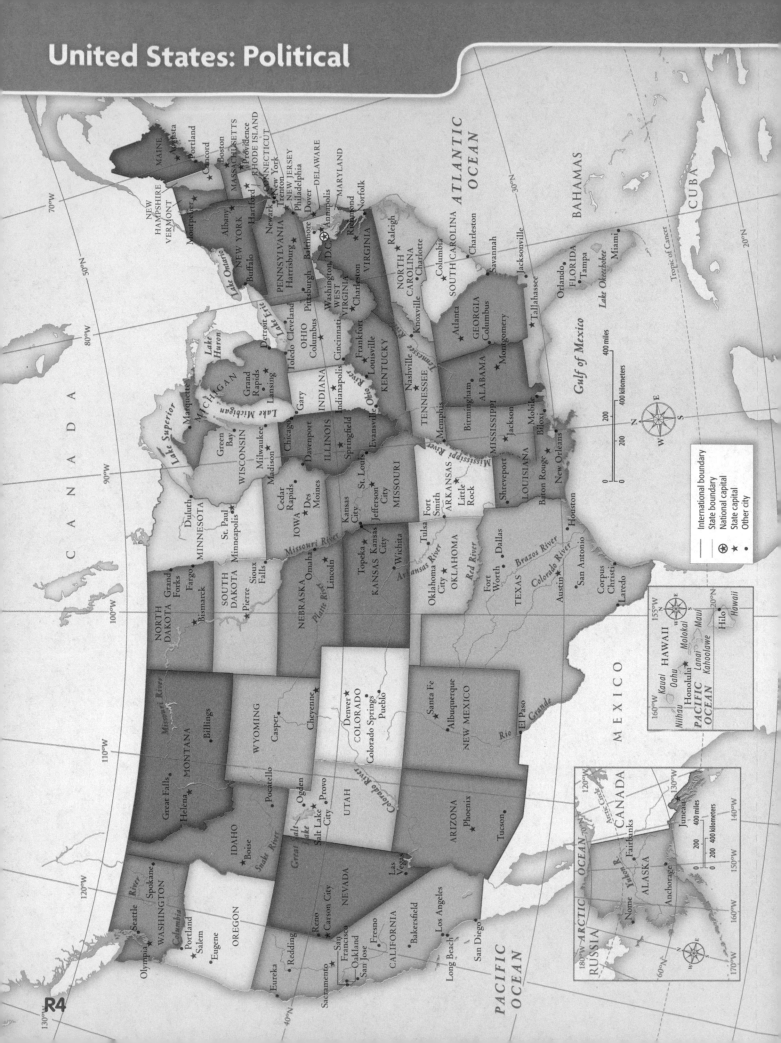

United States: Physical

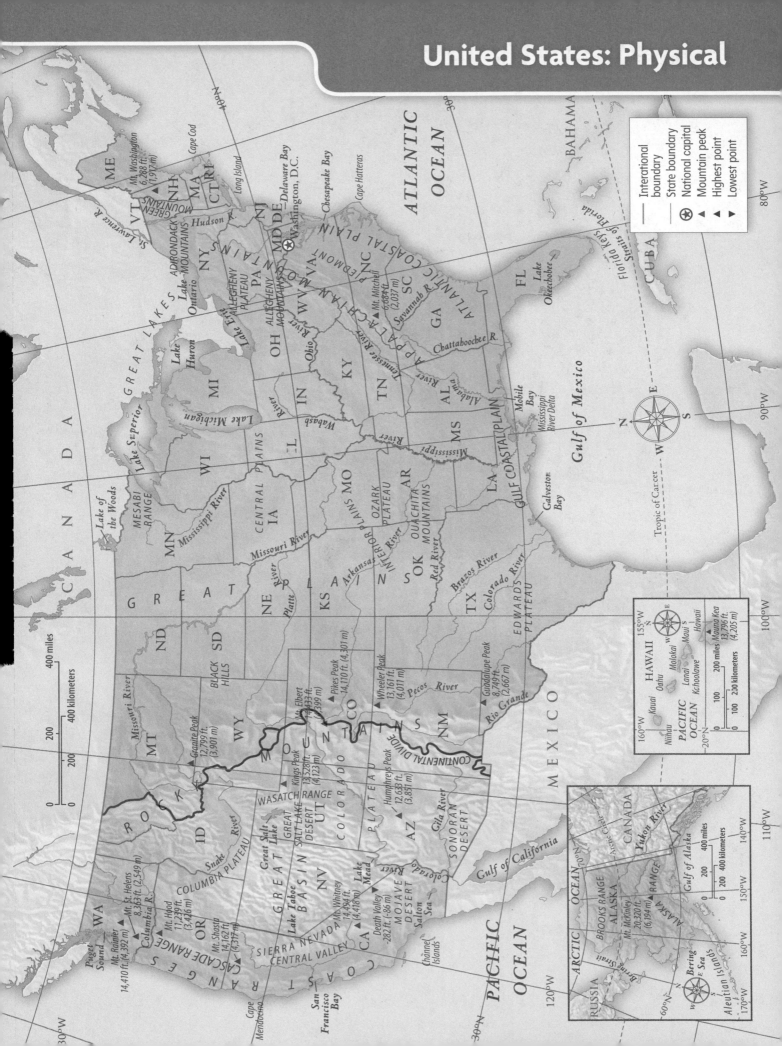

Legend
- International boundary
- State boundary
- ⊛ National capital
- ▲ Mountain peak
- ▲ Highest point
- ▶ Lowest point

ATLANTIC OCEAN

PACIFIC OCEAN

CANADA

MEXICO

Gulf of Mexico

BAHAMA

CUBA

States / Regions:
ME, NH, VT, MA, CT, RI, NY, PA, NJ, MD, DE, OH, WV, VA, NC, SC, GA, FL, KY, TN, AL, MS, LA, AR, MO, IA, IL, IN, MI, WI, MN, ND, SD, NE, KS, OK, TX, NM, CO, WY, MT, ID, UT, AZ, NV, CA, OR, WA

Mountains / Physical features:
- Mt. Washington 6,288 ft. (1,917 m)
- Cape Cod
- Long Island
- St. Lawrence R.
- GREEN MOUNTAINS
- ADIRONDACK MOUNTAINS
- Hudson R.
- Lake Ontario
- Lake Erie
- ALLEGHENY PLATEAU
- ALLEGHENY MOUNTAINS
- APPALACHIAN MOUNTAINS
- PIEDMONT
- ATLANTIC COASTAL PLAIN
- Delaware Bay
- Chesapeake Bay
- Cape Hatteras
- Washington, D.C.
- Mt. Mitchell 6,684 ft. (2,037 m)
- Savannah R.
- Chattahoochee R.
- Lake Okeechobee
- Florida Keys
- Straits of Florida
- GREAT LAKES
- Lake Superior
- Lake Huron
- Lake Michigan
- MESABI RANGE
- Lake of the Woods
- Mississippi River
- Missouri River
- Wabash River
- Ohio River
- Tennessee River
- Alabama River
- Mobile Bay
- Mississippi River Delta
- GULF COASTAL PLAIN
- Galveston Bay
- CENTRAL PLAINS
- INTERIOR PLAINS
- OZARK PLATEAU
- Arkansas River
- OUACHITA MOUNTAINS
- Red River
- Brazos River
- Colorado River
- EDWARDS PLATEAU
- GREAT PLAINS
- Platte River
- BLACK HILLS
- Pikes Peak 14,110 ft. (4,301 m)
- Mt. Elbert 14,433 ft. (4,399 m)
- Granite Peak 12,799 ft. (3,901 m)
- Kings Peak 13,528 ft. (4,123 m)
- WASATCH RANGE
- Wheeler Peak 13,161 ft. (4,011 m)
- Pecos River
- Guadalupe Peak 8,749 ft. (2,667 m)
- Rio Grande
- CONTINENTAL DIVIDE
- Humphreys Peak 12,633 ft. (3,851 m)
- COLORADO PLATEAU
- Gila River
- SONORAN DESERT
- Gulf of California
- ROCKY MOUNTAINS
- Missouri River
- Snake River
- COLUMBIA PLATEAU
- Great Salt Lake
- GREAT SALT LAKE DESERT
- GREAT BASIN
- Lake Tahoe
- Mt. Whitney 14,494 ft. (4,418 m)
- Death Valley -282 ft. (-86 m)
- Lake Mead
- MOJAVE DESERT
- Salton Sea
- Colorado River
- SIERRA NEVADA
- CENTRAL VALLEY
- COAST RANGES
- CASCADE RANGE
- Mt. Rainier 14,410 ft. (4,392 m)
- Mt. St. Helens 8,363 ft. (2,549 m)
- Mt. Hood 11,239 ft. (3,426 m)
- Mt. Shasta 14,162 ft. (4,317 m)
- Columbia R.
- Puget Sound
- Cape Mendocino
- San Francisco Bay
- Channel Islands

Scale:
- 0, 200, 400 miles
- 0, 200, 400 kilometers

Hawaii inset:
- HAWAII
- Kauai, Niihau, Oahu, Molokai, Lanai, Maui, Kahoolawe, Hawaii
- Mauna Kea 13,796 ft. (4,205 m)
- PACIFIC OCEAN
- 155°W, 160°W, 20°N
- 0, 100, 200 miles
- 0, 100, 200 kilometers

Alaska inset:
- ALASKA
- CANADA
- ARCTIC OCEAN
- Arctic Circle
- BROOKS RANGE
- Yukon River
- ALASKA RANGE
- Mt. McKinley 20,320 ft. (6,194 m)
- Gulf of Alaska
- Bering Strait
- Bering Sea
- Aleutian Islands
- RUSSIA
- 170°W, 160°W, 150°W, 140°W, 130°W
- 70°N, 60°N
- 0, 200, 400 miles
- 0, 200, 400 kilometers

Grid labels:
- 30°W, 40°W, 80°W, 90°W, 100°W, 110°W, 120°W, 130°W
- 30°N, 40°N
- Tropic of Cancer

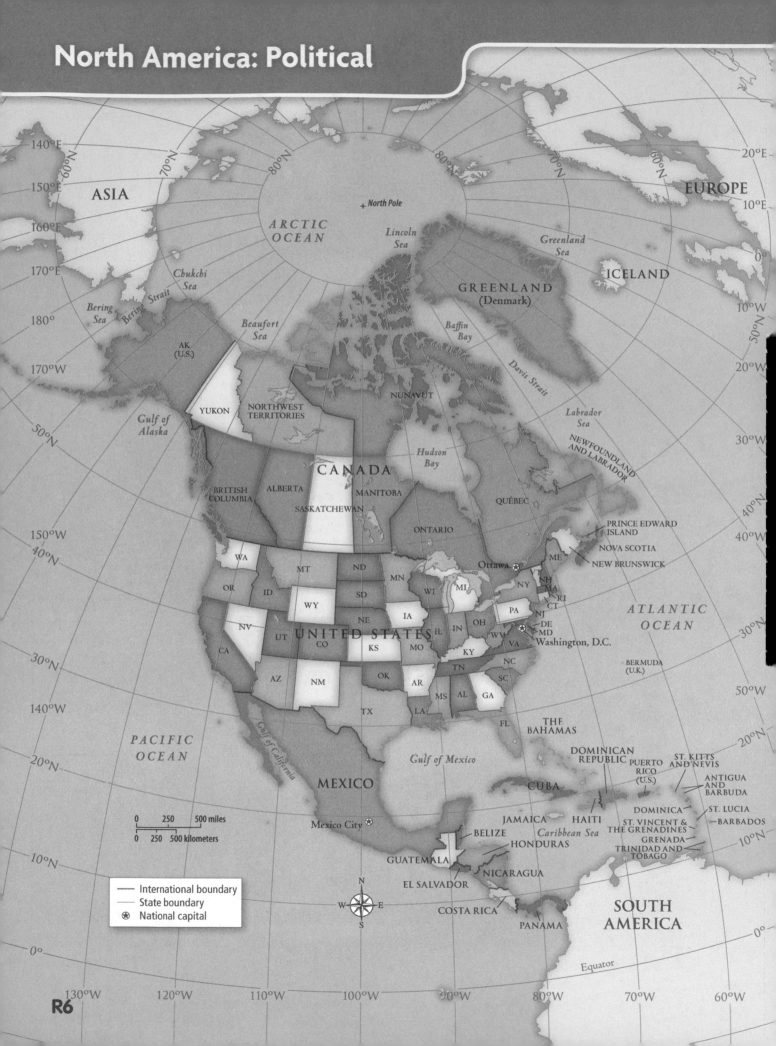

ASIA

EUROPE

140°E
150°E
160°E
170°E
180°
170°W
150°W
40°N
30°N
20°N
10°N
0°

ARCTIC
OCEAN

+ North Pole

Lincoln
Sea

Chukchi
Sea

Bering
Sea

Bering Strait

Beaufort
Sea

AK
(U.S.)

Gulf of
Alaska

YUKON

NORTHWEST
TERRITORIES

NUNAVUT

Greenland
Sea

GREENLAND
(Denmark)

ICELAND

Baffin
Bay

Davis Strait

Labrador
Sea

20°E
10°E
0°
10°W
20°W
30°W
40°W

60°N
70°N
80°N
80°N
70°N
60°N

Hudson
Bay

CANADA

BRITISH
COLUMBIA

ALBERTA

SASKATCHEWAN

MANITOBA

ONTARIO

QUÉBEC

NEWFOUNDLAND
AND LABRADOR

PRINCE EDWARD
ISLAND

NOVA SCOTIA

NEW BRUNSWICK

Ottawa ⊛

ME

WA

MT

ND

MN

OR

ID

SD

WI

MI

NY

VT
NH
MA
RI
CT

NV

WY

NE

IA

PA

NJ

CA

UT

CO

KS

UNITED STATES

IL

IN

OH

WV

DE
MD

Washington, D.C.

VA

MO

KY

AZ

NM

OK

AR

TN

NC

SC

MS

AL

GA

TX

LA

FL

PACIFIC
OCEAN

Gulf of California

MEXICO

Mexico City ⊛

Gulf of Mexico

THE
BAHAMAS

CUBA

JAMAICA

HAITI

DOMINICAN
REPUBLIC

PUERTO
RICO
(U.S.)

BELIZE

GUATEMALA

HONDURAS

Caribbean Sea

EL SALVADOR

NICARAGUA

COSTA RICA

PANAMA

BERMUDA
(U.K.)

ST. KITTS
AND NEVIS

ANTIGUA
AND
BARBUDA

DOMINICA

ST. LUCIA

BARBADOS

ST. VINCENT &
THE GRENADINES

GRENADA

TRINIDAD AND
TOBAGO

ATLANTIC
OCEAN

SOUTH
AMERICA

Equator

0 250 500 miles
0 250 500 kilometers

—— International boundary
—— State boundary
⊛ National capital

50°N
40°N
30°N
20°N
10°N
0°

130°W
120°W
110°W
100°W
90°W
80°W
70°W
60°W

North America: Physical

140°E · 150°E · 160°E · 170°E · 180° · 170°W · 150°W · 140°W · 130°W · 120°W · 110°W · 100°W · 90°W · 80°W · 70°W · 60°W

20°E · 10°E · 0° · 10°W · 20°W · 30°W · 40°W · 50°W

ASIA

EUROPE

ARCTIC OCEAN

+ North Pole

Lincoln Sea

Greenland Sea

Chukchi Sea

Point Barrow

Beaufort Sea

Greenland

Baffin Bay

Bering Sea

Bering Strait

BROOKS RANGE

Mt. McKinley
20,320 ft.
(6,194 m)

Yukon R.

ALASKA RANGE

YUKON PLATEAU

Mackenzie R.

Davis Strait

Cape Farewell

Gulf of Alaska

Mt. Logan
19,551 ft.
(5,959 m)

COAST MOUNTAINS

CANADA

Hudson Bay

Labrador Sea

Peace R.

CANADIAN SHIELD

Vancouver Island

ROCKY MOUNTAINS

Churchill R.

Saskatchewan R.

Lake Winnipeg

Newfoundland

Gulf of St. Lawrence

COAST RANGES

GREAT PLAINS

Snake R.

Missouri River

Great Lakes

Gulf of Maine

Cape Cod

Long Island

ATLANTIC OCEAN

GREAT BASIN

Mt. Whitney
14,495 ft.
(4,418 m)

Platte R.

UNITED STATES

Chesapeake Bay

Death Valley
-282 ft.
(-86 m)

Colorado R.

Arkansas R.

OZARK PLATEAU

Ohio R.

APPALACHIAN MOUNTAINS

Cape Hatteras

Bermuda (U.K.)

SONORAN DESERT

Mississippi R.

Red River

COASTAL PLAIN

BAJA CALIFORNIA

SIERRA MADRE OCCIDENTAL

SIERRA MADRE ORIENTAL

Rio Grande

Gulf of California

Gulf of Mexico

WEST INDIES

PACIFIC OCEAN

Orizaba
18,855 ft.
(5,747 m)

YUCATÁN PENINSULA

Puerto Rico (U.S.)

MEXICO

Caribbean Sea

CENTRAL AMERICA

Lake Nicaragua

SOUTH AMERICA

Isthmus of Panama

Equator

0 · 250 · 500 miles
0 · 250 · 500 kilometers

— International boundary
▲ Mountain peak

N W E S

R7

World: Political

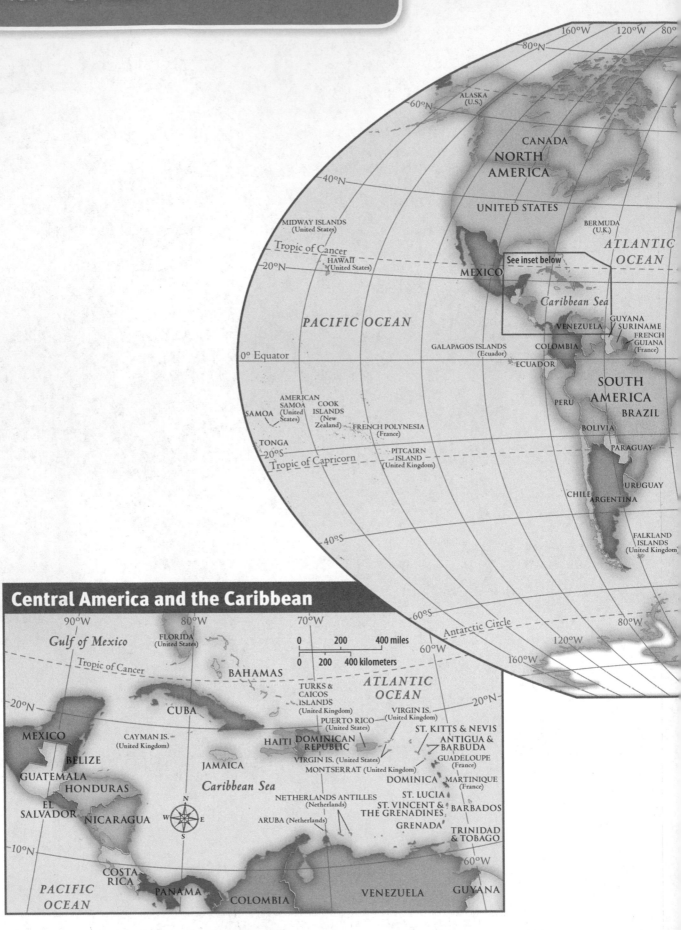

ALASKA (U.S.)

CANADA

NORTH AMERICA

UNITED STATES

BERMUDA (U.K.)

ATLANTIC OCEAN

MIDWAY ISLANDS (United States)

Tropic of Cancer

HAWAII (United States)

MEXICO

See inset below

Caribbean Sea

GUYANA
SURINAME
FRENCH GUIANA (France)

VENEZUELA

COLOMBIA

GALAPAGOS ISLANDS (Ecuador)

ECUADOR

PACIFIC OCEAN

0° Equator

PERU

SOUTH AMERICA

BRAZIL

AMERICAN SAMOA (United States)

COOK ISLANDS (New Zealand)

FRENCH POLYNESIA (France)

SAMOA

BOLIVIA

PARAGUAY

TONGA

PITCAIRN ISLAND (United Kingdom)

20°S

Tropic of Capricorn

CHILE

ARGENTINA

URUGUAY

FALKLAND ISLANDS (United Kingdom)

40°S

Antarctic Circle

160°W 120°W 80°N

60°N

40°N

20°N

20°S

20°N

40°S

60°S

80°W

120°W

60°W

160°W

Central America and the Caribbean

Gulf of Mexico

FLORIDA (United States)

90°W 80°W 70°W

Tropic of Cancer

BAHAMAS

ATLANTIC OCEAN

TURKS & CAICOS ISLANDS (United Kingdom)

20°N

CUBA

CAYMAN IS. (United Kingdom)

PUERTO RICO (United States)

VIRGIN IS. (United Kingdom)

MEXICO

HAITI

DOMINICAN REPUBLIC

ST. KITTS & NEVIS

ANTIGUA & BARBUDA

BELIZE

VIRGIN IS. (United States)

GUADELOUPE (France)

JAMAICA

MONTSERRAT (United Kingdom)

GUATEMALA

HONDURAS

Caribbean Sea

DOMINICA

MARTINIQUE (France)

NETHERLANDS ANTILLES (Netherlands)

ST. LUCIA

EL SALVADOR

NICARAGUA

ST. VINCENT & THE GRENADINES

BARBADOS

ARUBA (Netherlands)

GRENADA

TRINIDAD & TOBAGO

10°N

COSTA RICA

PACIFIC OCEAN

PANAMA

COLOMBIA

VENEZUELA

GUYANA

0 200 400 miles

0 200 400 kilometers

20°N

60°W

N
W   E
S

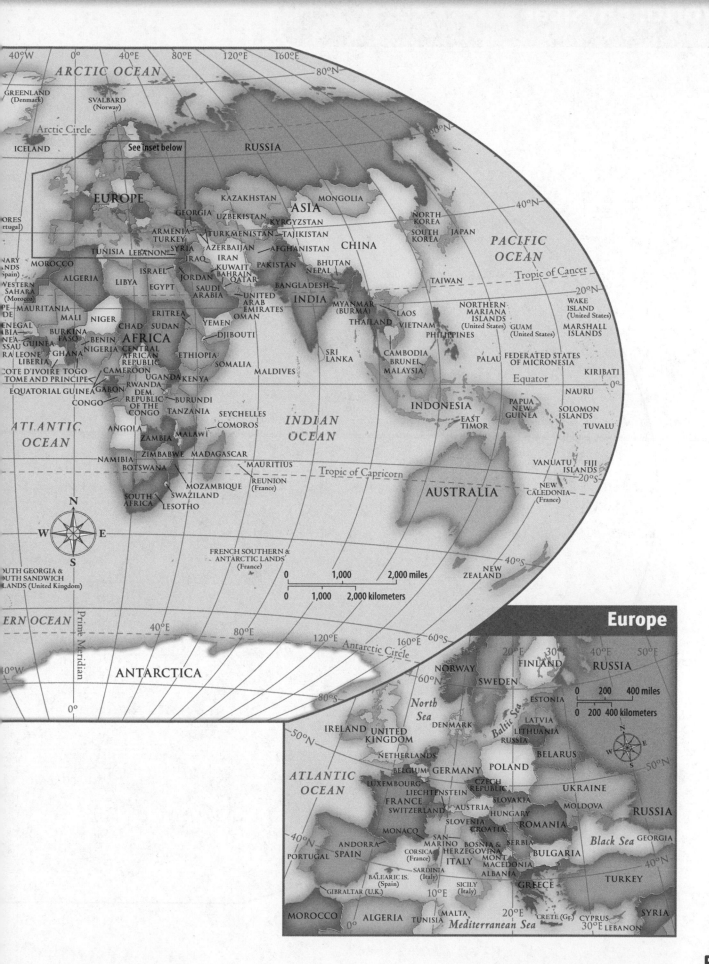

ARCTIC OCEAN

40°W   0°   40°E   80°E   120°E   160°E   80°N

GREENLAND
(Denmark)

SVALBARD
(Norway)

Arctic Circle

ICELAND

See inset below

EUROPE

RUSSIA

ORES
rtugal)

GEORGIA

KAZAKHSTAN

ASIA

MONGOLIA

ARMENIA
TURKEY

UZBEKISTAN

KYRGYZSTAN

NORTH
KOREA

40°N

ARY
NDS
pain)

TUNISIA LEBANON

MOROCCO

ALGERIA

LIBYA

SYRIA
IRAQ

TURKMENISTAN TAJIKISTAN

AZERBAIJAN

ISRAEL
JORDAN

AFGHANISTAN

IRAN
KUWAIT
BAHRAIN
QATAR

EGYPT

SAUDI
ARABIA

UNITED
ARAB
EMIRATES

PAKISTAN

CHINA

SOUTH
KOREA

JAPAN

BHUTAN
NEPAL

PACIFIC
OCEAN

TAIWAN

Tropic of Cancer

20°N

BANGLADESH

WESTERN
SAHARA
(Morocco)

PE
DE

MAURITANIA

SENEGAL
BIA
NEA-
SSAU
RA LEONE
LIBERIA

MALI

GUINEA

BURKINA
FASO

GHANA

NIGER

NIGERIA

CHAD

BENIN

CAMEROON

TOME AND PRINCIPE

ERITREA

SUDAN

AFRICA

CENTRAL
AFRICAN
REPUBLIC

ETHIOPIA

YEMEN

OMAN

DJIBOUTI

INDIA

MYANMAR
(BURMA)

LAOS

THAILAND

VIETNAM

SRI
LANKA

MALDIVES

NORTHERN
MARIANA
ISLANDS
(United States)

CAMBODIA
BRUNEI
MALAYSIA

PALAU

GUAM
(United States)

MARSHALL
ISLANDS

FEDERATED STATES
OF MICRONESIA

WAKE
ISLAND
(United States)

KIRIBATI

SOMALIA

UGANDA KENYA

Equator

0°

COTE D'IVOIRE TOGO

EQUATORIAL GUINEA GABON

CONGO

RWANDA
DEM.
REPUBLIC
OF THE
CONGO

BURUNDI

TANZANIA

ATLANTIC
OCEAN

ANGOLA

ZAMBIA MALAWI

SEYCHELLES

COMOROS

INDIAN
OCEAN

NAMIBIA
BOTSWANA

ZIMBABWE MADAGASCAR

MOZAMBIQUE

MAURITIUS

REUNION
(France)

Tropic of Capricorn

INDONESIA

EAST
TIMOR

PAPUA
NEW
GUINEA

NAURU

SOLOMON
ISLANDS

TUVALU

VANUATU FIJI
ISLANDS

20°S

SOUTH
AFRICA

SWAZILAND

LESOTHO

AUSTRALIA

NEW
CALEDONIA
(France)

N
W   E
S

SOUTH GEORGIA &
SOUTH SANDWICH
LANDS (United Kingdom)

FRENCH SOUTHERN &
ANTARCTIC LANDS
(France)

0   1,000   2,000 miles

0   1,000   2,000 kilometers

40°S

NEW
ZEALAND

ERN OCEAN

Prime Meridian

40°E

80°E

120°E

160°E

Antarctic Circle

60°S

40°W

ANTARCTICA

0°

80°S

Europe

20°E   30°E   40°E   50°E

FINLAND

RUSSIA

NORWAY

SWEDEN

60°N

0   200   400 miles

0   200   400 kilometers

North
Sea

ESTONIA

LATVIA

Baltic Sea

LITHUANIA

N
W   E
S

50°N

IRELAND

UNITED
KINGDOM

DENMARK

RUSSIA

BELARUS

NETHERLANDS

POLAND

ATLANTIC
OCEAN

BELGIUM

GERMANY

CZECH
REPUBLIC

UKRAINE

LUXEMBOURG

LIECHTENSTEIN

SLOVAKIA

MOLDOVA

FRANCE

AUSTRIA

HUNGARY

RUSSIA

SWITZERLAND

SLOVENIA

CROATIA

ROMANIA

MONACO

SAN
MARINO

BOSNIA &
HERZEGOVINA

SERBIA

Black Sea

GEORGIA

40°N

ANDORRA

SPAIN

CORSICA
(France)

MONT.

ITALY

MACEDONIA

BULGARIA

40°N

PORTUGAL

BALEARIC IS.
(Spain)

GIBRALTAR (U.K.)

SARDINIA
(Italy)

SICILY
(Italy)

ALBANIA

GREECE

TURKEY

CRETE (Gr.)

CYPRUS

SYRIA

MOROCCO

ALGERIA

TUNISIA

MALTA

Mediterranean Sea

LEBANON

ARCTIC OCEAN

160°W 120°W 80°W 40°W

80°N

GREENLAND

Mackenzie
River

ALASKA RANGE
60°N

Mt. McKinley
20,320 ft.
(6,194 m)

Arctic Circle

CANADIAN SHIELD

NORTH
AMERICA

40°N

ROCKY MOUNTAINS

APPALACHIAN MTS.

Mississippi River

ATLANTIC
OCEAN

PACIFIC OCEAN

Tropic of Cancer

Rio
Grande

Gulf of
Mexico

20°N

Caribbean Sea

Amazon River

0° Equator

SOUTH
AMERICA

20°S Tropic of Capricorn

ANDES MOUNTAINS

Mt. Aconcagua
22,834 ft.
(6,960 m)

ATLANTIC
OCEAN

40°S

PACIFIC OCEAN

Cape Horn

SOUTHERN OCEAN

60°S

Antarctic Circle

80°W Weddell
Sea

120°W Vinson Massif
16,067 ft.
(4,897 m)

160°W

40°W

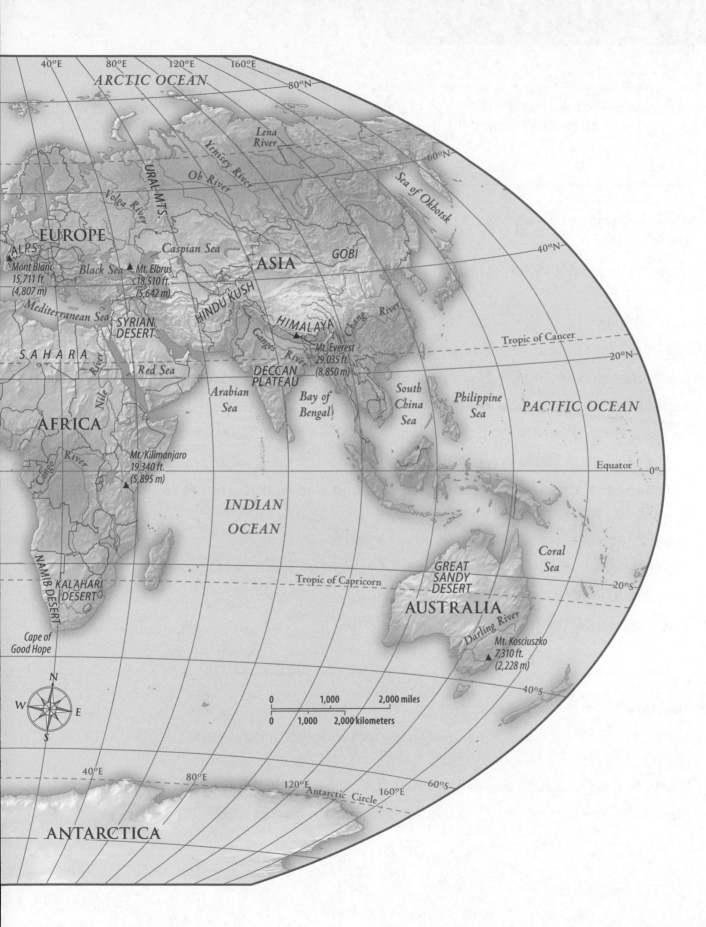

ARCTIC OCEAN

40°E 80°E 120°E 160°E

80°N

Lena
River

Yenisey River

Ob River

60°N

Sea of Okhotsk

URAL MTS.

Volga River

EUROPE

ALPS

Mont Blanc
15,711 ft.
(4,807 m)

Black Sea ▲ Mt. Elbrus
18,510 ft.
(5,642 m)

Caspian Sea

ASIA

GOBI

40°N

HINDU KUSH

Mediterranean Sea

SYRIAN
DESERT

HIMALAYA

Chang River

Tropic of Cancer

SAHARA

Red Sea

Ganges River

▲ Mt. Everest
29,035 ft.
(8,850 m)

20°N

River

Arabian
Sea

DECCAN
PLATEAU

Bay of
Bengal

South
China
Sea

Philippine
Sea

PACIFIC OCEAN

Nile

AFRICA

Mt. Kilimanjaro
19,340 ft.
(5,895 m) ▲

Equator 0°

Congo River

INDIAN

OCEAN

NAMIB DESERT

KALAHARI
DESERT

Tropic of Capricorn

GREAT
SANDY
DESERT

Coral
Sea

20°S

Cape of
Good Hope

AUSTRALIA

N

Darling River

Mt. Kosciuszko
7,310 ft.
▲ (2,228 m)

W   E

S

40°S

0   1,000   2,000 miles

0   1,000   2,000 kilometers

40°E   80°E   120°E   160°E   60°S

Antarctic Circle

ANTARCTICA

Glossary

This Glossary will help you to pronounce and understand the meanings of the vocabulary terms in this book. The page number at the end of the definition tells where the term first appears. Words with an asterisk (*) before them are academic vocabulary words.

A

abolitionist (ab • uh • LISH • uh • nist) was a person who wanted to end slavery in the United States

absolute location (ab • soh • LOOT loh • KAY • shuhn) the exact location of any place on Earth

act (akt) a law

ally (AL • eye) a political or military partner

amendment (uh • MEHND • muhnt) a change or addition to the Constitution

appeal (uh • PEEL) to ask for a case to be heard again

*application (ap • lih • KAY • shun) a way in which something is used

*appropriate (uh • RPOH • pree • uht) the right or correct thing to do; proper

*archaeologist (ahr • kee • AH • luh • jihst) a scientist who studies artifacts to learn about how people lived in the past

*aspect (AS • pehkt) a particular feature or characteristic of a group

assassination (uh • sas • uh • NAY • shuhn) is the murder of an important person

ssembly (uh • SEHM • blee) a lawmaking body

*. sume (uh • SOOM) to take for granted or as true

B

balance (BA • luhnts) an equal amount

barter (BAHR • tuhr) the process of trading goods for other goods, instead of using money

blockade (blah • KAYD) a barrier preventing the movement of troops and supplies

boycott (BOY • kaht) to refuse to buy goods or use services for a specific reason

R12

C

canyon (CAN • yuhn) a deep valley with steep sides

*characteristic (kare • ihk • tur • IHS • tihk) a quality that belongs to a person, thing, or group

*chart (CHAHRT) a document that shows where things are, such as stars

charter (CHAHRT • tuhr) an official document giving a person permission to do something, such as settle in an area

civilization (sihv • ih • lih • ZAY • shun) a culture that has developed complex systems of government, education, and religion

*claim (KLAYM) to declare ownership of something, such as land

*civil war ((SIV • uhl wawr) is an armed conflict between groups within one country. In the United States, it was the war between the Union and the Confederacy from 1861 to 1865

*code (COHD) a set of rules or laws

*common (KAH • muhn) often found

*conclusion (kuhn • KLOO • zhuhn) a well-thought out judgment or decision

*condition (kuhn • DIH • shuhn) the state something is in

*conduct (kun • DUHKT) to direct or lead an event, such as a ceremony

confederacy (kuhn • FEHD • ur • uh • see) a union of people who join together for a common purpose

*consequence (KAHN • suh • kwehns) the result of an action, an effect

constitution (kahn • stuh • TOO • shuhn) a plan for government

contiguous (kuhn • TIH • gyuh • wuhs) land that is connected by shared borders

cotton gin (KAH • tuhn JIHN) a machine that separates cotton from its seeds

covenant (KUH • vuh • nuhnt) a contract or agreement

culture (kuhl • CHUR) the beliefs, traditions, and language of a group of people

D

*debate (dih • BAYT) to discuss all points of view

debt (DEHT) the condition of owing something, such as money, to someone

*defend (dih • FEHND) to argue in favor of a person, action, or point of view

Glossary

delegate (DEH • lih • guht) a person who represents others at an important meeting

*demand (dih • MAND) to ask for with authority

desert (dih • ZUHRT) to run away or to leave someone in their time of need

*develop (DEE • vehl • uhp) to create over a period of time

*discuss (dih • SKUHS) to talk about

*distort (DIHS • tort) to stretch, twist, or bend out of shape

diversity (duh • VUR • suh • tee) a condition of having a great difference or variety among people or things

draft (DRAFT) is the selecting of persons for military service or some other special duty

due process (DOO PRAH • sehs) the idea that the government must follow the rules established by law

E

Emancipation Proclamation (ee • man • sih • PAY • shuhn prok • luh • MAY • shuhn) was an official announcement issued by President Abraham Lincoln in 1862 that led to the end of slavery in the United States

empire (ehm • PY • ur) a large area of different groups of people controlled by one ruler or government

*employ (ihm • PLOY) to hire or use

enslave (in • SLAYV) to force a person to work with no pay and without the freedom to leave

expedition (ehks • pih • DIH • shuhn) a journey for a specific purpose

F

federalism (FEH • duh • ruh • lih • zuhm) a system of government in which power is shared between a national government and states

forty-niner (FOR • tee NY • nuhr) a person who moved to California in 1849 in search of gold

free state (FREE stayt) a state where slavery was banned

frontier (FRUHN • tihr) the name given by colonists to the far end of a country where people are just beginning to settle

fundamental (fuhn • duh • MEHN • tuhl) basic

G

geographer (GEE • ahg • ruh • fur) a person who studies geography

Gettysburg Address (GET • iz • burg uh • DRES) was a speech made by President Abraham Lincoln at the site of the Battle of Gettysburg in 1863

guarantee (gehr • uhn • tee) a promise

H

hogan (HOH • gihn) a dome-shamed Navajo dwelling

I

immigrant (ihm • IH • grihnt) a person who lives in a country in which he or she was not born

impeach (ihm • PEECH) to put an official on trial for wrongdoing

impressment (ihm • PREHS • mihnt) the British practice of capturing American sailors and forcing them to serve on British ships

indentured servant (ihn • DEHN • shuhrd SUHR • vuhnt) a person who worked for someone in colonial America for a set of time in exchange for the voyage across the Atlantic Ocean

inflation (ihn • FLAY • shuhn) a rapid rise in the price of goods

*influence (ihn • FLU • ihns) to change or affect someone or something

*inform (ihn • FORM) to tell

*intent (ihn • TEHNT) the main goal or reason for doing something

interchangeable part (ihn • tur • CHAYNJ • ih • buhl PAHRT) parts of a product built to a standard size so that they can be easily replaced

*interpreter (IHN • tur • prih • tur) a person who changes words from one language into another

*intersect (IHN • tur • sehkt) to meet and cross at one or more points

irrigation (eer • ih • GAY • shuhn) to supply with water by using artificial means

J

jury (JUR • ee) a group of citizens who decide a court case

Glossary

K

kachina (kuh • CHEE • nuh) spirits that Pueblo people believe bring rain, help crops grow, and teach people how to live

L

latitude (LA • tuh • tood) imaginary lines on Earth that go from east to west and show a location's distance from the Equator

lodge (LAHJ) a home made of logs covered with grasses, sticks, and soil, which Native Americans of the Plains used when living in their communities

longhouse (lahng • HOWS) a home shared by several related Iroquois families

longitude (LAHN • juh • tood) imaginary lines on Earth that go from north to south and show a location's distance from the Prime Meridian

Loyalist (LOY • uh • lihst) a colonist who supported Great Britain during the American Revolution

M

manifest destiny (MA • nuh • fehst DEHS • tuh • nee) the belief that the United States had a right to expand its borders west to the Pacific Ocean and south to the Rio Grande

market economy (MAHR • kuht ih • KAH • nuh • mee) a type of economy in which individual producers decide what goods or services to sell, based on available resources and demand

mercenary (MUHR • suh • nehr • ee) professional soldiers from other countries

merchant (MER • chuhnt) a person who makes his or her living by buying and selling goods

migrate (MY • grayt) to move from one place to another

militia (muh • LIH • shuh) a group of volunteer soldiers who fight only in an emergency

missionary (MIH • shuh • nehr • ee) a person who tries to persuade people to accept new religious beliefs

Missouri Compromise (muh • ZUHR • ee KOM • preh • meyz) was an agreement in 1820 that allowed Missouri and Maine to enter the Union and divided the Louisiana Territory into areas allowing slavery and areas outlawing slavery

N

navigable (nav • IH • guh • buhl) deep and wide enough for ships to travel on or through

navigation (nah • vih • GAY • shuhn) the science of finding direction and getting ships from place to place

neutral (NOO • truhl) not expressing strong opinions or feelings; not connected with either side in a war

nomad (NOH • mad) a person that moves from place to place and doesn't have a permanent home

O

occupation (ah • kyuh • PAY • shuhn) the work that a person does in order to earn a living; a job

overland wagon (OH • vuhr • lahnd WA • guhn) wagons that pioneers used to carry all of their possessions along the trails to the West

P

Patriot (PAY • tree • uht) a colonist who supported the colonies' fight for independence in the American Revolution

persecution (puhr • sih • KYOO • shuhn) the act of causing someone to suffer because of their beliefs

*persuade (puhr • SWAYD) to win over with words

pilgrim (pihl • gruhm) a person who travels to a place for religious reasons

pioneer (PY • uhn • eer) a person who settles a new part of the country

politics (PAW • luh • tihks) the process of choosing government leaders and running the government

potlatch (PAWT • lach) a special Native American celebration in the Pacific Northwest at which guests, not hosts, receive gifts

prairie (prehr • EE) flat or gently rolling land covered mostly with grasses and wildflowers

press (PREHS) members of the news media, such as reporters and columnists

*previous (PREE • vee • uhs) coming before, earlier

*primary (PRY • mehr • ee) first; main

proclamation (prah • kluh • MAY • shuhn) an official announcement

Glossary

profit (PRAH • fuht) the money made on goods or services that is more than the cost of production

profiteering (prah • fuh • TIHR • ihng) to charge high prices for goods that are in demand during a war or emergency

proprietor (pruh • PRY • uh • tuhr) a person who owns property or a business

R

ratify (RA • tuh • fy) to approve and adopt

reaper (REE • pur) a machine that cuts grain for harvesting

relative location (REH • luh • tihv loh • KAY • shuhn) the location of a place in relation to other landmarks

repeal (rih • PEEL) to cancel something, such as a law

*response (rih • SPAHNS) something that is done as a reaction to something else

responsibility (rih • spahn • suh • BIH • luh • tee) something that people must do because it is their job or duty

S

secede (sih • SEED) is to withdraw from the Union

slash-and-burn (SLASH UHND BUHRN) to cut and burn trees to clear land for farming

slave state (SLAYV STAYT) a state where slavery was allowed

slavery (SLAY • vuh • ree) the practice of owning people and forcing them to work without pay

spy (SPEYE) a person who secretly watches people or things in order to get information

stagecoach (STAYJ • kohch) a large carriage pulled by horses that was used to carry passengers

steam engine (STEEM EHN • jihn) a machine that uses steam from boiling water to create power

submit (sub • MIHT) to offer for approval

T

*technique (tehk • NEEK) a way, or method, of doing something

teepee (TEE • pee) a cone-shaped tent made from animal hides and wooden poles used by Native Americans of the Plains territory (tehr • IH • tor • ee) an area of land that is under a country's control and protection, but is not part of the country

tolerate (TAH • luh • rayt) to allow something to be or be done without trying to stop it

totem pole (TOH • tuhm POHL) a log that is carved and then painted with symbols, called totems, of animals or people

*translate (trans • LAYT) to change words from one language into another language

treaty (TREE • tee) an agreement between nations, such as for peace

tributary (trihb • YOO • tehr • ee) a river or stream that flows into a larger river or lake

*typically (TIH • pih •klee) what is normal or expected of a certain place, person, situation

tyrant (TY • ruhnt) a person who uses power in a cruel or unjust way

U

union (YOON • yuhn) a group of states or nations that are ruled by one government or that agree to work together

V

veto (vee • toh) to reject a bill

W

wagon train (WA • guhn TRAYN) a line of wagons led west by an experienced guide

wampum (WAHM • puhm) polished beads made from shells strung or woven together and used in gift-giving and trading by Native Americans

War Hawks (WAWR HAHKS) members of Congress that supported the war against Great Britain during the War of 1812

Index

This index lists many topics that appear in the book, along with the pages on which they are found. Page numbers after a *c* refer to a chart or diagram, after a *g* to a graph, after an *m* to a map, after a *p* to a photograph or a picture, and after a *q* to a quotation.

Index

Index

Index

Index

Index